ZIMBABWE:

A Hitchhiker's Guide to a Failed State

MAX CHISVO

ISBN 978-184426-439-1

Printed by Lightning Source

Zimbabwe: A hitchhiker's guide to a failed state.

The UN, at least during the tenure of Kofi Annan, had become nothing more than a third-world debating club, long on meaningless resolutions and very short on any action.

Contents

"You should free yourselves from the unreasonable demands of your Government, which exacts from you actions contrary to your moral teachings and consciousness. Only adhere to that liberty which consists in following the rational way of life... and of themselves will be abolished all the calamities which your officials cause you. You will free yourselves from your officials by not fulfilling their demands and above all, by not obeying you will cease to contribute to the oppression and plunder of each other". Leo Tolstoy, 1899.

Introduction

Other presidents in the region, such as Julius Nyerere of Tanzania, were envious of the jewel one Robert Gabriel Matibili-Mugabe, the Prime minister of The Republic of Zimbabwe had inherited. "The delay of Zimbabwe in attaining independence was a blessing in disguise. Zimbabwe has the entire required infrastructure (for development). Ourselves, when we got independence in 1964, we had no such advanced infrastructure... Look after it," Nyerere advised Mugabe in 1980.

Firstly it should be pointed out that it makes no sense for Africans to pretend that criticising a corrupt murdering African tin pot dictator openly is tantamount to betraying the 'black race'. After all, it is we the ordinary black Africans all over Africa who are suffering the most out of tyranny, corruption, torture and state murder. Refusing to help fellow Africans rid themselves of leadership that causes them suffering is wrong. The job of fixing Africa is in our African hands, rather than those of rock stars, NGOs (Non-Governmental Organisations) and Western politicians.

Africa tells a very strange story to the casual passer by. Africa is a continent so full of contradictions and extremes that sometimes just the fragments tell their own story about the situation. Africa itself is a continent so dark that political leaders admitted to the abundance of mineral wealth, much of it still to be tapped, but accuse Europe of 'stealing' the minerals; were leaders view targeted sanctions against themselves as sanctions against the whole country because they think they are the nation state. A continent were circumcision to limit the physical capacity of a woman to enjoy sex is common yet the continent has the highest birth rate in the world.

This is a place were crooks shout for Europeans to keep to Europe and leave African elites to abuse their resources the way they want. These 'scholars' deny the existence of good white men or evil black persons simply because we were at one time victims of racism and slavery. They also seek to deny that man is a relatively free moral agent who can act contrary to the wishes of his or her government. This 'school' ultimately seeks to deny the possibility of individual penance and forgiveness and can envisage only Armageddon between whites and blacks in the end.

Here in Africa you will also find those who believe God did not create bad human beings. In every bad human being was a good human being struggling to come out. Such people believe racist Rhodesia's Ian Douglas Smith was also a good person, with difficulty expressing himself in a way other people could understand him. The problem was his language bore too many similarities with the language of another man in history, Adolf Hitler. Years later, both Smith's and Hitler's language would be like that of another man of history, Robert Gabriel Matibili-Mugabe.

These crooks' most distinguishing trait is hypocrisy and double standards. They would rather talk about the squalor of Harlem in the US than the plight of people dumped by their own government in Hatcliffe Extension and Whitecliff farms; they prefer talking about Abu Ghraib and Guantanamo detainees than Zimbabwe's deplorable prison conditions and the high HIV infection rates. They demand reparations, "something tangible", from Europe. But they are wrong. The apology would get a lot of people preoccupied with irrelevancies for a continent ravaged by civil wars, hunger, irresponsible political leaders, corruption, ignorance and superstition long after the end of colonial rule.

The second point addressed here is that the Zimbabwe crisis has nothing to do with 'race'; it is not a 'black versus white' conflict as Robert Matibili also know as Robert Gabriel Mugabe, affectionately called Uncle Bob, demented President of the Republic of Zimbabwe, would like the world to believe. Zimbabwe's is a conflict between right and wrong, democracy versus tyranny, black upon black cruelty and disrespect. When one points out this truth, it should not be construed to be an attempt to 'impress the West', but a genuine concern by an African for Africans.

We have picked out the Zimbabwe scenario, the latest scene of African chaos of ruining a once prosperous country because it perfectly reflects what is wrong and right with Africa; the struggles that we go through at the hands of a predatory, corrupt ruling class. It is one thing to be independent. It is another to be free.

Zimbabwe is a small African banana republic just north of South Africa. For all its abominable acts, colonial rule left Zimbabwe semi-developed (more like Brazil) and an agricultural base without parallel on the continent outside South Africa. There was enough wealth underground and above ground to move the country forward. The country was infect a functioning nation state with working government structures. Since independence, Britain had provided more than £500 million in bilateral support for development and in total and the wider donor community had provided over two billion dollars in assistance since 1980. Twenty years later it was US$7bl in debt and an economy that no longer functioned.

While Zimbabwe may be a nation of docile citizens, they are not imbeciles by any stretch of the imagination. Africans and Zimbabweans in particular are a resilient people and up until 1995, the country had developed a relatively large pool of professionals. Be it in farming, banking and government, Harare was the envy of the rest of Africa, as it became the central African hub with every foreign expatriate and diplomat preferring to be officed in Harare's glass and clean sky scrappers. Its nationals were even envied by Western countries as the country's universities and colleges disgorged thousands of fine trained nurses, teachers, doctors, accountants and journeymen.

What really impressed most foreigners was the quality of Zimbabweans of all races, their spirit, enterprise, work ethic, moral values, respect for their fellow countrymen and the rule of law. The country's beauty was startling; it's sporting courage and proud tradition amazed and most fall in love with the country and have adopted it, proudly calling it home. Foreigners are overwhelmed by what has been built in little over a hundred years.

Its leader since independence in 1980, one Robert Gabriel Mugabe (a.k.a Robert Matibili of Malawian extraction), a former peasant teacher, had several honorary degrees and doctorates from various international Universities was revered throughout the world and the country boasted the most educated cabinet in the world.

The country's ruling elites had indeed inherited a jewel with all the trappings of a fine tuned economy, bureaucracy, judiciary, farming community and finite natural resources that included the Victoria Falls, Kariba and Great Zimbabwe Ruins, unrivalled African tourist magnets and a host of precious minerals as the jewels in its crown.

For many years after independence Zimbabwe appeared to hold a lofty position at least among the largely deteriorating nations of Africa. Zimbabweans felt special to the point of looking down upon neighbours that appeared to have got it wrong politically and economically such as Zambia and Mozambique. Zimbabweans felt different and even wondered how other countries in Africa could let one man rule the country for more than two decades. This supposedly "superiority complex" remained with Zimbabweans, so that when problems began to show, they turned largely to the international community to assist in resolving the crisis with the belief that Zimbabwe was special and different from other African countries. They expected something to be done for them by someone, taking themselves out of the equation and without accepting that it was in fact their own responsibility to free themselves of black oppression.

In general and on the average, Zimbabweans are a fair skinned, literate, hardworking, fairly loud, proud and gullible Hottentot (Bantu) people and a handful of whites, Chinese and Indians. Besides Christianity, ancestral worship is the most practiced non-Christian religion which involves spiritual intercession. On a fair day, an average Zimbabwean is a mild racist and tribalist who believes in his superiority over other Africans but feels inferior to white people. Soon after 1840 when the Ndebele King, Mzilikazi invaded, Zimbabweans developed a collective inferiority complex; that they were victims, powerless and expected others (as Cecil Rhodes had done earlier) to feel sorry for them and therefore to take decisions and actions on their behalf.

Further, because of this inferiority complex, for the generality of young black Zimbabweans, beauties lies on the lighter end of the complexion scale. Skin lightening cosmetics like Movate, Bu-tone and Ambi that contain skin-damaging substances like hydroquinone and mercury were banned in Zimbabwe and were classified as dangerous drugs. Their side effects, including cancer, are usually seen after years of use yet many educated middle class, city dwelling Zimbabweans risked their lives plashing these Chinese sourced creams to look a bit more 'white' and hence 'beautiful'.

Given a good manager and a good day, a Zimbabwean will excel and is generally capable. Arranging huge funerals, weddings and parties comes natural as it does to nearly all Africans. But the problem comes when required to run multi-faceted tasks like huge corporations. South Africa's Deposit Protection Institute chief executive John Chikura said of Zimbabweans, "We have a corporate governance crisis in both private and public sectors stemming from a complex mixture of directorial ignorance, strategic incompetence and greed. This is despite the country boasting of robust and highly educated boards as well as a high literacy rate in Africa".

Yet despite all these advantages, by end of 1999, 20 years after independence, Zimbabwe had become a rogue and failed state, with the international community, especially the West imposing targeted sanctions on Mugabe and his Zanu cronies and their families and companies that propped them up. A once self-reliant and proud people was subjected to humiliating and degrading food handouts, or worse, left to scavenge in Johannesburg, Botswana and UK.

Since 1995 the cases of Zimbabwean torture had risen exponentially, both in terms of numbers and in severity; peaking in 2007 when respected opposition leaders lay in hospital fighting for their lives with their skulls bashed in by police and an elated Mugabe claiming responsibility cheered on by regional leaders.

Security forces caused chaos, beat customers, shut down bars and businesses perceived as hotbeds of a popular albeit chaotic opposition. Undercover police eavesdropped on conversations in cafes, hotels, buses and on the Internet. Striking kids where shot dead in the townships and entire communities destroyed. This became undeclared martial law as the demented dictator relied more and more on the security forces. It tore whole communities apart as the middle class migrated or was crushed mercilessly by the ruling classes supported by the financial elites in the Western suburbs of Harare and the military.

Direct foreign investment had evaporated, expatriates threw their arms up in surrender, packed their bags and left for crime ridden South African and donors practically started to maintain the country. As of February 1999, Zimbabwe's foreign debt repayments ceased. Yet despite these troubles, billions of US$ were spent in the country's senseless involvement in imperial wars, purchase of Chinese fighter aircraft armaments and lavish galas were hosted in praise of a failed revolution, presidential birthdays and weddings.

There was no doubt that without some form of peaceful United Nations intervention there was no prospect of Zimbabweans being able to recover from the catastrophe they found themselves in. All the signs were already there. Fundamentally the failure to respect the rule of law acts like a cancer in any society. From 1995 onwards Court judgements were ignored with impunity. The law in Zimbabwe was applied selectively like a spider's web that lets through big animals and only catches small insects.

In May 2005, for two hours, the most powerful financier in the country, a former tea boy called Gideon Gono, the Zimbabwe Reserve Bank Governor's presentation was broadcast live on national television. He described utter chaos in the economy while his audience of Ministers, bankers and businessmen, a.k.a Zimbabwe's elites, laughed and feasted on a huge breakfast while the country starved. The Governor, who awarded himself a doctorate degree while vice chancellor of a local university, spoke about resettled farms where people who were supposed to be farmers were cutting down orchards to sell for firewood, selling timber plantations and chopping coffee plantations in order to plant a few maize stalks, stripping assets, destroying infrastructure and selling immovable property.

Gono talked about people leaving the country by air with suitcases literally bulging with US dollars, by road with foreign currency stuffed in false fuel tanks under their cars and of unauthorized private aircraft coming in to collect smuggled gold, diamonds and other precious metals. He spoke of massive environmental degradation and a rape of the land so widespread that there was to be nothing left for Zimbabwean children to inherit. Almost every sentence contained words like corruption, indiscipline, hoarding and abuse. In short he spoke about greed that knows no bounds.

By 2004, the aging and by now illegitimate president Mugabe had started his insane demolition of houses and businesses as he increasingly look liked Pol Pot reborn; cash-strapped public schools were requesting pupils to bring along chairs and desks; patients in hospitals had no drugs and walked around death stinking corridors naked. In fact, the Minister of health happily unveiled ox-drawn ambulances! From a jewel in the African crown, Zimbabwe was a sad litany of failure, brought to its knees by an old man gone mad on his own perceived importance, grudgingly supported by his neighbours.

Trying to simplify the continent's problems with the fiction that it was Blair (UK) and Bush's (USA) fault as some African scholars do, is deceitful and downright stupid. It makes Africans blind to our own responsibilities. We need African leaders and citizens who are bold and courageous enough to adopt tough measures in an environment with different and difficult dynamics; leaders with the courage to face present realities in the face and lead us (Africans) out of the mess we are in, guide us and care for us as their children; feed, house, clothe and educate us; leaders who are like Moses, who will take us to the promised land and not enter Israel to enjoy the fruits of the land themselves.

Zimbabwe didn't need to reinvent the wheel, to ruin all the farming and industrial infrastructures to free themselves of neo-colonialism. After all, the ruling elites hadn't rejected other European inventions like the Mercedes Benz 600L stretch Limousines which they had turned into status symbols and didn't regard as bonds of servitude to their colonial past. The failure of Zimbabwe to grasp the moment and make massive strides toward a predominantly middle-class nation is testament to the unbelievably poor, non-statesman leadership Zimbabwe had been subjected to for too long. Mugabe didn't have to be as wise as Nelson Mandela to make his nation work; he just had to avoid being a madman.

Indeed, it seems that to many people across the world, the behaviour of the Zimbabwe government was nothing out of the ordinary considering the history of poor governance and abuse of power in Africa. The mention of Africa conjures images of fly-infested, pot bellied naked children surrounded by poverty and gun-totting youths. Not much attention was paid to the decline in those other countries. In each of those cases the people appealed to the amorphous international community, with minimal results except in the few cases where perhaps there was full-blown war and interests of the 'international community' needed safeguarding. Why then do Zimbabweans seem to feel that theirs was a special case? Zimbabwe was simply travelling a well-trodden path.

The "dark ages"

"It is easy to blame these (African) ills on the past and on outsiders. The depredations of imperialism and the slave trade, the imbalance of power and wealth in a flagrantly unjust world. But that cannot absolve us, the Africans of today, from our own responsibility to ourselves," Koffi Annan, UN Secretary General, 2006.

The word Africa can be traced to the Phoenician "afer" (plural "afri"), "a black man," or in Latin and Greek, Aphrike. The original Africa was a progressive Roman province on the southern coast of the Mediterranean, roughly equivalent to the modern Tunisia, not the whole continent. Yet if it is true that human life started with black-skinned people in the place we now call "Africa", it must be true also, that it never had an 'original' name except "Home", in whatever language we might have spoken originally.

Scientists have been working continuously to discover the origins of the black race. There is no evidence of the Bantu (Negro) race anywhere on earth before 20,000BC. Initially and according to archaeologists, the African continent was home to the Pygmies only, the distant cousin of the ones you find in the Congo area today. 500BC Herodotus tells a story of Nasamonians who met Dwarfs only around the Niger River. Sataspes, also recorded by Herodotus, sailed down the West African coast and at the furthest point he sailed he met 'a dwarfish race' that wore a dress made from palm tree". Aristotle wrote of "....dwarfs or Pygmies living in the region of the lakes in which the Nile has its source." The point is up to 500BC there appears no other race on the west coast of Africa except the Pygmies.

Archaeology points to 15,000 BC as about the arrival time of Caucasian people from Asia into North East Africa were they introduced agriculture and the domestication of animals. It looks like by 10,000BC the Caucasoid element from Asia had been completely absorbed by the majority dwarf hybrid. Hence the Hottentots 'Bantu' race is a hybrid of inter-breeding between the Pygmies and immigrants from Asia and their colour is derived from the Pygmies. Further inter-breeding with the Khoi-San, Indians and Chinese brought in colour, facial, hair and height differences. The Egyptian civilisation was in actual fact mainly made up of Black Africans (46%) and all the earlier Pharaohs were indeed black Africans. All early Egyptian statues and drawings depicted people with African features, e.g. the Narmer Hathor, Thutmose etc.

Hence between 10,000BC and 8,000BC it is safe to conclude that every African on the continent was a Mulatto. The word Bantu signifies a group of people with similar dialects and with time the word Negro (Latin word Niger which means Black) became reserved for American slaves and not resident Black Africans. The first people to use the word 'Bantu' was Earl Grey and Bleek who had observed a common peculiarity in the languages spoken by Africans, the root "Ntu" in reference to being human.

Slavery

When evaluating the predicament of sub-Sahara Africa in the 21st century, one has to take into account the repercussions and astounding horrors of the slave trade on the continent. Though this is a tired story everyone has heard thousands of times and one that bores a lot of liberals, it will help in briefly re-telling the story of the total collapse of many African states.

That the slave trade is very central to what is happening today in Africa is true, as it robbed Africa of its best and brightest, its farmers, teachers and workers; brought about acute economic stagnation, which is still haunting the continent today.

Firstly lets take away the mirth of the 'dark continent'. Besides the famous Egyptians up north, the Ashanti, Ghana's largest tribe, were one of the most religiously intricate, commercially astute and militarily adventurous civilisations on the continent trading in gold, ivory and slaves. Early Europeans described well planned cities with clean wide streets, schools and carefully planted trees and houses with toilets flushed with boiling water. Before the arrival of the white men the Ashanti Empire ruled itself with a monarch and participatory democracy just as the UK does today.

Further south, the Mwene Mutapa Empire (Owner of the Conquered Lands and Peoples), mentioned in the bible and basis for the King Solomon's mines myth, had its capital at today's city of Masvingo in Zimbabwe and encompassed other cities such as Sofala and Tete. Zimbabwe itself housed over 40,000 dwellers at its peak and its boarders stretched from modern day Botswana to the Indian Ocean. The kingdom produced gold for export and had schools, roads and ships that crossed the seas to India. The Kings' children were educated in India at Goa and some even travelled as far as China spreading the Christian gospels. The kingdom traded peacefully with the Arabs, Indians and Chinese for hundreds of years before the white men landed at Cape Town.

Timbuktu was an economic and cultural capital equal in historical importance to acclaimed cities like Rome, Athens and Mecca. Timbuktu was founded around 1100AD as a camp for its proximity to the Niger River. Great mosques, universities, schools, and libraries were built under the Mali and Songhay Empires, some of which still stand today. Timbuktu's golden age ended in the late sixteenth century, when a Moroccan army destroyed the Songhay Empire. Africa was dotted with numerous such advanced kingdoms which contrary to white beliefs, were civilised and existed in the most, peacefully with each other.

Slavery is widely practiced and deeply rooted in African culture, even long before the arrival of Europeans and long after they left. When the 15th century Portuguese began sailing down the coast, they met long-established slave traders keen to sell off surpluses. Europeans almost never went on slaving expeditions into the interior. They bought slaves from dealers, which means that slaves taken from Africa were first enslaved by other Africans. By 2008 Sudan was still practicing slavery and even in modern cities like Harare young girls were still working for food and a pair of shoes a month and prisoners were made to work for free on government ministers' private farms. These modern day enslavers were never criticised.

Hence slavery was aided and abetted by the role of West African warlords who sold their captives into slavery. Luckily senior citizens like former President Joaquim Chissano were able to pick up on these obvious omissions when he said: "I wish I had the mandate to ask for forgiveness as well, because most of the sins committed by Europeans were not committed by them alone."

After 1650, African exports, chiefly controlled by Europeans and abetted by corrupt local elites, become a monoculture in human beings; impoverishments as the slaves were men and women who would otherwise create wealth for Africa, the strong who could withstand the rigours of the trip across the jungles and the seas. Between 1441 and 1880 over 14 million Africans were ripped from their families and turned into slaves in the new world while millions more were taken but died walking hundreds of kilometres to the ports and crossing the Atlantic.

Although a profitable enterprise for Europe and their African stooges, the slave trade destroyed Africa and eviscerated its people and empires. For more than 400 years Africans were forcibly removed from their continent by the Portuguese, Dutch, British, French and other European enslavers and spirited away 10,000 kilometres away, where they had to confront a different culture, economy and politics.

This first contact between the three continents produced three victims; slaves, moral corruption of whites and blacks and the physical denigration of Africans. This contact was based purely and simply on barbarity and terror inflicted by Europeans and experienced by Africans; a violent collusion of cultures and endless in its consequences, an association of the powerful and the powerless and greed of the white men and the corruption of African rulers.

Slavery is a past that shocked and paralysed an entire breed of people, rendering them directionless for ages into their future; a past that is so dark and shameful that the perpetrating races try by all means to deny and rub it out of their conscience. To say that the trade created great instability is an injustice as entire functioning peaceful kingdoms, states and nations were subverted in the fight to control the trade and new artificial ones formed based on foundations of corruption and disobedience to tradition. In this relationship the European has remained dominant, feeding the continent's rulers with dirty money and toys in return for cheap minerals, moral support at the UN and cheap raw materials.

Africa has had an arduous time recovering from the economic and social vacuum formed by the forced removal of its best citizen and strongest genes from their communities. Though slavery and slave trade were most probably the first widely recorded contact between Europeans and Africans, it was sadly not the last, as many equally or more devastating contacts were to visit the two very different communities in the future.

Colonialism

The demise of the slave trade triggered the emergency of still another negative aspect to the Africa/Europe relationship; the imposition of colonial rule. This book will not dwell much on the evils of colonialism, because much has already been said; it is the past and Africa must forge ahead. However, a discussion such as this would not be complete without a brief mention of the colonial legacy and the effect it has had on modern-day African states.

By 1805 Europe began to ban slavery and also simultaneously began to industrialise; the interior of African began to open up to European explorers; European monarchs organised official claims to large swaths of the continent and imperialism become once again a very financially and personal competitive game with its own corrupt imperial interests paramount. The search for raw materials and at times personal fiefdoms was fierce and Africa had these in abundance. The map of Africa was redrawn by people who had never set their foot on the continent, who did not intent to reside there, where not the least interested in the mechanisations of the continent and who hated everything African.

Africa was thrown into a violent collusion with the most self-righteous and best-equipped colonial bulldozer in world history. Europeans with a pronounced conviction of their own cultural, biological and technological superiority poured onto the continent and set up police states complete with a new language, religion and norms. The states were set up to subjugate, not serve the citizenry; they were vehicle of plunder and no middle class was ever set up to believe in the Bill of Rights or two-term presidency or democracy.

In disrupting pre-colonial political systems that worked for Africans and imposing alien models, colonialism laid the seeds of political, social and financial crisis. Perhaps the most crucial aspect was the arbitrary drawing of boundaries, which cut across age-old tribal borders, forcing people of different ethnic backgrounds and in same cases of different races such as the Arabs and the Berbers to become a nation. Imagine, for example, the complexities and chaos that would result if, suddenly, a new country was created incorporating part of Holland, part of Germany and part of France; it led to two world wars and still causes confusion in the Balkans and middle east.

By redrawing the map of Africa, throwing diverse people together, ethnic conflicts were created that are now destabilising the continent. A third of the countries in Africa have populations of less than 10 million and almost 90% of African borders are artificial, created out of the needs of the European imperialists rather than African states; with ethnic groups often divided between territories because a river or mountain served as a demarcation point.

Often British colonisers selected one tribe to work with and to serve them, creating dependence and a feeling of superiority, while other tribes were economically and politically marginalized and the selected tribes went on to become the 'ruling elites' at independence; creating resentment among the marginalized, leading to civil wars which today still tear apart the continent.

This was the divide and rule tactic based on the theories of English philosopher Edmund Burke. His gradualism theory made colonial management easy. Nothing was supposed to happen. The interaction of coloniser/colonised was based on racism traceable to the slave trade as colonialism entailed removing the colonised from history, usurping the colonised's political, economic, personal and cultural objectives by destroying their humanity and socialising by manipulating them to accept the fact that they were inferior.

In Australia and America, the British embarked on a genocidal massacre of Aborigines and red Indians, reducing present day populations and the survivors into hopeless alcoholics and objects of pity and tourism. As a result, the vanquished natives are now in the minority whilst their murderers have multiplied to become the majority. Australians are decedents of criminals from Britain, who the British wanted to send out of their country.

Belgium was and is a special case as it remains today; their colonial policy was based on open racism, was genocidely deadly and killed millions in the Congo, treating it's colonised as though they were little unthinking kids. Education was ignored and the trauma left has vanquished Congolese societies and individuals up to today. Belgium unofficially accepted the blood diamond trade on their territory and provides little viable assistance to their former colonies and participated in the genocide in Rwanda. They left colonies poorer and more traumatised than they found them.

The colonial educational systems produced social types who were culturally removed from the cultures from which they sprung. The first and most important vehicle for the removal and alienation of the educated African from his or her original cultural moorings was the use of the colonial language, English, French or Portuguese and the Bible. Africans were taught to be ashamed of their own religions and languages. This pattern of education and knowledge production was inherited with only minor revisions by the post-colonial state.

Indeed, in post-colonial Africa, apart from weak attempts in Tanzania and Madagascar to use African languages as languages of education at the post-primary levels, no African country has made any serious attempt at developing African languages as the basis for the production and reproduction of knowledge. In the case of both Tanzania and Madagascar, after some years of half-hearted trial and error the policy of using indigenous languages consistently in the educational system has been, in both cases, abandoned.

It is however interesting to note that in all societies that are able to advance forward scientifically and technologically, primacy is vested in the development and use of languages indigenous to the people. This is true not only for non-Western societies like China, Japan and Thailand, but is equally true for countries, in the West like Denmark, France, Britain or Germany.

For just about wherever Britain and the West have been involved, from the Horn of Africa to the Cape of Good Hope, Africa bears scars. Nowhere are the consequences of Western misjudgement more evident than Southern Africa, where the denial of responsibility is at its loudest. Britain was as complicit in the consolidation of White power in Rhodesia in the early 1960s, as surely as it helped create Iraq's fearsome armoury.

It was Britain that imposed the Central African Federation of Rhodesia and Nyasaland on the voteless African majority. And it was Britain that presided over its dissolution, on terms that gave the bulk of the armed forces to white-ruled

Rhodesia, soon to declare illegal independence, triggering a 10-year civil war that killed 250,000 innocent civilians. It was Britain that jailed the leaders of African nationalism (some progressive) in nearly every one of its colonies.

Not only were African labour and resources exploited, the continent's ability to develop was undermined. Guyanese historian Walter Rodney in his book 'How Europe Underdeveloped Africa' contends that under colonialism "...the only thing that developed was dependency and underdevelopment." As far as Rodney and other critics are concerned "...the only positive development in colonialism was when it ended."

Under European imperial rule, African economies were structured to be permanently dependent on Western nations as they were consigned the role of producers of primary products for processing in the West. The terms of trade in the Western controlled international market discriminated against African nations who were unable to earn enough to develop their economies. Hence in disrupting pre-colonial political systems that worked for Africans and imposing alien models, colonialism laid the seeds of political, financial and social crisis.

It is impossible to say what would have been the shape of modern African history had colonial rule never taken place. Japan, China and parts of Southeast Asia were never colonised, yet they are today major world economies. These Asian nations had more educated labour forces and were technologically more advanced than Africa; their ruling classes were more ideologically committed to social progress and economic development.

However, had Africa not been colonised, (parts of Ethiopia and Liberia were not colonised) the likelihood is that its elites and rulers would still have wanted to consume the products and services of Western industrial nations just as they do today. If during the slave trade, rulers and traders happily waged wars and sold fellow African humans to buy mirrors, sugar and second-hand hats, one can only imagine what they would have done if faced with offers of BMWs, TVs, IBMs, yachts and planes. Undoubtedly, without colonisation African societies would still have sought industrialisation and Western type modernisation at that, as have peoples in virtually every other region in the world.

As there is no basis to assume that Africans would have independently and been first to develop electricity, computer software, the motor and aeroplane engines and other products of advanced technologies, it is fair to suppose that if Africa had not been colonised, Africa would have needed to import Western technology and therefore would have had to export something to pay for it. Like other pre-industrial societies, African nations would invariably have had to trade minerals and agricultural commodities for Western manufactures.

To believe that colonization thwarted the economic development of Africa is to believe that indigenous societies were on their way towards prosperity but were brutally shoved off course by Europeans. Slavery was widely practiced, and deeply rooted in Africa culture long before the arrival of Europeans. There is no reason to think that, left to themselves, Africans would have risen from the primitive conditions which at times they still practise even today. So Africa's position in the international economy, particularly as a producer of primary products for industrialised countries, should not be blamed solely on colonialism. Just take a brief look at Ethiopia.

However, it is, of course, a presumption that modernisation is desirable. The fact that Western society is more complex than traditional African society does not necessarily mean that it is better. Pre-colonial African societies were materially less developed than societies in other regions of the world, but there is nothing to say they were no less balanced and self-contained than elsewhere. Who is to say whether people living in agrarian societies are less developed as human beings than inhabitants of industrialised ones?

There were huge shortcomings to colonial rule but in some instances the overall effect was somewhat positive. Sure, the colonial powers exploited Africa's natural resources big time, but on the balance, colonialism slightly reduced the economic gap between some Africans and the West. Colonialism laid the seeds of the intellectual and material development in Africans; it suppressed slavery, it brought formal education and modern medicine was brought to people who have, in some instances, limited understanding or control environment.

The introduction of modern communications, exportable agricultural crops and some new industries provided a foundation for economic development. Africans received new and more efficient forms of political and economic organisation. Warring communities were united into modern nation-states with greater opportunity of survival in a competitive world than the numerous mini entities that existed before. Some parts of Africa are in political and economic turmoil today because they failed to take advantage of their inheritance from colonial rule. It was, and it's sad to say, to some extend, Africa's inadequacies that made slavery and colonisation necessary and possible.

There are nations that are political, post-colonial contemporaries of Zimbabwe's that were surging forward inexorably even as Mugabe tirelessly worked to pull Zimbabwe in the opposite direction. Those who contend that colonialism made no positive impact are as dogmatic as those who present it as the salvation of Africa. What is unequivocal is that it was an imposition of unwanted and resisted alien rule. Whatever may have been its pluses and minuses, the common result is colonialism was a dictatorial regime that denied peoples' right of self-determination. It brought death, pain and humiliation to millions of its victims.

The cold war and the bones of independence

A dog can chase a car, but when it catches it, it doesn't know how to drive the car.

"The state that claims sovereignty deserves respect only as long as it can protect the basic rights of its subjects. When it violets them, the state's claim to full sovereignty falls," Hoffmann.

When two elephants fight the grass suffers.

The apparent "victory" of Western ideology and practices, encompassed in the democratic market economy, over Marxist-inspired central planning is part of what is known as the "end of the cold war". Thus there is now high levels of economic interdependence between the "East" and the "West" as cold war politics have given way to Western efforts to assist the East's transformation using not least huge financial loans and at stake is the avoidance of a return to conflict with a potentially isolated Russia. A partial cause of the East's collapse was its inability to remain at high levels of economic isolation from the West.

As the cold-war came to an end, central governments in Africa once reliant on free Eastern and Western military aid to fight their internal class and social battles found themselves adrift and the poorer quasi-states forced to cope in a new austere climate, resulting in some cases partition (Ethiopia and Eritrea) and in others in further crumbling of empirical statehood (DRC, Somalia). Infect the plight of some, like Zimbabwe, had become so catastrophic that they were described as failed states; entities totally deficient in internal order and utterly unable to sustain themselves as members of the international community.

Development studies in the 1950s and 1960s usually assumed that, once colonialism had shaken these underdeveloped countries out of their traditional stupor, they would embark on a process of "modernisation". Considerable empirical work was produced indicating the idea being that once a trend had been identified it could then be deliberately introduced or manipulated through aid schemes to initiate the growth process. In this scenario, the centre stage was occupied by selected elites (rulers) guided by the aspirations of nation building and development, aided by foreign military support.

But by 1966-67, Fanon was to provide the characterisation of a socio-psychology of a "comprador bourgeoisie" class, essentially "born senile and decadent before scaling the heights of enlightenment and industrial revolution". At best, he said, Africa could have "lumpen bourgeoisie", "dependent capitalist" or, worse, "drone capitalist". Such descriptions pointed to one fact, namely, that the African state was not up to its "historical mission" of ensuring capitalist accumulation. Such a ruling class could not produce the "captains of industry" needed for the mobilization of resources and acquisition of technology.

The end of the second world war saw a remarkable growth in the number of states, from about 60 to about 180 by 2000, ranging from tiny states like Gambia, and the Holy See up to huge ones like Sudan, India and Russia. For a state to be called a state there are common characteristics, of which a territory, a sovereign government and a subject population are the most important and the existence of a common culture and a sense of national identity, a minimum level of political stability and order as other prerequisites. Most if not all these seem to be non-existent in Africa.

States cannot survive on their own. They require the international community to be able to sustain whatever it is they want to achieve. Take for instance economic issues were the ability of the sovereign state to pursue policies of its choice has been fundamentally challenged by globalisation. On the subject of populations; here the problem is that some populations have often been compelled to escape the state in which they are contained as a result of the state displaying a poor sense of overarching national identity as in the case of Zimbabwe. The usually subordinate position of the population is viewed as demeaning and the only proper course of action is self-determination and hence the construction of its own state through military means or they become foreign based as in the Diaspora.

As colonialism was coming to an end in the 1960s, relations between coloniser/colonised having taken root and seemed smoothed over, most African states gained independence, the USA and Russia moved into the vacuum left by the imperialists and extended the ethnic divisions to better serve their interests. One superpower would buttress the corrupt ruling elites empowered by the colonialists while the other power backed the opposition often with disastrous implications for the common people.

The cold-war implied pouring billions of dollars worth of weaponry into client states and training the local elites to use them to support the superpower's interests and counter indigenous forces taking power. The USA was preventing the spread of communism being spread by Russia. The two powers fanned the fires of ethnic diversity and frustration and alienation with the ruling classes easily spread and the violence that accompanied the ensuing struggles for superpower hegemony was awesome and destructive.

It is of interest to note that the cold-war superpowers, USA, Nato, France, China and Russia, pursued their own interests irrespective of the internal political dynamics of the African states and internal politics did not interest them at all as long as their concerns converged with those of the ruling elites. All the billions worth of weaponry donated to Ethiopia and Somalia for example was subsequently used in internal civil wars and did not kill a single white imperialist. In Zimbabwe armaments purchased from China were used heavily to intimidate its own citizens and those inherited from Rhodesia and 'liberation forces' were used mainly against local Ndebeles in the mid-80s and in the black imperialist wars in Mozambique and the DRC. In general, it can be said the weapons were mainly directed at other Africans and not to end imperialism as the wars left dead Africans only.

In essence the Western and Eastern block adversaries acted in Africa like nothing more than war criminals. In this regard, the West and East should pay reparations to Africa as a realisation that in fact they must pay. However it must be noted that reparations are not going to compensate for the paralysis imposed on Africa nor will they take Africa out of the paralysis. Only Africans can do this.

Africa's problems, as pervasive and ghastly, are not the final score of a doomed continent; rather they are preliminary readings from the world's messiest experiment in socio-cultural and political change. Africans were bullied into this experiment by looting Europeans and corrupt African rulers. The Europeans curved the continent into weirdly shaped money making countries and then administered them from the top down for about 100 years then left murdering elites to do as they please. With the sudden collapse and subsequent withdrawal of such imposed influences, Africa has progressively slipped back into a form of tribal feudalism that allows a few elites to dominate and in fact use the legacies of colonial administration to loot national resources in the pursuit of personal wealth.

Sub-Saharan Africa inherited from the pre-colonial and colonial eras a political-economic configuration that left little room for the construction of viable national economies or robust national states. Attempts to build these against all odds did not on the whole get very far in spite of the considerable legitimacy that they enjoyed at the time of independence. At that time the incidental core agenda of African nationalists comprised three basic strategies: de-racialising civil society, detribalising the Native Authority (via force in most cases) and developing the economy in the context of unequal international relations.

Tribal custom was stranded, overtaken by Western style education, jobs and welfare. Africans were forced to reconcile within themselves without any tradition to guide them to leap centuries forward yet divorced from each world. For example, 'modern' Africans across the continent still believe that birth into a tribe entails privileges and duties that have nothing to do with free will. In this regard an African can no more wish away his tribal duties than he can wish away the laws of gravity. These urbanised traditionalists who live in Johannesburg, Harare, Nairobi or Lagos all their lives but still insist that a small hut in a remote village of their ancestors is their only home have fundamental decisions of life to make.

This is a continent were childless women are blamed for illness and death in a village; Were Juju murders afflict modern Africa in a way that school children shooting sprees afflict the USA. Abhorrent, unpredictable and typical though the violence may be it happens often to be a symptom in Africa as in America. In need of a spiritual edge over competition in business, an African goes shopping for a fresh human head just as a grudge infected drugged American goes shopping for an AK rifle and goes on a Rambo-style massacre.

Hundreds of millions of Africans are today lurching between an unworkable Western present and a collapsing tribal past. Their loyalties are stretched between predatory governments and disintegrating tribes, between corrupt government demands and the demands and pleadings of relatives; between bible commandments and obligations to their ancestors.

While nationalist regimes of all political persuasions made major strides in deracialising civil society, they did little or nothing to detribalise rural power. This is the reason why development ultimately failed. Nevertheless, the fact that African elites needed to detribalise the social structures they inherited from colonialism if they were to create viable states did constitute yet another handicap in the intensely competitive environment created by the global crisis of the 1970s and the preferential treatment that the United States accorded its East Asian allies in the early stages of the Cold War. This preferential treatment played a critical role in the 'take-off' of the region's economic renaissance.

As an aside, the true dimensions of this generosity are revealed by the fact that nearly $13 billion (in 10 years) in US economic aid to South Korea compare with a total of $6.89 billion for all of Africa for the same period. Equally important, the USA gave the exports of its East Asian allies privileged access to the US domestic market while tolerating their protectionism, state interventionism and even exclusion of US multinationals. Perhaps aside from China, the only country that appears to have benefited unambiguously from the trend towards open markets worldwide is the United States, where a huge inflow of capital has allowed Americans to spend more than they save, and to import more than they export.

Hence, unsurprisingly, decolonisation of Africa, the failure to detribalise and the international economic arrangement, resulted in battles for self-determination pursued with a force that rendered whole African areas effectively beyond state jurisdiction as a large number of the states had boarders and patterns that failed to conform to patterns of population distribution. This is very common in Sudan, the DRC and Angola were central government totally lost control of whole stretches of the countryside ruled by mobs like the Janjaweed and Huturahamwe.

Unlike in Asia, patronage of tyranny and tolerance of corruption have long been at the heart of Western policy across Africa, from Kenya under Daniel Arap Moi, to Zaire under Mobutu Sese Seko and Liberia under Samuel Doe to Robert Mugabe of Zimbabwe. Today, for all the protestations to the contrary, commercial interests or strategic concerns continue to take precedence over principles: West Africa, for example, is expected to provide 10% of USA oil imports, a forecast that buys political leeway for some of Africa's most venal, barbaric and mismanaged governments.

This patronage doctrine will prove to be a two-edged sword, and provoke what Europeans see as a perverse and irrational solidarity among the weak. Britain at least should know better. It has more experience after all. Yet far from recognising that Africa's past still shapes current events, the British government appeared to believe that it could start afresh, without the baggage of history. For those in Britain who determine foreign policy, it seems that the continent's history began when Labour won office in 1997.

On the other hand, at independence former colonies became "free" nations, able to chart for themselves whatever course they had the ability and determination to follow. They could have, as some did, nationalise foreign owned corporations. They could have stopped primary commodity exports and ended imports from the West. They could easily have traded amongst themselves.

Of course, such radical policies would have consequences. They did not because it was not in the interest of their rulers to do so and not because they were shackled by neo-colonialism. If Cuba, only a few kilometres from the capitalist mega-power, the USA, could pursue an independent economic agenda and survive, there is no reason why African nations could not have done the same. In 1974 Nigeria had US$100 billion in cash reserves and they squandered it all within 10 years on Champagne and golden bathtubs.

Hence by 1990, essentially no independence had really arrived in Africa. On gaining independence, most new African presidents were content that nationalism had little appeal to the new elites and a few who did appear like Nkruma and Nyerere rapidly found themselves out of power or favour. Africa remains slave to foreign demands and even after the cold war, it was abandoned by both superpowers and its rulers failed to thrust the continent onto a level international playing field.

Post 1990 Africa found itself in isolation as the West absolved itself of any responsibility for its past dealings and left the corrupt ruling elites, killers and marauders to do as they liked. An individual would take control of a country via violence and mercilessly cling to it, calling it his own (Mugabe, "Blair keep **your** England and I'll keep **my** Zimbabwe!"). Starvation, drought and plagues raged through a population on the move as they fled advancing armies, militia and rebels, millions perishing in the process, hacked down by hunger, disease, bullets, HIV/Aids and fatigue.

In some parts, since independence in 1960, not a single kilometre of road/rail has been added, not a single dam, bridge or telephone, in some towns one cannot even access the Internet by 2007. Some states were in a more precarious state than they were during colonial time, yet were left with functioning democratic bureaucracies, a fairly large educated population, a fairly advanced economy with functioning banks etc. But within 20 years, corruption, greed and neglect had wasted away all this and replaced it with chaos and anarchy.

Western educated African ruling elites, with mountains of degrees, ravaged entire economies until they where on their knees. State assets, tender boards, banks, taxes, all fertile agricultural land were personalised and distributed among cronies and any opposition was ruthlessly crushed, with the tacit approval and help of Western and Eastern nations. Dictators had privatised Africa and were clinging to their prize.

"Why not simply privatise whole African countries?" asked Robert Wheelen in September 1996. Wheelen argued that multi-national companies should be invited to bid for the right to run African nations under leases of up to 21 years. They would undertake to provide specific services and bring about efficiency and discipline in return for pre-set tax revenue.

The footballer George Weah, apparently exasperated by the anarchy and hopeless condition of his homeland, told the New York Times in May 1996: "The United Nations should come in and take over Liberia, not temporarily, but for life. To make Liberians believe in democracy, to make us believe in human rights."

The tragedy of Africa's situation is that as absurd as these proposals by latter day imperialists sound, there are many Africans who would support some degree of direct governance by external agents to straighten out their countries. For instance, Liberians called for their war-battered nation to become a trust territory of the United Nations. For his outspokenness, two of Weah's cousins were raped and his house burnt down.

Weah's comment was naive but understandable. Blaming Africa's woes on bad leaders has become the hymn of many people concerned about the continent's future. A change in government, preferably through democratic means, is viewed as the main pre-requisite for making a fresh start and attracting economic investment. Analysts focus their minds on how bungling African leaders can be got rid of. The tendency is to view Africa's woes in terms of the excesses of individual dictators and their cronies.

Why not just move the boundaries just a little bit so they reflect more closely tribal and religious reality and cut huge ungovernable countries like Sudan into two? The answer lies with the African Union (AU), which had been unanimous and inflexible (except for Eritrea) as they felt this would open up old tribal and religious grudges leading to uncontrollable wholesale slaughter. Further, most African rebels have resigned themselves to the task of overthrowing existing national governments not creating new ones.

Blaming all of Africa's problems on slavery and colonialism and the machination of neo-colonialists strikes a cord with many educated Africans angry with the West. Western bashing also played on the guilt of white liberals like the former British Prime Minister Tony Blair, who were happy to bear the burden of the historic sins of their ruling classes. Some right wing whites, still regretting the end of the "...empire", may be flattered by it because it acknowledges the all-embracing supremacy of the white man.

But it remains unquestioned for example, why is it that a peasant farmer in ice-cold Russia or in the deserts of Australia can get a higher return on investment than an African, in warm tropical Africa where there is no winter and it rains much of the year round. You will wonder why it is that people who live in a perfect farming climate are starving to death year after year, while others, who live in snowfields or in deserts can provide for themselves.

Considered for example the contrasting fortunes of Malawi and South Korea. In the mid-50s, Korea had been devastated by war. What was left of the economy of this underdeveloped ex-Japanese colony was based on peasant cultivation of rice. GDP per head was under US$100. Meanwhile in Africa, when they became independent in 1964, Malawi and Tanzania could count on a fairly decent legal and physical infrastructure, a capable Asian, African, European business class, a steady Western and Eastern donor assistance and modest but thriving economies.

It is not as though Western countries had neglected Africa. Since the 1960s, they have poured more than $300 billion in aid into the continent. Tanzania, a favourite target for Scandinavian largess, received $8.6 billion between 1970 and 1988. By 1988, Tanzania's annual per capita GNP was lower than at independence in 1964. Within 30 years, Malawi and Tanzania managed to be the world's least-developed nations. After decades of dictatorship during which the Asian business class was dispossessed, the economy stagnated.

Meanwhile, Korea, with massive help from the USA, industrialised and increased its GDP per capita from virtually nothing to around £9,000. The first thing the Koreans did was to get rid of their unproductive peasant agriculture; precisely the kind of backward economy that the "fair trade" lobbies and NGOs wished to entrench in Africa.

There is nothing wrong with African land, people, climate or soil. Africa is heaven-on-earth and most of its people use common sense and logic. The problem is the African ruling elites. The World could give until it hurt, and they would still be amazed at how little they managed to help. At every African Union summit, crooks such as Moi, Kaunda, Mobuto and Mugabe who had looted their nations' coffers were applauded for speeches that mixed cries against regional marginalisation and criticism of the IMF with insincere pleas for African unity and calls for debt forgiveness.

These leaders only had to spice their speeches with some anti-imperialist rhetoric to be acclaimed at home and abroad as defenders of their people. As long as black nationalists verbally attacked Whites and the IMF they qualified as militants. It does not seem to matter that some of these so-called black radicals were reactionary in relation to other African social groups, including abusing women and children, denying the starving food aid and HIV/Aids drugs; were down-right crooks who exploited the poor and for whom politics was merely an opportunity for individual gain and power.

Africa's poor gained little or nothing from colonialism but its elites and rulers bloomed as a result of it. African millionaires, who today live on the upper layers of the pyramid with fat bank accounts in Western capitals, certainly owe their fortune to slavery and definitely to colonialism and the blind and patronising assistance of Western "friends".

A praise singer for failed African leaders, former President Mkapa got used to that while working so long for Julius Nyerere, first as one of his editors then as one of his ministers. After the disastrous Nyerere years, Tanzania was left bankrupt after decades of Ujama 'self-reliance' policies. Mkapa had to pick up the pieces and start all over again without de-constructing the myth of Mwalimu Nyerere. Mkapa did that job brilliantly while privately acknowledging that Nyerere had been badly 'misled' by a collection of "idiotic intellectuals" from Western universities playing out their political and economic fantasies in an African Disneyland.

All Western aid agencies and Live-Aid singers needed to do was realise that Mkapa was not rich before he was president and his salary was not that significant; but he was very rich when he stepped down; not rich in African terms, but really, really rich even by Western terms. You don't need to be very clever to know where Mkapa got his wealth from; yet after 10 years Mkapa left Tanzania worse off than he found it.

Perhaps Mkapa had been taking lessons from one of his heroes, Robert Matibili-Mugabe. "For us in Tanzania, Zimbabwe is more than a friend. We are brothers in the struggle for justice and freedom, for human rights and democracy," Mkapa said at a dinner in Harare 2005. "A new leadership is emerging in Africa that cannot accept tutelary relationships with our erstwhile colonisers, a new leadership which would rather listen to its elders, such as Comrade Mugabe." The spectacle of one of Blair's allies flattering one of Africa's worst tyrants highlighted the perils of changing the continent and countries.

As Ghana's JJ Rawlings stepped down after 19 years in power, what was his contribution to Ghana and to Africa? Did he bring peace and prosperity to what was a chaotic and corrupt country? Or was he simply a ruthless military thug in civilian disguise keeping dissent at bay through fear, intimidation and murder? Ghanaians fell victim to the longest playing economic fizzle in Africa. Being the first independent African country the government had US$1 billion in reserves, a well educated bureaucracy, was the world's biggest cocoa producer and had productive gold mines. Nkruma and JJ Rawlings managed to pool these advantages, mixed in megalomania, naiveté, avarice and socialist rhetoric and engineered a classic model of how to collapse an African country.

As the international community tire more and more of Africa, investment would decrease even further and poverty, more wars, and more chaos would ruin the continent and Africa as a whole would move backward. Instability and conflict within one African country had a destabilising impact on its neighbours and an unsettling effect on potential investors. There would be AIDS-induced poverty and AIDS-induced famines with no progress at all, with the world looking on aghast and unbelieving that all the billions they poured into Africa came to nothing.

There are few signs of this enlightened 'new African leadership' that Western leaders speak of. The fact that more African countries were run by ostensibly elected governments instead of military dictatorships obscures just how structurally similar the new administrations remained to what went before. The elites that had adapted to the times, learning to play the democracy game with flair. Africa's lazy and corrupt ruling elites had just reinvented themselves but there's only one game they knew how to play very well. Former African Leaders interim chairman Joaqim Chissano on the scope of their operations: "Our activity has no limits, apart from our principles of not causing offence to the current leaderships."

The culture of criticising the leadership never really took root in Africa, since the culture of subservience is well entrenched in African culture. Criticising African leaders is considered "disrespectful". They thrive on fear, not respect. Leaders routinely use troops, police, personal militias and soldiers to terrorise citizens who criticise or challenge them.

"Emperor Bokassa" had school children killed for refusing to put on uniforms printed with his face. The psychopath, Idi Amin Dada, literally took matters into his own hands, while apartheid thug John Vorster had school children shot dead in June 1976 for refusing to learn Afrikaans. Jerry Rawlings once beat up one of his ministers, and Kenneth Kaunda once told an accredited professional journalist: "You're stupid! Sit down!" just for asking a question. Kamuzu Banda simply locked up his critics and threw away the key. A Nigerian president once called one of his ministers an idiot, while Mugabe said he had degrees in violence, and had already proved it on many occasions. Kenya's wrinkly first lady 2005 invaded the newsroom of The Nation newspaper, confiscating journalists' equipment, mouthed obscenities and slapped a photographer. This is just but a few of the examples of African rulers gone mad.

The South African media had failed dismally because inexperienced reporters could not properly analyse the nuances of any political situation. Trends such as the "juniorisation of newsrooms" due to political and commercial pressures had caused news bulletins to move away from serious political reporting. There was also a lack of mentorship, because editors were holding themselves accountable only to those who held the purse strings, mainly advertisers and politicians. The South African government outlawed statements sparking "public panic". Mbeki's ruling African National Congress (ANC) faced frequent charges of being intolerant of criticism especially from the media, whom Mbeki had accused of having a racist agenda.

African insanity and the continent of dictators

"Those who support the MDC must watch out because death will befall them," Mugabe 16/3/2000

"We will move door to door killing like we did Chiminya. I am the minister responsible for defence therefore I am capable of killing," Mahachi, Minister of defence, Zimbabwe 2/6/2000.

President Robert Mugabe, opening a crucial party congress (8/12/2000) urged black Zimbabweans to unite against whites. "Our party must continue to strike fear in the heart of the white men, our real enemy."

A dictator is an absolute ruler with no legal, constitutional, social or political considerations to restrict his latitude. Dictators exert their power without any regard to the moral or ethical consequences of their actions and they survive out of the fear that grips their people. Dictators often use armed force, propaganda, torture and arbitrary detention to enforce their will and usually suppress any opinion which runs counter to their own.

Traditional dictators seize control through force, while constitutional dictators hold office through voting fraud or severely restricted elections, and are frequently puppets and apologists for the military juntas that control the ballot boxes. In any case, none have been democratically elected by the majority of their people in fair and open elections.

Dictators usually grow rich, while their countries' economies deteriorate and the majority of their people live in poverty. Western tax dollars and US-backed loans made billionaires of some, while others were international drug dealers who also collected CIA and KGB pay cheques. Rarely are they called to account for their crimes. And rarely still, are Western governments held responsible for supporting and protecting some of the worst human rights violators in the world.

Some dictators also thrive on the political loneliness the West or East inflict and in some cases appear to seek more of it. The pariah treatment suited Bashar Assad, Kim Jong-il and Robert Mugabe just fine. Fidel Castro was another dictator who had flourished in isolation. Every time the USA considered lifting its embargo, Castro unleashed a provocation designed to ensure that the USA don't normalize relations.

Rape, electrocution, severe beatings on the body and the soles of the feet, forced nakedness, witnessing the torture of family members and friends and mock executions were all part of a long list of horrifying state-sanctioned acts with which huge numbers of Zimbabweans were all too familiar. 30,000 of the citizenry had been murdered in Matebeleland under operation Gukurahundi led by Mugabe, Perence Shiri, Enos Nkala and Emerson Mnangagwa.

Unsurprisingly, coups were the most common way of changing African national governments and civil wars spawned the worlds' largest refugee population. During the 80s alone, there were at least 98 attempted and/or successful military takeovers in sub-Saharan Africa, affecting 29 countries. Governments of Ghana and Benin had been toppled at least 5 times each with six coups in Nigeria. More than 200 Presidents for life had come and gone and the continent continued its downward spiral.

The big Man's face hangs on every wall, every office and clothing and ministers wore pins with his photo. Streets, stadiums, schools, dams were named after him and he insisted on being called names such as the teacher, The national miracle, the messiah, Doctor, conqueror, the wise, comrade etc. He appeared as headline news everyday of the year and he slept with daughters of powerful people in government, including his bodyguards (male or female didn't matter) as a subjugation ritual. He paralysed government policy by suddenly shuffling ministers and banned all political activities, emasculated courts and stifled academia. He packed government with his tribesmen, manipulated exchange controls to benefit himself but weakened foreign companies and he was the richest man in the country who went to church.

These are democratic America's undemocratic allies. South Africa's apartheid regime was quietly supported by the US government, despite a UN boycott and Congressional efforts to reduce investment there. Ronald Reagan significantly increased military expenditures in the country that imprisoned Nelson Mandela, massacred innocent school children and killed Steven Biko. But few Americans realized that Botha's total strategy against blacks had turned his nuclear armed nation into a ruthless aggressor that assassinated President Samora Machel, invaded Angola and used a nuclear device there and carried out state terrorism against its own indigenous majority black people.

When Portugal withdrew from its colonies in Mozambique and Angola, Botha, claiming he wanted to strengthen capitalism on the continent, financed the Mozambique National Resistance Army (MNR) against the country's popular government. The MNR (RENAMO) cut off the ears, noses, limbs of civilians and used civilians as human shields in combat. After killing their parents and raping young women in front of 10-year-old boys, they recruited these boys to fight. In 1989 P.W. Botha suffered a stroke, later resigned and died without ever being prosecuted for these crimes.

Earlier, Emperor Halie Selassie may have been a better king to the animals of Ethiopia than to its people. In 1973, during the height of a drought in which 200,000 Ethiopians died of starvation, Salassie fed beef to his Great Danes. As a young provincial governor, Selassie took 50% of his peasants' crops while other governors were taking 90%, and in the 1950s as many as 100 political prisoners were tortured in his jails at one time. Under his long rule, Ethiopia remained in the dark ages. Just after his overthrow in 1974, the annual per capita income was $90, the literacy rate was 7% and Ethiopia was the poorest nation in Africa and on earth. It was never colonised.

Under Selassie, Ethiopia received more US aid than any other African country and Washington purchased a $2 million yacht for the Emperor. When Selassie faced an uprising in the province of Eritrea, the US sent advisors and arms to help him smash the revolt. In return for that support, Selassie provided the United States with a naval oasis in the Red Sea and a place for a strategic communications station.

Selassie's kindness to his animals was his downfall; he was overthrown when photos of him feeding his dogs during the 1973 famine were circulated among his outraged troops. Mengistu Haile Mariam marked his arrival in power in Ethiopia in

26

1974 by sending the existing government to the firing squad. Halle Miriam Menghistu was hugely financed and armed by the Soviets.

Mengistu sought to right the wrongs made by his feudal predecessors but in the end he committed far greater wrongs than they did. At the height of his power, Mengistu himself frequently garrotted or shot dead opponents, saying that he was leading by example. Family members who went to morgues to collect bodies of loved ones were asked to pay for bullets that killed them. The Soviet Union poured $18 billion in military support into Ethiopia as President Mengistu built Africa's largest standing army. For months in 1984, Mengistu denied that famine was ravaging Ethiopia's north as he flew in planeloads of whisky to celebrate the anniversary of his revolution while Bob Gildorf sang himself horse to raise money for the starving. 2 million people starved to death.

By any standards Mengistu should have faced up to the consequences of his actions, but by evil chance the coward chose another mad dictator as his saviour. Mugabe arranged for Menghistu to become a consultant to the Central Intelligence Organisation (CIO), his dreaded secret intelligence police. No doubt the CIO could benefit from his wide experience in suppressing dissent and torturing opponents.

The Ethiopians were starving not because of Bob Geldof's Live Aid millions or the West and East lent them money and where demanding large repayments, but because their mad dictator had butchered at least 1.5million of them in imposing his Marxist dictatorship. Then he launched a series of external wars, with the help of Cuban tanks lent by his equally odious fellow dictator, Fidel Castro. And much of the food aid paid for by Live Aid ended up being stolen by Mengistu. Never mind, it made Geldof famous, even if it didn't help the Ethiopians.

Africa's bloodiest war was fought over a barren and inconsequential patch of wasteland separating Ethiopia and Eritrea between 1998 and 2000. Both nations are among the least and last 10 developed nation on earth but fought trench warfare, air and tank combat that left both economies in total tatters. It involved billions of dollars, over half a million combatants and over 200,000 field casualties and millions of refugees.

President Isaias Afwerki of Eritrea and President Meles Zenawi of Ethiopia were indeed brothers. They belonged to the same Tigrean ethnic group and Isaias and Meles were also Comrades-in-Arms as rebels fighting for the overthrow of Ethiopia's Marxist dictatorship. With the overthrow of Mengistu, Isaias Afwerki became the president of an independent Eritrea and Meles Zenawi assumed power in Addis Ababa. Relations were cordial until Eritrea started to behave like a real independent country by adopting policies such as introducing its own currency.

Eritrea, though a small country, had proven quite cantankerous. Since 1993, it had gone to war with Sudan, Yemen, Ethiopia and had also threatened its smaller neighbour, Djibouti. Both Ethiopia and Eritrea also found time to support rival rebel groups in Somalia. The war coincided with acute famine that threatened millions brought on by drought in both countries.

Still earlier, one Ian Douglas Smith promised the whites who elected him Prime Minister of Rhodesia in 1965 that he would keep Rhodesia white, at any cost. To stop the black guerrilla fighters trying to overthrow his regime, Smith rationed food spiced with birth control formulas for Africans whom he believed were feeding the guerrillas. This cruel measure only served to starve the already undernourished black population. Over 90% of Rhodesia's black children were malnourished and nutritional deficiencies were the major cause of infant death. Smith rounded up blacks into conscription camps he called "protective" villages. Believing that ignorant people were less likely to revolt, he cut funding for black education, spending $5 on each black child compared to $80 on each white child.

His all white Parliament passed a law protecting officials who took actions for the suppression of 'terrorism', enabling the police and military to commit atrocities. An international trade boycott against Rhodesia arose, but while the USA publicly condemned the government, it continued to do business there. In 1971, President Nixon lifted the chrome embargo against Rhodesia at a time when there was a surplus of chrome in the USA. The fact that this tired, humiliated, diseased and malnourished black population went on to briefly become successful after independence is more than a miracle.

In early 1970s Uganda, during the rule of Idi Amin, a practising Moslem who declared himself King of Scotland, animosities that were fundamentally tribal led to the wholesale slaughter of 250,000 people and sent millions into camps and thousands of Indians into exile, their properties and businesses confisticated and distributed to Amini's relatives.

Amin's willingness to obey orders had brought him a long way from the tiny hut of a bullying Kakwa tribesman of northern Uganda in 1928 to a blood thirst semi literate lieutenant in the Uganda army by 1960. His career took off more robustly after independence when he became deputy commander of the army under a drunkard called 'President' Milton Obote. Amin's first act was to flex his muscles, not against whites, but against fellow blacks; 150,000 Buganda died. On 25 January 1971, with the help of Britain, Amin staged a coup against Obote and within three months 10,000 people of the Acholi and Langi tribes had been slaughtered, including anyone whose name started with 'O', a common characteristic of Acholi names.

While pursuing this genocide, Amin's government was receiving funding and recognition from the UK and Israel amongst others. He was invited, dinned and danced with Prime Minister Edward Hearth and the Royals who took him on a tour of his favourite Scotland. On this trip he requested for, but was politely denied an order of Harrier Jet Fighters "...to bomb Sudan and Tanzania." Though, like Mugabe, he adored the British and aped their style, he took a special delight in tormenting England yet practised Juju.

Amin had a harem of wives and thirty children. When one of his wives, Kay, died aborting a bastard child, he ordered surgeons to cut her up and reassemble her with arms and legs swapped. He kept the heads of Jesse's (his other wife) former husband, that of Ruth Kobusinje (his girlfriend he suspected of infidelity), and six others in a freezer at his house. Why he did these things, no one knows but soon after visiting the British Queen, he suddenly switched sponsors and fell into the hands of a young and eccentric Qaddafi; he proclaimed, "I'm the greatest politician alive. I've shaken the British so much I deserve a degree in Philosophy". He killed so many that he's equalled only by Bokasa of CAR and Robert Mugabe of Zimbabwe. Amin was eventually crashed by the Tanzanians and fled first to Libya, were he had some unpleasant business with Qaddafi's fourteen-year-old daughter and was chased away to Saudi Arabia were he died in 2003.

After Amin, exiled Milton Obote returned after living comfortably in Zambia, slaughtered another 250,000 out of fervour Uganda and millions again went into camps. Even under 'three terms' Museveni, millions of Ugandans died or remained in camps as war ravaged northern Uganda and boys were still forced into the military to carry out atrocities unimaginable. Museveni, in power for over 20 years 2005, ensured Uganda more misery as he amended the constitution to allow him to rig yet more elections.

Africa's only self-styled emperor of Central African Republic (CAR), mentally retarded Jean Bedel Bokasa, had his memorable 48 hours with a coronation that cost US$20 million, faithfully replicating Napoleon Bonaparte's coronation yet spent weeks watching queen Elizabeth's coronation on TV, practising her royal wave. During the coronation itself, 2,500 invited foreign guests unknowingly dinned on human flesh and danced the night away.

An established alcoholic, Bokasa decreed that all school children wear French school uniforms printed with his head and manufactured by his wife. When general unrest spread due to this decree, the army was sent in, 100 kids were rounded up, taken to Ngarabo prison were they were raped, beaten then killed in front of the emperor himself. The killings spread and tens of thousands died some ending up on Bokasa's dinner table.

The only state leader ever to be tried and convicted of cannibalism escaped initially to Libya (the rest home for people nobody wants) in 1979 while the French carried out a coup, dragged one David Decko out of bed in Paris and still half asleep, thrust him into Bokasa's palace where he continued his snooze. Bokasa eventually ended up in France, broke with no water, telephone or electricity and his three children arrested for shoplifting, he headed back to Bangui prison. He had 50 children and died of a heart attack in November 1996.

Time moved on and by year 2000 Africa was the devil's bandit country; Ivory Coast, once wealthy and stable, metamorphosed into perilous space. Guei, who had rigged an election but went on to lose, dissolved the election commission and declared himself president. Thousands took to the street and Guei relented only for Gbagbo, who had won the election, to declare Himself president; got challenged by one Outtara, but supported by France, Gbagbo refused to hold new elections setting off mayhem between Moslems and Gbagbo's Christian supporters who rampaged through the street with catastrophic and deadly results as thousands died. In the process Gbagbo attacked French "peace keepers" who retaliated by destroying Ivory Coast's entire air force.

By 2000 Sierra Leone was the worst place on earth. It all started in 1990 when a band of desperados led by Sankor entered the country from Liberia, armed and financed by the cocaine addict 'president' Charles Taylor. By 1994 they controlled the diamond trade there, burnt villages turning a million people into refugees. Sankor's brutality is legendary. Then Kabbah took control reaching a short-lived accord with Sankor to jointly rule the country. At that point Koromah overthrew both and the country once again collapsed into civil war, drawing in the Nigerians via ECOMOG. Koromah was neutralised and Kabbah reinstalled but then the RUF swarmed Freetown murdering all in sight. Besides the human toll, the crisis was an economic and social calamity. All indicators were negative up to 2008. The USA national interests lay somewhere else and did not do enough to assist Sierra Leone. Sierra Leone, Liberia and Rwanda cases were total madness and a shame to Africans.

One of the most appalling Big Man of Africa was Samuel K. Doe of Liberia (he insisted on being called Doctor) called "that fool" by another fool called Jerry Rawlings of Ghana. Doe, the youngest and lowest-ranking soldier to seize power, had nothing to compromise and broke all records on secret execution, public cannibalism (he believed eating bits of a warrior's body would make him stronger), rigged elections, minting 'Doe dollars', a habit enthusiastically picked up by Idi Amin and Robert Mugabe. After coming to power American aid to Doe totalled US$500 million mainly to buy protection for their investment in Liberia.

What they actually bought was Doe's legitimacy, weapons to coerce loyalty, his promises of going back to the barracks, which he never did, and a poisonous level of tribal hatred that eventually blew up killing millions. Doe's Krahn tribe took part in killings, torture, public mutilation, rapes, and floggings yet Liberia is the closest America came to establishing a colony in Africa.

When Doe realised that he was under age to stand in the elections, he changed his birth certificate and went on to declare himself the winner of American sponsored elections, which he had lost. Every year or two Doe staged a phoney coup that justified killing his opponents. Later America did nothing to help Liberia where the Mandinga and Krahn tribes were raped and slaughtered for being perceived to be Doe's supporters.

Military dictators for most of its independent life have ruled Nigeria, the colossus of African politics and cultures and the biggest West African economy. Africanism revolves around Nigeria. Infect the whole Africa seems to revolve around Nigeria. Nigeria contributed nearly 4% of the USA's energy to increase to 10% by 2010. If Africa is going anywhere, Nigeria was likely to get there first just because of its size and wealth. It is the most populous Black Country in Africa (the most populous black country is not in Africa) though no reliable census has been taken since 1960 due to religious differences.

Nigeria was not a banana republic; it was the world's ninth largest oil producer and has 3 million university-trained graduates. Nigeria is dirty, noisy, dishonest and vulgar but Nigerians do not tolerate Big Man rule. They talk loud about how important they are and drive just as fast yet Big Man are ridiculed, overthrown and worse murdered. For most of its independent life, Nigeria had been ruled by civilians for less than 15 years as they refused to be subjugated to tyranny. It is no fluke that half the books and half the journalist on the continent are Nigerian.

Nigeria had a bruising civil war 1967 to 1970 and after that, had an avalanche of money; US$100 billion in ten years to be précis, yet after the oil boom, Nigeria was US$20 billion in debt, a spoilt population addicted to luxury, huge crime ridden cities and farmers who had forgotten how to farm. In the late 1970s 15% of the world's merchant ships were waiting to off-load at Nigerian ports and the country was the biggest importer of Champagne, golden bathtubs and Rolls Royce cars. Yet it was Nigerians who set fire to government buildings that contained records linking them to corruption. But the importance of this legacy is not what it bought but what it taught. The squandering of Africa's biggest fortune sobered Nigeria leaders to the folly of too much government.

After countless coups and counter coups, with all the trauma Nigeria had had up to then, nothing had prepared them for what happened next; for the most ruthless and vicious despot encountered thus far had emerged. Abacha was a Muslim of Kanuri extraction. As a young man, he was trained at various Nigerian and British military colleges. In 1993, general Sani Abasha ousted the interim civilian governments and proceeded to virtually destroyed the country along with its oil-rich economy.

Comparable only to Idi Amin, Jean-Bedel Bokassa, Mobuto Sese Seko and Mugabe, Abasha ran Nigeria not so much as a country but a personal business, siphoning out billions of US dollars into overseas bank accounts, while millions of Nigerian fled abroad. Newspapers were closed down, poverty deepened, trade unions were banned while intellectuals, activists, journalists and opponents, real or imagined were jailed or eliminated. Ken Soro-wiwa, a courageous activist, writer and television personality of the Ogoni people was hanged for demanding financial compensation for the poverty and environmental devastation inflicted on the region by imperial companies BPShell, ELF and Agip. Abacha eventually died of a Viagra overdosed, 1998, while in the company of two Indian prostitutes.

The Democratic Republic of Congo (all 'democratic' African countries are democratic in name only), potentially and arguably the richest place on earth in per square kilometre terms degenerated into chaos soon after independence and has yo-yoed between peace and war. In modern day DRC is enveloped in the ethos of the African dictator who reinvented the Congo and made up predatory rules by which it is still ruled.

Joseph, Desire Mobuto transformed himself into Mobuto sese Seko (meaning the all-powerful warrior who will go from conquest to conquest leaving fire in his wake) a.k.a. The guide, father of the nation, the helmsman, the messiah and whose mother was compared to the Virgin Mary and local TV showed him descending from the clouds like a god. Under Mobuto, Zaire did not build a single hospital. In the ones that still remained from colonial rule, nurses and doctors had to be bribed to do their work

Mobuto was fabulously rich with approximately US$5 billion stolen from the people and neatly starched away in Switzerland; had 11 palaces, renamed everything in the Congo (Zaire is actually a Portuguese mispronunciation of the ancient Kikongo language "nzere" meaning the river that swallows all rivers) and had an assortment of fancy houses in Europe and the USA and built himself a small city in his birth village called Gbadolite.

Mobuto was born on 14 October 1930 and grew up poor and was booted out of school at 19 for 'proclivity, delinquency and burglary'. He was sentenced to 6 months in prison and 7 years in the army, which proved to be less of punishment to him. He quickly rose to sergeant major while making some useful connections with "good" French and CIA members and remained so with Ronald Reagan calling him "a voice of good sense and good will". He was rewarded by the West for being less crooked with US$600 million 1983-87 and received 6 years grace on debts.

Sese Seko proved he had more staying power than any other African tin pot dictator and made sure he would never be poor again. He used his vast wealth in keeping himself powerful while keeping his tribally fractious nation peaceful. This is until it all exploded in 1996 when, with massive support from Rwanda and Uganda, playboy and illiterate Leurette Kabila's army marched on Kinshasa as dying Mobutu fled to Morocco in 1998.

President Yoweri Museveni of Uganda and President Paul Kagame of Rwanda were the best of friends and Comrades-in Arms. When Museveni was a rebel in the Ugandan bush fighting for the overthrow of Milton Obote, he employed Kagame, a Rwandan waTutsi exile living in Uganda as his Chief of Staff. Once in power, and no longer a rebel, President Museveni returned the favour; General Paul Kagame became the life President of Rwanda and Rwanda became the only other African country ruled by alien minorities. The other was South Africa.

But, Kagame and his minority waTutsi government in Kigali had a problem. The waHutus whom he overthrew had fled to Zaire and they posed infinite danger to him. In fact Mobutu kept the body of the late Rwandan waHutu President (whom Kagame forces had shot down), in a fridge in one of his estates in Zaire for future burial in Rwanda. Thus, Kagame and Museveni again united to support the illiterate Laurent Kabila who eventually caused Mobutu to flee to Morocco. Once in power, Kabila did not prove amenable to the interests of either Museveni or Kagame. Kagame and Museveni clashed over the spoils of the huge Congo natural resources.

At this juncture all hell broke loose as madmen of Zimbabwe, Angola, Burundi, Namibia, CAR, Uganda, Chad plus a dozen other rebel forces of all sorts and ideologies all entered into what became known as Africa's First World War. Hundreds of 1000s died as millions marched through the inpenetratable jungle, running away from the advancing and retreating armies, ravaged by disease, famine and bullets. Entire brigades disappeared and billions worth of military machinery wasted and renewed, more than 90% of the 85,000-mile road network the country inherited from Belgium turned into bush. The Congolese, ever the bourgeois, fly.

The next potentially richest place on earth is next-door Angola ruled by a quiet Portuguese-African; a sly old fox called Mr Jose dos Santos. It was only in 2002 that a peace agreement ended 27 years of a brutal civil war that left millions dead or maimed. However, the track record of the ruling MPLA, led by dos Santos, was much longer than that. President dos Santos had been in power longer than Zimbabwe's Mugabe and as the later despot, did not seem to be going anywhere.

Angola's diamond industry was in the gift of the president. The biggest cellular company was a Presidential family concern, as were some of the largest banks. The Angolian economy's most significant feature was the lack of an effective banking system. This was a dollarised, cash economy much like Nigeria's. There were no credit cards and State control was strong.

With 2-million barrels of oil produced a day this placed Angola on a par with Kuwait and potentially Africa's greatest hope. Reserves were huge and the country was the largest supplier of crude oil to China and had also become the seventh-largest oil supplier to the US, which explained the renewed CIA interest. It was no surprise then that China and Europe were throwing money at Angola, building infrastructure and providing export-import bank financing to the tune of $14bn. In addition to oil, Angola has large reserves of gas and other precious minerals. The population is about 13-million, most crammed into Luanda to escape the 70s and 80s civil war. Two-thirds of the people lived below the dollar-a-day poverty line. Top-down corruption was rife with over 2 billion dollars unaccounted for every year. Though life remained hard for most Angolans, the economy as a whole was buoyant with 95% of the wealth in 5% of the population's corrupt hands. This $40bn economy enjoyed 24% growth by 2007.

Further north, Sudan was Africa's biggest and longest-festering open wound. National government barely existed outside Khartoum the capital. Even there it afflicted rather than govern, where starving people were so desperate that they sold their children into slavery and government authorities refused to let Western relief agencies operate unless they paid fat bribes. Even then, aid convoys were often attacked and pillaged by government soldiers who then sold relief supplies for their own profit.

The economy, before the Chinese came for oil was literally camel meat, sesame seeds and gum Arabic. The country uses sharia Islamic law, which in itself is not bad, but in Sudan it allowed crucifixion as a punishment. The complexity of Sudan's problems is only rivalled by its size; it's the largest African country with the largest inaccessible swamp and the rest is desert. The desert inhabitants are Dinka tribes who rely solely on cattle blood, milk and cheese, dung (as plaster, insecticide, tooth paste and fuel), urine to tan leather. They rarely kill cows. However this peace and tranquillity the Dinka had known came to an abrupt end when the Turco-Egyptions invaded from the north and brought in slavery and eventually ruled Sudan after independence.

The southern tribes fought bravely with spears but more often fought among themselves and only the British intervention brought peace after 15 years of hard work and the banning of slavery. However the British policy was to seal off the Dinka and isolate them from the Islamic north making it a closed district in the 1920s. Marriage or trade was banned between the northern and southern districts and southerners were not allowed to wear djellabas. The British purposely kept the districts ignorant of each other and drew up a constitution for independence without consulting southerners who up to today accuse the Northern rulers of racism.

The result was one of Africa's longest and bloodiest war with over 3 million Sudanese going into exile. Nimeri, one time hero of the southern district tribes suddenly swerved and introduced nationwide Islamic law, banning beer, which the Dinka feel is their human right. John Garang, a Dinka, assembled dinka deserters in Ethiopia and proclaimed themselves the Sudanese People's Liberation Army (exclusively Dinka). Today the desert and the swamps are literally littered with unburied human skeletons killed in the war and unmarked mass graves victims of northern soldiers atrocities. Garang's army attacked and stopped oil drilling in the south and shot down a civilian plane killing all 60 passengers onboard and called the North extremist. The north called Garang a terrorist and after making Garang co-vice president of Sudan, the northerners shot down his helicopter, killing him barely days on the job.

Another winner in the moral sweepstakes was the small Republic of Congo (not DRC), run by a man who militarily overthrew an elected government in 1997. The African Union once vowed to shun anyone who took power militarily. Yet, 2006 the continent's supreme political body chose thug Denis Sassou-Nguesso as its chairman. The world was also kind to Sassou-Nguesso, writing off $2.9bn of Congolese debt. To his credit, the nefarious World Bank president, Paul Wolfowitz, tried to block this measure on learning that Sassou-Nguesso had chalked up an US$81,000 bill at a New York brothel. He was overruled.

In tiny Gambia, the President was a self-proclaimed medicine man publicly specialising in managing HIV/Aids complications using the Koran, banana leaves and herbs. He administered it himself promoting unscientific treatment that could have dangerous results.

Ethiopian fugitive, Mengistu Haile Mariam, was on an indefinite state-sponsored, uninterrupted tour of Zimbabwe; Milton Obote had seen successive governments come and go in Zambia; war criminal Charles Taylor was on trial; and diminutive Jean Bertrand Aristide was president without a country in South Africa. Privileged senile Rhodesian Ian Douglas Smith badmouthed a leader who never had the same privileges under his UDI regime; PW Botha's lot quietly lived on in South Africa as though they didn't do anything wrong. Slobodan Milosevic and Saddam Hussein must have cursed themselves for not having been leaders in Africa.

It can be more accurate to say the end of the cold war had permitted the world to be more aware of the significance of ethnic conflict as the end of ideological war unveiled conflicts that were basically ethnic. Further, the cold war had mixed effects on African states as they intervened and counter-intervened in their competitive involvements and arms sales led to protracted wars. Hence the end of the cold war made it possible to end some of these wars e.g. Angola. But in some cases it also provided for an opportunity for the suppressed populations to surface into violent conflicts e.g. DRC.

The sources of Africa's problems are varied, as they are complex. Kenya for example has at least 41 tribes with the Kikuyu (5 Million) being historically the most powerful and favoured. The second largest and historically frustrated are the Luo (3 Million) and these two tribes have many reasons, ancient and contemporary, to hate each other. Kikuyu are Bantu agriculturalist and the Lou Bantu pastoralists migrated from up north. The Kikuyu circumcise and the Luo find this barbaric; the Luo remove the lower teeth and the Kikuyu find it disgusting (Tetanus or lockjaw is common in Africa and in case of infection a toothless gap large enough to pour milk can keep a Luo or Dinka alive). The fundamental responsibility of a Luo clan is to bury its dead and they see the Kikuyu as denatured, money-hungry good-for-nothing so-and-sos aping Western values.

To Luo, Kikuyu and come to think of it, most of Africa, women are there to cook, bear children, fetch water, gather firewood, wail for the dead and keep their noses out of men's affairs and the women believe it too. It legitimises their existence (infertile women are pitied). What differs is the extend to which these norms are enforced but then hundreds of millions of Africans are born and raised in tradition governed villages before they escape to the cities or overseas.

When Europeans drew up colonial boarders in Berlin in 1884 these two, the Kikuyu and Luo, became reluctant countrymen with the Kikuyu monopolising political and economic power and to entrench themselves they had to be corrupt and ruthless.

In the 50s a Mau Mau uprising started in the Kikuyu highlands. These highlands are among the most suitable land in Africa for Europeans to steal; were the days are warm, the nights cool and there are no mosquitoes. The insurrection was reported as a murderous spree against white people but after 6 years of violence the death toll was 32 European civilians, 53 European soldiers and over 12,000 Mau Mau combatants and civilians killed. In the end the war led to Kenya's independence. But the Mau Mau are up to today regarded as blood thirst marauding terrorists who butchered whites because they were white.

So why is it that, African tyrants tend to seem more powerful and entrenched at the point when their political record is at its worst? When an economy collapses or is in crisis, the few parts of it that are still working are almost always in the hands of regime officials and supporters. The opposition supporters have nothing, and therefore they can't fund anti-government politics. The opposition needs an economy that is doing well to thrive. The only problem with that is there may not be enough anger to cause enough people to kick the government out at elections. And by the time matters are bad enough and there is sufficient anger, there is no economic infrastructure to support rivals.

In situations where people have nothing, the ground is fertile for armed rebellion. Therefore, if people don't take up arms or resort to drawn-out street action (as in Kenya during Daniel arap Moi's rule), then the strongman will survive. Militant action brings results partly because there is a limit to how long hungry soldiers can dig in against rebels.

There is a view that people who have endured the long and painful history of slavery, which then gave way to colonialism, have a strong tendency toward self-preservation. For that reason, of all the people in the world, the African is the least likely to be a suicide bomber. An offshoot of this is that many Africans cannot easily be persuaded to put their necks on the line and die in the process. Hence the ruling elites have it easy.

Corruption and men of dishonour.

Consider this: Sub-Saharan Africa has received an estimated $114 billion in bilateral and multilateral aid from 1995-2008. Yet African countries have consistently ended up at the bottom of the United Nations Development Program's Human Development report, which measures life expectancy, gross domestic product per person, and literacy. So you may ask the billion-dollar question: Where did the money go?

In Malawi a gleaming new building in Blantyre, symbolises just the kind of tangle that makes many aid experts wince at the doubling to £37 billion of the global aid budget to Africa. 2006 China pledge even more aid and debt forgiveness, to the applause of the ruling elites as, "...Christmas is here at last". The hotel belongs to Friday Jumbe, Malawi's former finance minister and a close associate of Bakili Muluzi, who retired as president of Malawi May 2004.

Three years before that, Jumbe was the boss of the state Agricultural Development Marketing Corporation. He sold all Malawi's grain reserves just before a drought. Jumbe was subsequently arrested, as he was about to fly to South Africa with a bagful of loot and charged with having pocketed £2.1m; £420,000 of which had allegedly been used to build the hotel. Jumbe had failed to come up with any explanation as to how he came by the money.

In Angola, the IMF remained at loggerheads with the government over the disappearance of £2.2bn in oil revenues in a country where 90 per cent of the 14 million people live in abject poverty. According to the African Union's own estimates, corruption is costing Africa at least US$150bn annually.

In broad terms, political corruption is the misuse of public office for private gain. Political corruption encompasses abuses by government officials such as embezzlement and nepotism, as well as abuses linking public and private actors such as bribery, extortion, influence peddling and fraud and can be petty or grand, organized or unorganised. All forms of government are susceptible in practice to political corruption.

There are two types of corruption, grand and petty. Grand corruption occurs when heads of state and/ or their political entourage abuse and misuse their position for personal gain. Petty corruption, on the other hand, relates to payments solicited by low-level officials with the objective of fast-tracking decisions thereby flouting administrative and bureaucratic procedures and regulations. This type of corruption adversely affects the poor and the weak to the extent that they pay for services they are entitled to anyway.

As corruption discourages investment and the growth of the economy, its eradication is crucial in developing an enterprise culture and democratic societies. More importantly corruption undermines the smooth functioning of markets in three ways: as a tax, as a barrier to entry and by subverting the legitimacy of the state and its ability to build institutions that improve the productive efficiency of the economy. As a tax, corruption distorts the choice between activities and lowers returns to public and private investments. As an entry barrier, corruption discourages new entrants to an economy and hence it damages its growth and development prospects.

The end-point of political corruption is kleptocracy, literally rule by thieves, as in Zimbabwe and the DRC.

Professionals from many fields often enable corrupt transactions. Corrupt intermediaries link givers and takers, creating an atmosphere of mutual trust and reciprocity; they attempt to provide a legal appearance to corrupt transactions, producing legally enforceable contracts and they help to ensure that scapegoats are blamed in case of detection.

Corruption has a direct and causal relationship with centralization of power and despotism. Corruption in elections and in legislative bodies reduces accountability and representation in policy making; corruption in the judiciary suspends the rule of law; and corruption in public administration results in the unequal provision of services. More generally, corruption erodes the institutional capacity of government as procedures are disregarded and officials are hired or promoted without regard to performance.

Since it is a nefarious secretive activity that in its most direct form occurs between two consenting parties, corruption is therefore often wrongly referred to as a "victimless crime". In many ways, policy makers concerned with fighting corruption are fumbling in the dark as they devise policy in an almost near vacuum of information about the nature and extent of the problem. In the absence of other credible attempts at measuring corruption, educated guesses and perceptions of the extent of corruption are nevertheless important as demonstrated by the annual Transparency International Corruption Perception Index, which ranks countries according to perceptions of businesspeople engaging with such countries.

It is important to underscore that while the developed countries have traditionally seen national governance and corruption as particularly daunting in poorer countries with rich countries generally viewed as exemplary, the reality is more complex. Even rich countries are corrupt and yet emphasis on narrow legalisms often subtly obscures manifestations of mis-governance that afflict rich countries as well.

Because corruption in Africa is actively entrenched at the top and not reported on, it easily filters to the shop floor. African leaders and their cronies faced three alternatives when nearing the end of their term; namely relative poverty, term extension or corruption. By the African Union's own admission, it is widely accepted that no business ever gets done in Africa without a present changing hands, from a bottle of Vodka slipped under the desk to facilitate a traveller's speedier entry through customs to the bigger "cuts" made to state officials by conniving Western multi-nationals in exchange for lucrative state tenders.

Self-serving declarations by Africa's post-colonial political elites to fight corruption have not been backed by any action exemplified by Zimbabwe's Gedeon Gono and Dydmus Mutasa's rhetorics. Kenya's chief anti-corruption official, John Githongo, resigned because of lack of political backing in his anti-corruption effort. Nuhu Ribadu, the head of Nigeria's anti-corruption watchdog, expressed his determination to stamp out corruption in Africa's most corrupt country. He told reporters he would even bar the former military ruler, Ibrahim Babangida, from his bid to succeed Obasanjo because the former allegedly salted away billions while in power. Ribadu was summoned by Obasanjo, a close friend of Babangida, and ordered to apologise for his remarks, which had received wide media publicity.

Why are Europeans not a problem to themselves to the same degree that the African is a problem to himself? Is this born from a black genetic coding and black culture that is simply inferior to say the genetics and culture of whites? Is it the case that Africans were naturally given to corruption? Why is it that an ordinary Swede could not countenance being corrupt, yet it seems to come so easily to Africans? It couldn't be that corruption could be accounted for by poverty or the specific circumstances on the continent because even Africans who had good jobs and rich say in Europe were corrupt. Is the problem born from less ethics and morality in the African culture relative to others, resulting in a higher occurrence of corruption in Africans? Is it that African culture, ethics, morals, though natural to Africans, are seen as corrupt by other people?

Some Europeans had even put forward the proposition that the problem with African leaders was that their views of power and politics "often have more to do with consumption than with transformation". To some Europeans, African power is inseparably associated with metaphors of "food" and "eating". Some of this could be laughably biased; until you look at examples of recent African excesses: Mobutu Sese Seko, Idi Amin, Jeano Bedel Bokassa, Macias Nguema and others.

African scholars are right to respond to this scandalous portrayal of African leadership with a massive "Oh, yeah? What about Attila the Hun, Hitler, Mussolini, Stalin, Nicolae Caecescu and Slobodan Milosevic?" In other words, despotic or corrupt rule is not peculiar to Africa. Yet the one continent that can ill-afford such luxuries as unbridled corruption is Africa, because it is way behind the other continents and will not catch up with them if it persists in squandering opportunities to improve its delivery of service to the people.

The Danish government was spending a lot of money to "help fight corruption" in Uganda as a large portion of the costs of running the office of the anti-corruption were met by the Danish government. The Danish Minister of Taxes, Mr Koch, spoke of blacklisting African countries "with a tradition of corruption", yet was unable to name a single country with a tradition of corruption. Could Koch's failure to name a corrupt country be construed as fraud and hence corruption?

Africans are economically passive and certainly we cannot blame the West by claiming corruption is a legacy of colonialism. Because if we are saying African corruption is not really African then in the same vain Colombian drug trade isn't entirely Colombian and American imperialism isn't entirely American.

When it comes to the wholesale theft of national resources and the subversion of the rule of law and democracy, African leaders are in a league all by themselves. They have become adept at manipulating the media and foreign governments and the multinational agencies such as the World Bank and the UN. To this long list perhaps should add the G8 leadership and the boring singer Bob Geldof. African leaders are allowed to strut across the platforms of the world stage as if they were acting in the real interests of their people and not acting simply as self-serving tyrants.

In truth, the people of African nations are mostly ignorant about what their government is doing behind the scenes. This ignorance born from the inability to bare witness makes the masses dependent upon others to tell them what the government is doing. How many Africans bare witness to the Swiss Bank accounts of their leaders, to know that they are corrupt? Usually it is Western nations who make the claims of corruption, and when confronted, as Mugabe did, to reveal these accounts, usually "..none are found".

Quite frankly until African leaders themselves put their own houses in order there should be no talk of international Government-to-Government assistance of any kind. Some donors have taken a hard line against corruption, such as DANIDA (Danish International Development Agency), which cut off aid to Malawi and Kenya as a consequence of blatant corruption. It is ridiculous that Ethiopia with its rich agricultural resources has been supported by massive food aid for all its life and is still in a mess. Just take a look at Nigeria and Cameroon; oil giants of the world yet threatened with instability and rising poverty that belies their wealth and status.

Nigerian President, Olusegun Obasanjo, then accused European countries of "sitting" on much of the stolen money stashed in European banks and in this case demanded Abasha's loot back. There was little action from Europe. European countries and banks providing a safe haven for stolen African money had to share the guilt. Obasanjo said Africa needed a watertight international convention to allow money hidden in foreign bank accounts to be repatriated. Obasanjo had been forced into a deal with the family of his late predecessor, Sani Abacha. The family handed over $2bn looted from Nigeria but retained $100m. Of the $2bn only $26 million found its way to Nigeria. European banks had insisted on proof the money was stolen, although the Abachas had no business that had a $2bn profit after tax.

Swiss banks had co-operated in investigations into the assets held abroad by the late Congolese strongman Mobutu Sese Seko and fallen Mali dictator Moussa Traore. Over 20 years, Switzerland alone had returned nearly US$1,3 billion in loot! Though this was a welcome development it was just a tiny fraction of loot they where holding, and handing back to new crooks.

"Yes, we can fight poverty, but poverty will always be with us. Not even Jesus Christ could end poverty," said one African dictator. But then nowhere in the Bible is it stated that Christ's mission was to end poverty. The time for the blame game is over: African corruption is as much a barrier to trade as rich-nation subsidies. Simply getting a truckload of goods from Ghana to Nigeria requires paying "exorbitant" bribes. Abdoulaye Wade, Senegal's president, called corruption the lack of qualified managers and the reluctance of African leaders to criticize each other the major obstacles to the continent's success. We "...accuse our partners but we are the ones wrong," he said and more and more Africans believed he was right.

The theme in all of the African leader's life is that a career in politics is the quickest road to wealth; all were poor when they got the top job, all were filthy rich within 2 years in office. To want to be wealthy is not necessarily wrong, but the tendency for politicians to become numb to the poverty and suffering around them seems to be part of the package. Most African countries are largely Christian nationalist Socialist/Marxist in their outlook; they do not encourage business or proper investment and the leaders are corrupt control freaks and murderous thugs.

Socialism was introduced by the white priests who accompanied the initial white adventurers. Socialism destroys personal initiative, it kills business, and it stifles and holds back those individuals who would do great things for society. It kills off business ideas and entrepreneurs who could bring many benefits and employment and this plays a big role in countries ending up on the rubbish heap.

The African extended family cuts into the hearts and pockets of every African. It operates on a smaller and more intimate stage populated by blood relatives and close 'friends'. The extended family is like a day-care, social security and welfare system all lumped into one. It feeds the lazy, unemployed and gives refuge to the old, infirm, disabled and sick by re-distributing resources between the haves and have-nots and does not follow the free market concepts or rule of law. Blood ties, tradition and guilt govern it. This system is the glue that holds the poor continent together, economically and politically although Africans accept both traditional and modern values without making strong moral commitments to either.

The extended family has undermined the importance of doing the job in relation to doing it and it hobbles the careers and limits the achievements of individual Africans. Jealousy relatives often harm each other, gossip, curses and witchcraft are aimed at successful relatives. Relatives demand a share of and influence over a spending relative's income. In these circumstances it is impossible to distinguish between one's own property and that socially owned. This thwarts the individual's initiative and creativity and interference with efficiency and creates corruption at lower levels.

In this flow, he who holds the slightest cover of public authority uses it illegally to acquire money, goods, prestige or to avoid obligations. The right to be recognised by a public servant for anything is all subject to a tax, which, though invisible, is known and expected by all. Sese Seko created this Kleptomaniac state, which henceforth was copied and implemented in every African state; a state not held accountable to voters, to legislature or to courts of law. Mobuto did not make any enemies that could threaten him nor was he repressive; his power was based on palaver, compromise and buying off potential problems.

Mali's Moussa Traore's personal fortune in Swiss Banks was equivalent to Mali's external debt. When he was forced out of office by the people of Mali, he ordered the army to fire on peaceful demonstrators, thus slaughtering hundreds of innocent people. This seems to have appealed to Mugabe, who 2007 ordered his police to shot to kill any demonstrators.

And this heartlessness starts with seemingly innocent comments. Julius "Mwalimu" Nyerere, had some of Africa's rulers in mind when he likened running an African government to riding a famished tiger: "You have to hold fast and remain on its back otherwise the moment you let loose and fall off, it will devour you." Mwalimu, himself an icon of simplicity, retired to his rural home in Butiama village on realising that his socialist Ujama experiment had dismally failed to uplift the poor peasants from crushing poverty.

Mobutu Sese Seko left a legacy of three palaces, the largest of them a three-story marble-clad building. At Kawele, outside Gbadolite town, he built two palaces within a walled compound. One, which gave Mugabe ideas, is a village of Chinese pagodas, with tall roofs of jade and orange glazed tile that surround ponds. It was built by the Chinese and used primarily as a residence for Mobutu's family and guests.

Gbadolite is a town in northern Equator province of the Democratic Republic of the Congo. It was the ancestral home of Mobutu Sese Seko. Mobutu ensured that the people of Gbadolite enjoyed many of the spoils the rest of the country didn't have, such as reliable electricity, water and roads. Mobutu built Gbodolite into a luxurious town often nicknamed "Versailles in the Jungle". He built a hydroelectric dam on the nearby Ubangi River, an international airport that could accommodate the Concorde, which he often hired. As a result, the people of the town had no trouble finding jobs, often as servants.

Mugabe's cheaper copy was a Chinese palace that cost at least US$5 million to build. The sprawling residence had 25 bedrooms with bathrooms and spas offering more than three acres of accommodation, mostly on three floors, including two-storey reception rooms and an office suite. The Chinese-style roof is clad with midnight blue glazed tiles from Shanghai. Arab craftsmen decorated ceilings. Set on 44 acres of heavily wooded land, the property is made up of three separate title deeds. Instead of the proverbial "love thy neighbour" policy, Mugabe gave notice to homeowners around his mansion that their properties now fell under a designated security area and would be confiscated by the state. Mugabe had several such homes all over the country including a thatched eight-bedroom mansion in his rural hometown of Zvimba, another in Mazvikadei, Mutare and in South Africa and Namibia. Zimbabwe's taxpayers picked up the tab for building and protecting the properties.

The former cannibal Emperor of the Central African Republic (CAR), Jean Bedel Bokassa, had a huge fortune and invested in castles in France. Bokassa was a close friend of the former French President, Giscard d'Estaing. The former French President supplied the Central African Republic with much financial and military backing. In exchange, Bokassa frequently took d'Estaing on hunting trips in Africa, and supplied France with Uranium, a mineral vital for France's nuclear weapons program. Also billions of Francs that were stolen from the Central African Republic were lost to the benefit of fat creditors of the Western world.

Bokassa is an interesting historical figure for he symbolizes perhaps more than any other puppet in world history, the extent to which colonial powers were in a position to empower useless, uneducated and perhaps even mentally retarded Africans to maintain their domination. When the former French President, General Charles de Gaulle died on the 9th of November 1970, Jean Bedel Bokassa was seen on French television crying uncontrollably for his deceased master.

The French oil giant Elf Aquitaine were in the habit of paying commissions to leaders of African countries where it did business, the company's former president testified. Loik Le Floch-Prigent said the money was funnelled through intermediaries to the leaders of Gabon, Cameroon, Congo and Angola. Le Floch-Prigent was one of 37 former top officials on trial for allegations that Elf, once France's largest company, paid and received enormous commissions and used inflated bills and other devices to enrich a chosen few. He was Elf's president from 1989 to 1993, during which the state-run company allegedly misused more than $145 million in public funds.

How could Omar Bongo, president of Gabon support an electioneering campaign in France when people don't have food to eat in his own country, when there is only one road in Gabon and 80% don't have electricity? Omar Bongo, who had been in power for four decades, was popular for his love of the high life. He had a reputation of flying French call girls from Paris, to lavish parties that he frequently hosted at his palace in the Gabonese capital, Libreville.

Even the late former Senegalese president, Leopold Sedar Senghor, who was credited as a democrat and an intellectual with clean hands, used public funds for his personal comfort and to fund members of the ruling party and a host of political clients. He imposed a one-party regime and violently crushed several student protest movements.

The late President Felix Houphouet Boigny of Ivory Coast was a confident major sponsor of Jacques Chirac's maiden campaign in which he lost to Francois Mitterrand, whilst many Ivorians were and still are hungry. Houphouët-Boigny moved the country's capital from Abidjan to his hometown of Yamoussoukro, and built Africa's largest church there, the Basilica of Our Lady of Peace of Yamoussoukro at a cost of $300 million. He also built a presidential palace at great cost. In 1989, UNESCO created the Félix Houphouët-Boigny Peace Prize for the 'safeguarding, maintaining and seeking of peace'. He is believed to have diverted significant government funds for his personal use and for patronage.

South Africa's corruption scaled dizzy heights when Mandela left office while the African National Congress inner circle was sometimes called the Xhosa Nostra took over the reigns of power. Jacob Zuma, South Africa's deputy president was 2005 implicated in a long-running corruption trial. The judge found "convincing and overwhelming evidence of a corrupt relationship" between some convicted businessmen and Mr Zuma arising from the bribes paid by a French company bidding for a large defence contract. The fact that this trial could proceed was an encouraging sign that judicial independence was alive in South Africa albeit it made Mbeki very unpopular within the part of the ANC that is corrupt and African 'political correctness' trends.

South Africa's former Director of Public Prosecutions, Bulelani Ngcuka, was subjected to vicious character assassination and was forced to resign for initiating the probe into the financial scandal and influence peddling. Zuma, who admitted in court to having unprotected sex with a friend's HIV positive daughter, was eventually indicted for the irregularities, but Ngcuka, who was hounded out of office for doing so, paid a high personal price.

In Kenya, tribal rivalries had been less gory but were as important in explaining the country's political structure and its intractable problems. Tribalism figures heavily in the process of governing African countries where one-man doctorial rule over a stew of competing tribes ensues that they had to balance tribal interests if they want to stay in power. Most of the time the president's job was to play tribal hatreds against each other.

However in Kenya's case, Moi was actually from one of the smallest tribes; the Kalanjin. Jomo Kenyatta chose him Vice-president because he was presumed daft and hence corruption was an essential option to a lack of popularity. Like most African rulers Moi had no salary; the central bank wrote him a blank cheque every year to spend as he liked and hence his wealth was equal to or more than that of Mobuto Sese Seko of Zaire. He frequently gave visitors to state house wads of cash and his generosity was reported every night on TV. Yet he was not popular and used to torture people, imprison opponents without trial, cowered courts and was downright corrupt to remain in power.

Moi proved himself a cunning tribal gamesman and after a short time had acquired more power over the whole of Kenya than Kenyatta ever had. He quickly realised that he could ill afford to alienate either Luo or Kikuyu so he used to throw bones to them to fight over to ensure that the two tribes never admire each other and come up with a joint candidate to rival him. "I would like ministers and others to sing like a parrot after me. That is how we can progress", Moi said in 1984.

Moi eventually lost the plot and was replaced by a labour grouping led by one Kibaki. The very first law Kibaki's parliament passed rewarded politicians with a 172% salary increase. MPs' take-home pay increased to £65,000 per annum and a fat package of allowances included a £23,600 grant to buy duty-free cars, together with a monthly £535 fuel and maintenance allowance. The new government spurned its corrupt predecessors' Mercedes E220 models and upgraded with the purchase of 32 new vehicles for top officials, including seven for the Office of the President. Most of these were new E240s, while the minister in charge of Kenya's dilapidated roads, Raila Odinga, went for a customised S500 at a probable cost of £100,000. Not to be outdone, Kibaki got himself the S600L limousine.

According to John Githongo, Kenya's former anti-corruption tsar, Kenya's Anglo-Leasing and related scandals presents a case in point, where the misappropriation of public funds was enabled through fraudulent contracts using sophisticated shell companies and bank accounts in European and off-shore jurisdictions. And according to TI Kenya's Kenya Bribery Index, bribery costs Kenyans about US$1bn each year, yet more than half of the population live on less than US $2 per day.

An extraordinary 1,244 Benz limousine cars were need for the Sudanese 2006 AU summit. 237 were reserved for the presidents themselves and another 669 were set aside for their assortment of sidekicks and no less than 338 were held in reserve. Since Mercedes Benz produced the stretch 600 Pullman, for Africa's Big Man, it was love at first sight. Idi Amin snapped up three, Jean Bedel Bokassa more when he crowned himself emperor in Central Africa. Zaire's Mobutu Sese Seko bought many and kept six for his summerhouse on Lake Kivu. Liberia's Sergeant Samuel Doe had 60. Since those days Africa has been through 196 coups, 66 wars and eleven million dead, and the Mercedes has been ideal, both for conveying dignity and for getting out of trouble, fast.

The boy King, Mswati III of Swaziland went for a £264 000 Maybach 62 for himself plus a fleet of BMWs for each of his 10 wives and three virginal fiancées selected annually at the football stadium 'dance of the impalas'. The boy king changed his mind about Mercedes and roared up to his rubber-stamp parliament in a new S600L limo. The total bill was about £1 million yet 70% of Swazis languish in absolute poverty and four out of 10 have HIV/Aids, the highest rate in the world. The boy king went on to build palaces for his 12 'queens' at a cost of US$45 million.

Mercedes Benz gifted Nelson Mandela a bullet proof S600L, and he accepted it. In 2001 the ANC chief whip Tony Yengeni was charged and later jailed for accepting a Mercedes ML320 at a 48% discount in return for lobbying on behalf of Daimler-Chrysler companies in the European Aeronautic Defence and Space consortium. Most shocking of all President Thabo Mbeki himself had been given an S600L armoured limousine for a test drive. He kept it for a full six months. The following year the wrinkled face of Brother Muammar Gaddafi of Jamahiriya Libya gave Mbeki an S600L as a replacement present.

The late Hastings Kamuzu Banda demonstrated how leaders endowed with acquisitive instincts go about acquiring vast financial empires in the midst of commonplace poverty. Banda's business empire encompassed breweries, distilleries, food processing industries, textiles and metal products manufacturing, tourism and hotels, wholesaling and retailing. He built expensive houses for members of the women's league who excelled in dancing and praising him. He even purchased planes to ferry dancing and singing troupes of women to his meetings. Banda built 11 sumptuous official residences across Malawi with government funds such as the Sanjika Palace and luxuriously furnished them and then rented the properties to the state. One took 20 years to build and cost US$100 million.

At that point Britain promised to increase its aid to Malawi to £52,4 million in a single year specifically to help the 65% of Malawians existing on less than 50 pence a day. Malawi's government celebrated by purchasing 39 top-of-the-range S-Class Mercedes Benz at a cost of £1,7 million. In 2005 Malawi's new anti-corruption bureau launched an investigation into how £53m in international donor cash landed in the private bank accounts of Bakili Muluzi, the country's president from 1994 until he stepped down 2004.

In office Muluzi generously handed out the state's money through his extensive patronage network. While ostensibly governing the country, he acquired a vast fortune built on a business empire of petrol stations, TV and radio stations, banks, office complexes, shopping malls and the country's top football team. In December 2003, Kalonga Stambuli, a former business associate and government adviser to Muluzi, researched and circulated a dossier of Muluzi's extensive holdings. Shortly afterwards, Stambuli was poisoned, strangled and murdered. Under Muluzi, it is alleged that British and other aid funds were skimmed. But when questions were asked in the House of Commons and the then British high commissioner, George Finlayson suggested that the implicated ministers step down, one Malawian minister simply replied: "We don't resign in Malawi."

Even Mluzi's predecessor President wa Mutharika, whose anti-corruption drive was being backed by Britain and other Western countries, had made some questionable moves. His first act on achieving power was to throw MPs out of parliament in Lilongwe and make the building, with 300 air-conditioned rooms set in 555 hectares of gardens, his personal palace. The MPs had to conduct state business in hotel conference rooms. He abandoned the palace claiming it had ghosts. Schizophrenia?

Wa Mutharika, who also owned a derelict farm in Zimbabwe, protected from land invasion by Robert Mugabe's regime, awarded himself a 353% pay rise, scarcely a year after coming into office. His education minister, Yusuf Mwawa, was arrested on charges of using public funds for his lavish wedding ceremony. For many Malawians, wa Mutharika's anti-corruption drive came as a surprise, not least because he was seen as a stooge of Muluzi, but because some of the missing government millions that landed in Muluzi's accounts were almost certainly spent on wa Mutharika's election campaign.

But as the anti-corruption tussle continued between Muluzi and his handpicked protégé, Malawi Law ensured that Muluzi was not legally obliged to explain how he got his vast wealth. And that is Africa's whole problem. Many anti-corruption laws do not obligate people to explain wealth that is disproportionate to their income.

At the sometime one notoriously corrupt Malawian, Robert Matibili-Mugabe, appeared to be strengthening his alliance with corrupt regional leaders and particularly with wa Mutharika, as 8 security agents from Zimbabwe had been hired to guard the presidential palace. The deal came about when wa Mutharika's Zimbabwean wife, Ethel, fired her guards after a major disagreement, precipitating 15 Malawians being sent to Zimbabwe to train with that country's notorious army and the dreaded murderous CIO. Zimbabwean 'cooks' were preparing meals at the state house in Malawi.

Wa Mutharika's thank you was to name a high way financed by the European Union linking Malawi to Mozambique ports as Robert Gabriel Mugabe Road; the EU was not very pleased for obvious reasons.

Western aid had corrupted generations of African politicians, as it was the fastest route to riches for the local elite. The problem was how to break the perpetual cycle of charity enfeebling sub-Saharan Africa, funding its civil wars, corrupting its politicians and making Africans hate Westerners for their patronising Western ways.

Even sentimental and likable Kenneth Kaunda of "one Zambia one nation" was an example of bad economics, disastrous development, corruption and cronyism that saw one Zambia two nations and yes, he did many indecent things. When his father died Kaunda had to wash dishes for the white missionaries to pay for his way ending up a teacher and scout master and a short spell in prison for possessing and handling "The African and colonial world," a socialist pamphlet. Emotional and very public, Kaunda always carried a white handkerchief were he frequently wept into when making speeches about the "tribulations of Africa". Though mildly corrupt himself, the same could not be said about his wife who was in control of the Zambia poaching mafia that caused havoc in neighbouring Zimbabwe nor his son's plunder of fertilizer for resale at staggering profits in Malawi. Kaunda, as Mugabe had Malawian ancestry.

However as all other Big Man, Kaunda eventually turned bad as copper ran out and he dragged his feet on selling off parastatals that were keeping him in power via cronyism. White Kerchief or not, the Big Man uses muscle eventually in direct proportion to the economic worries and in this case Indians and Pakistanis were at the receiving end. By the end of his reign Zambian prisons were literally busting at the seams as the Big Man utilised a had-me-down colonial law that allowed him to detain anyone without trial and tortured them. Common in Zimbabwe, Kenya, Tanzania, Malawi, Angola, Cameroon, electoral laws were changed arbitrary to ensure he was the only candidate on the ballot and the currency, the Kwacha had his picture on it.

Most if not all the looted funds are invested abroad and the little money used within the country is often spent on marriage and birthday ceremonies, activities or goods and services that hardly benefit the economy or those in dire need of government assistance. Lavish palaces like Cameroon's Unity Palace and a new presidential plane spent over FCFA30 billion and where successive regimes have misappropriated Southern Cameroon's' financial and economic structures that formed the lifeline of the region.

Where did they get all this money? Most African leaders amass wealth not as a privilege, but a birthright. Money is political power since patriotism is for sale to the highest bidder; the African Big Man has to control most, if not all, income within his reach. And he makes secret deals with mining conglomerates to be paid part of the profits directly into his Swiss account.

There had been much concern at the international level over the use of corporate vehicles for illegal activities, which included money laundering, corruption and bribery. The problem of beneficial ownership and control arises in situations whereby a person uses a corporate entity or individual as a front to obscure his real identity in commercial transactions or holding assets. An illustration in the case of Zimbabwe is where two farms had been allocated to a trust and the wife of a cabinet minister. He claimed that legally he had no farm at all, that the two farms were owned by his wife and the trust whose beneficiaries were the children. On the face of it and at law the minister had no farm yet in reality he was the beneficial controller of both farms.

In the construction industry the rules state that all cabinet ministers are prohibited from having any financial interest in projects. However, ministers disguise their identities behind shelf companies. The shareholders of the companies were nominees with no obvious connection to any of the ministers. The small company got into a partnership with a foreign company were they received massive bribes, which were paid to the local company as 'consultancy fees'. The consortium bid for the contract that the ministers were key decision-makers in the awarding of the contract. They claimed that it was the company, not them, which was a party to the contract. The proceeds, which were essentially products of corruption, ultimately reached the ministers although the apparent legal arrangement did not show them to have any stake in the consortium. The crafty ministers stashed their looted proceeds of corruption in foreign countries that have strict bank secrecy laws, in the names of those corporates.

Lack of data makes it difficult to quantify exactly how much is lost through corruption. SADC countries lose money to diamond, gold, platinum, cobalt and zinc smuggling all connected to the elites. Seizures of several tonnes of narcotics worth millions of dollars in Kenya and South Africa show that Africa was increasingly becoming a hub for drug trafficking. Mauritius, Botswana and South Africa have the best laws in the region to tackle financial crimes and smuggling, but many others are lacking such laws and sometimes, even the agencies to enforce them. And those that have agencies often find that they have no backing from their governments, leading to ineffectiveness. The problem is especially acute with anti-corruption bodies, which have to depend on the very governments they investigate for staffing and funding, leaving them open to sabotage.

As long as African political rulers and administrators are drawn from predators, no amount of preaching the virtues of good governance or tuition on public administration will fundamentally alter the quality of governance. This is not to say that constitutional reforms and increasing civil society infrastructure are not important. They are. But they are not the key to solving the problem of bad governance.

Good governance is the effective exercise of power and authority by government in a manner that serves to improve the quality of life of the populous. This includes using state power to create a society in which the full development of individuals and of their capacity to control their lives is possible. A ruling class that sees the state solely as a means of expropriating the nation's limited resources is simply incapable of good governance. More specifically, such a class will, by its character and mission, abuse power.

An underlying cause of many of the manifestations of bad governance, including political repression, corruption and ethnic sectarianism, is the endeavour by the ruling classes to be and remain part of the global elite despite their nation's poverty. The competition for national resources leads to conflict and repression. Bad governance is not mainly a problem of ignorance or lack of infrastructural capacity or even of individual dictators. States in Africa are incapacitated as instruments of development because ruling classes, including people in and outside government, are motivated by objectives that have little to do with development and transformation.

For example corruption became so rampant in Zimbabwe that some people began to believe that it promoted development. Their argument was that a corrupt person used the proceeds to go into business and create employment. Corrupt army and police officials were among some of the most "successful" business executives though no one was asking how they got their starting capital.

No other evidence of petty corruption can beat the admission by a long haulage truck driver who openly declared in the glare of television cameras: "I would rather bribe a policeman at a road checkpoint than pay a million dollars for a traffic offence. My boss will reprimand me and take me for an idiot for failing to part with Zw$100,000 to avert a million dollar fine." Neither had Mugabe heeded calls in the past by student unions that routinely paraded the streets in protest against corruption in high places. Instead, he had given a free rein to baton wielding riot police, unleashing them on the students for daring show him publicly their disdain for commonplace graft.

Of all the weaknesses inherent in the Zimbabwean strongman, allowing crony capitalism to flourish was the most obvious. That weak trait had nourished an entourage of party hangers on and other petty government officers whose pet whim was to abuse their authority and swindle well-intentioned government programmes. Studies indicate that governments lacking legitimacy and a strong framework of good governance, the rule of law and adequate banking regulations while clinging on to unsound investment decisions, provide fertile grounds for corruption to thrive. Zimbabwe had all those ingredients.

There were no major casualties after the plunder of the War Victims Compensation Fund were Mugabe's Vice-president managed to secure compensation for 85% mental disability and the Air Force Marshal secured his via 105% disability! The tender for the construction of the new Harare International Airport went to the president's bankrupt nephew, despite glaring anomalies that amounted to palm greasing. And those who made millions through corrupt oil procurement at the National Oil Company of Zimbabwe (NOCZIM) are still free. All the culprits arrested after the massive corruption at the Grain Marketing Board, including then Agriculture Minister Kumbirai Kangai, got away. Those who corruptly obtained land also got away with it. How do you explain an ex-traffic policeman running a fleet of buses and haulage trucks; a former district administrator running a chain of hotels in just 4 years? But more importantly, how do you explain how some of the most wanted executives skip the country when the net is closing down on them and then the Governor of the Reserve Bank pleading for their forgiveness?

How do you explain a deal whereby Zimbabwean flamboyant businessman Philip Chiyangwa, who was implicated in a high-profile espionage case in which his co-accused were sentenced to jail terms ranging from four to five years, was removed from remand, then sold off Midiron Enterprises, which warehoused his leather and footwear industry assets, to Attorney General's (AG) family?

The intimate involvement of important political figures in business, officially and informally, weakens the will and capacity of government to combat corruption. In spite of the occasional official inquiries into corruption, and judicial exposures and condemnation, Zimbabweans are relatively highly tolerant of deviance in public office. In 2004 Zimbabwe was ranked 121 most corrupt out of 146 countries. Corruption would disappear from government departments if the incumbents and their superiors had to account fully to the general public for their conduct and the salaries and perks they receive for the work they are supposed to be doing. But any move in that direction would be crushed by the persons concerned because of its implications for good governance, and they have means of crushing it.

A free press plays a vital role in curbing corruption. Freedom of the press simply did not exist in most of Africa. Everything was under government control, from the licensing of the media and journalists down to the content of articles. Television and radio were a state monopoly and out side broadcasts were routinely jammed. Police and the judiciary ensure that dissenters live in terror or endure the constant battering of relentless harassment. Geoff Nyarota, who was then editor of the Bulawayo based paper, The Chronicle, was unceremoniously removed from his newspaper job and "promoted" to a public relations position after he had authored and published an expose on a vehicle acquisition and profiteering scandal involving government ministers and ruling party officials. He ended up in exile in the USA and blacklisted as an enemy of the state.

Dydmus Mutasa, of "we-are-better-off-with-6-million-Zanu-supporting-citizens" appeared on a television programme, Face the Nation, to discuss how his new ministry would go about fighting corruption. Looking straight into the TV cameras without a hint of irony, appealed to all those who knew they were involved in corrupt activities to voluntarily come forward and "confess their sins" to his ministry! If such wrongdoers gave themselves up before the Anti-Corruption Ministry went after them, Mutasa said with a straight face, their sins would be forgiven. Naturally, Mutasa left the ministry without announcing any successes and went on to hound magistrates who had been appointed to hear his friends' corruption cases. For over 25 years, Zimbabwe's resilient lot had to watch helplessly as their quality of life took a dive from the 'good old days' when their living standards were the envy of many on the African continent to the depths of utmost despair.

The belief that a nation can be redeemed by removing a set of crooked leaders inspired the killing of Nigeria's first post-independence civilian rulers by idealistic army majors. But the coups only succeeded in shifting power to another set of ineffectual corrupt leaders. Despite the changes of governments, the Nigerian state remained corrupt and ineffective and the country no better. Throughout Africa, changes in leadership have not lessened corruption or quickened the pace of economic development.

Some put the persistence of African mismanagement down to a lack of capacity for good governance. One result of this view is the explosion of capacity building programmes initiated by donor and multilateral agencies. The aim of the schemes is to help African countries put in place structures and reforms that will strengthen the rule of law, support democracy and promote greater accountability and transparency. In effect, the aim is to do now what should have been done by the colonisers before they relinquished power. That is, teach Africans how to govern themselves as Westerners do.

Certainly African nations suffer from poor administrative, inadequate judicial infrastructure and insufficient numbers of expertise. But these shortcomings cannot explain the abuse and misuse of state power in the continent. For instance, Nigeria has 100s of thousands of highly trained professionals, including accountants and constitutional lawyers. Laid down budgetary procedures, include provisions for checks and balances are adequate. But the fact remains that Nigerian rulers have ignored the provisions of the constitution and laid down administrative procedures are irrelevant to the actual workings of government.

Similarly, we should not see reactionary economic policies and practices of African governments as stemming mainly from lack of knowledge of economic theory and management. Zimbabwe's economic ministers, all fine graduates of fine Western universities, continued to produce some of the best economic budgets that could easily have pulled the country out of its slumber, but never consulted anyone in industry in producing these documents and hence were mere academic thesis. There is reason in the anarchy.

The practice of rewards also takes place among big business people who were awarded state contracts or access to cheap money from government in exchange for their unwavering support for the establishment. There were traits of this insalubrious practice inbuilt into the ruling elite in Harare. Mugabe had been very adept in ensuring that key people across the social spectrum were adequately catered for in cash and property. It was a practice that ensures that strategic partners get prime positions at the feeding trough. It was a system that sort to hoodwink the public into believing that the state was benevolent and keen to correct colonial imbalances by redistributing resources. At the end of the day, deserving cases had been elbowed out of the queues and those who should benefit from the state's welfare system were as poor as ever.

There were senior civil servants and military, police and security officials who had become very rich because of this patronage system. They got expensive new executive cars every year and went on to abuse the system at Willovale (a local car manufacturer); they got military disability allowances they did not deserve; War pensions funds were looted; they were allocated productive and well-equipped farms during the resettlement exercise; they accessed cheap loans from government and parastatals; they were in the government scheme to acquire subsidised tractors and irrigation equipment; they had not repaid loans but they still got the opportunity to have another helping even though there was a long list of hungry Zimbabweans locked outside; they were the same people who looted funds from the Pay for Your House Scheme in the mid-1990s.

Zanu praising traditional chiefs and other junior traditional leaders had been given 4x4 cars they couldn't drive and their houses electrified when district hospitals did not have ambulances or running water. These chiefs abused villagers, women and children and forced them to work on their fields for no payment and then forced them to support Zanu. There were also scraps for the selected lot lower down the social ladder. These came in the form of 2 bags of seed and fertiliser, preferential treatment in accessing relief aid and even a party T-shirt with a portrait of Mugabe emblazoned on it. All these beneficiaries formed various layers of support for the establishment because their collective consciences had been bribed.

It is important to be clear-headed about the causes of Africa's dismal economic performance in the years since independence. Certainly, diseases, ruinous levels of international debt and unfair trading rules wreaked havoc. But corruption and grotesque mis-governance of the sort that scars Zimbabwe are critical factors. Until African leaders themselves get angry about these abuses, many in the northern hemisphere will remain cynical.

In his testimony before the U.S. Senate Foreign Relations Committee in September 2004, Ghanaian Professor George Ayittey from the American University documented the following amounts of grand embezzlement among African leaders: General Sani Abacha of Nigeria: US$20 billion, President Félix Houphouët-Boigny of Ivory Coast: US$6 billion; General Ibrahim Babangida of Nigeria: US$5 billion, President Mobutu Sese Seko of Zaire: US$4 billion, Robert Mugabe US$3 Billion; President Mousa Traore of Mali: US$2 billion, President Henri Bedie of Ivory Coast: US$300 million, President Denis N'guesso of Congo: US$200 million, President Omar Bongo of Gabon: US$80 million, President Paul Biya of Cameroon: US$70 million, President Haile Mariam of Ethiopia: US$30 million.

In total, Nigerian President Olusegun Obasanjo estimated, "...corrupt African leaders have stolen at least US$140 billion from their people in the four decades since independence." Corrupt leaders do not discriminate between foreign aid and other revenue (such as oil wealth) when stocking their Swiss bank accounts, so it is nearly impossible to discern how much pilfered loot came directly from development funds. There are multiple factors that cause corruption. They include greed, desire and selfishness. The material world is very corrupting. Universally man worship material things and would do anything to acquire them to the detriment of others.

A continent of honey and milk

"Let it never be asked of any of us, what did we do when we knew another was oppressed" Nelson Mandela.

"Africa needs a leadership that is politically and personally as gracious, honourable and magnanimous in defeat as in success. We need the leadership that acts as much as for today as it does for the future as well as the leadership that generates trust, goodwill and confidence. Africa needs a leadership that lives by the tenets of consultation, persuasion, accommodation, and cohabitation." Khoza chairman of South Africa's Eskom power utility (2005).

Why do some nations, often in adverse locations, prosper? Why are some, with lush soils and huge mineral resources, destitute? Humanity prospers when people can swap their goods and wares and services without control, regulations and taxes. How do we ensure freedom of trade and contract? By legislation being impartial, predictable and capable of generalisation. Who is top of the league of such virtues? Hong Kong, Singapore, Ireland, Luxembourg and Iceland. Who is bottom? Zimbabwe, Myanmar, Iran, North Korea, Sudan, Iraq and Congo don't even rank, as they are so lawless. What has Iceland got? It is cold, dark and barren. Yet it has freedom. It thrives.

People have often asked, "What is this democracy? There is no democracy even in the UK, so how do you think we can ever have it in our own countries? There is no freedom in the UK for us Africans."

Democracy is an African concept as old as time. Contrary to common beliefs, the Ashanti of Ghana may have been the first to rule themselves democratically and hence this is not a Western construct, as many believe. 'Chivanhu', African way of life, is constructed on the notions of participatory decision-making. Democracy is the doctrine that the numerical majority of an organized group can make decisions binding on the whole group. Democracies require that their governments be limited, not that they be weak. Democracies have demonstrated remarkable resiliency over time and have shown that, with the commitment and informed dedication of their citizens, they can overcome severe economic hardship, reconcile social and ethnic division and, when necessary, prevail in times of war.

It is the very aspects of democracy cited most frequently by its critics that give it resiliency. The processes of debate, dissent and compromise that some point to as weaknesses are, in fact, democracy's underlying strength. In the end, a government resting upon the consent of the governed can speak and act with a confidence and authority lacking in a regime whose power is perched uneasily on the narrow ledge of military force or an unelected party apparatus. One of the most important contributions to democratic practice has been the development of a system of checks and balances. As a general term, checks and balances have two meanings: federalism and separation of powers.

Freedom of speech, debate and enquiry: This is the principle of democracy because it is essential to the open debate upon which a vibrant political culture is founded and maintained. It's been said that the strongest power is that which can forbid its own mention. Anybody who attempts to suppress any form of debate should be suspected of trying to defend illegitimate power.

The national mass media is crucial to the national democratic process. It is the national mass media that forms and validates most people's understanding of what is 'real'. It is the national mass media that holds the key to reaching the millions of voters. It is essential therefore that the mass media is: Open and transparent so we may know the people behind it and their agenda; Accountable to the public, so we may acquire a remedy when it is inaccurate. The 'freedom of the press' must be balanced with its accountability; Diverse in the sense that media monopolies should not be allowed to develop and dominate. The best way each of us can help build a diverse media is to support alternative media projects.

Liberalism is a political view that seeks to change the political, economic or social status quo to foster the development and well being of the individual. Liberals regard the individual as a rational creature who can use his or her intelligence to overcome human and natural obstacles to a good life for all without resorting to violence against the established order. Again Liberalism may also mean a political system or tendency opposed to centralization and absolutism.

The notion of development prominently implies the improvement and upliftment of the quality of life of people that they are able, to a large measure, to attain their potential, build and acquire self-confidence and manage to live lives of reasonable accomplishment and dignity. It can be understood as a process of social transformation in which the exploitation of resources, patterns and strategies of investments and capitalisation, the ethos and direction of technological advancement and attendant institutional adaptation are in relative harmony and facilitate both current and strategic potentials to satisfy the needs and aspirations of members of the society concerned.

In this regard African leaders have always been aware of the need for some "nationalist-cum-developmentalist" ideology for both nation building and development. The quest for an ideology to guide the development process inspired African leaders to propound their own idiosyncratic and often incoherent "ideologies" to "rally the masses" for national unity and development. The centrality of "development" was such that it acquired the status of an ideology ("Africanisation") that provided the ideological scaffolding of "development plans". If such ideologies are still absent it is not for lack of trying.

Although the Bretton Woods institutions (BWIs) have managed to convince many that African leaders' objection to structural adjustment programmes (SAPs) was because these would undermine their corrupt practices, there are well-documented developmental arguments against SAPs, advanced by African bureaucrats. The Economic Commission for Africa has over the years regularly codified these positions, which were often dismissed peremptorily by the BWIs.

Further, too often skyscrapers, beautiful residential areas, cinemas and hotels are seen by some to represent development. The availability of champagne and whisky, ham and sausages and Mercedes-Benz cars are equated with evidence of development. Ironically, the champagne and caviar life style in Africa invariably coexists with sprawling, disease-infested shanties pervaded by unspeakable stench spawned by open drains and sewers. The elites have been content to gorge themselves on the latest choice commodities of Western consumer culture, and for as long as the availability of consumer-goods are assured, the song and dance and the make-believe of "Africanised" development rhetoricians continues.

Why did Asia perform so much better after colonialism than Sub-Saharan Africa? At least part of the answer is that, through the 1970s, Latin America and Sub-Saharan Africa had become far more dependent on foreign capital than East or South Asia that were favoured by USA loans. As the re-direction of capital flows towards the United States gained momentum, such dependence became unsustainable. Once the Mexican default of 1982 dramatically revealed how unviable the previous pattern had now become, the 'flood' of capital that Third World countries had experienced in the 1970s turned into the sudden 'drought' of the 1980s. In the case of Africa, the literal Sahelian drought made things considerably worse, reducing Africa's capacity to cope with subsequent natural and man-made disasters.

Hence, a Western television viewer can be forgiven for concluding that the entire African continent is misgoverned, and characterised by massacres, internecine warfare, fear, failure and want. To them Africa is universal gloom and doom. The West hears very little about the good news of growing democracy on the continent, points of economic achievement, of social progress, new cultures of tolerance and respect for human rights in some cases.

The African Union now has a human rights commission (which they hate and don't listen to) and there is a renewed commitment to finding answers to Africa's long-running crises. The protocol on women's rights to the African charter of human rights, that came in on November 25, 2005 bounds by law all AU members to non-discriminatory education and labour practices, to prohibit female genital mutilation and underage marriage and forced military training for youths.

If, by 2005, on the political side things looked gloomy, the economic side was faring a little better. Despite its history and in the face of numerous challenges, there was reason to be optimistic with the future of this "dark continent". A new era was dawning as the number of warring countries in Africa had decreased, the number of children enrolled in primary schools had increased by more than 50 percent, and the economic growth of 24 African countries had exceeded five percent.

Big Man rule has not always been disastrous to Africa though it depended more on luck than anything. But those that seem to succeed owe their success to the steady hand of a shrewd but benevolent Big Man. Felix Houphouet-Boigny of Ivory Coast shunned big projects and focused resources onto farms making sure that peasants were taught good techniques, given quality seed and fertilizer and paid a handsome price for their produce though he pocketed 20% of the proceeds. As a result the country blossomed into the world leader in cocoa production and earned itself a whopping 65% increase in per capita income in two decades. Houphouet-Boigny daftly managed corruption, bought ethnic peace with government jobs and was fabulously rich with billions in his 'Swiss accounts'.

Apart from China and India, African countries were the only ones growing exponentially more than any other countries in the world driven especially by oil and diamonds. In South Africa, Namibia and Botswana, press freedom was comparable to what prevails in European countries. In Benin, Cape Verde and Mali, the governments showed their journalists some respect and no significant violations were registered in 2004. Their growth was positive. And the situation continued to improve steadily in Angola after years of a devastating civil war despite the ruling party's drastic shift to the left. There was a clear trend in recent years for African countries to fall into line with modern democracies and decriminalise press offences.

The often-vaunted example of successful development in Africa is Botswana. As compared to the Asian experience, Botswana was a society awash with revenue from diamonds and which had provided lavishly for its elites to live and express themselves materially in a style largely incomparable on the whole continent. Botswana is one of the major beef producers in the world. Botswana beef has a lucrative market in the European Union. The semi-feudal Mafisa (cattle-loaning) system was still prevalent. Botswana, with a population of about 1.25 million, had reserves totalling about $7 billion invested in US government bonds and had a 15% stake in De Beers diamond company. Such reserves could transform the society, if transformation was measurable by or a factor of US dollar revenue.

Contrary to the African stereotype of oppression of women, some countries had made significant advances in the field of gender empowerment. Liberia elected Africa's first woman president. South Africa had a woman vice president and so did, believe it or not, Zimbabwe. With Zimbabwe's retired army general Solomon Mujuru's camp dominant in both the lower and upper chambers of the august House, Vice-President Joice Mujuru had an edge over other presidential aspirants in both Zanu and the government.

The family unit is terribly important in all African cultures. Old people in Africa are highly respected and cared for within the bosom of the community until they die and this seemed to be extending into the future as the newer generation absorbed this culture. Though continually battered African values endure and that's the reason why the continent is not hopeless or even a sad place. It's a land where the bonds of family keep old people from feeling useless and guarantee no child is an orphan; it is a place were true friendships exists and life long loyalty can be felt; a place were children can play outside and parents are not afraid; marriages still work and nature sits side by side with man.

It's the smiles that actually shock you at being greeted with a smile by a bank teller in Lusaka or Harare! Or the surprise at a senior bank official in Dakar who actually responds to your email. African countries were beginning to be at peace with themselves. They had their problems but they were calmly working on them to the best of their abilities. There was no tension in the air in a number of countries and one did not automatically assume that a soldier or a police officer was an agent of oppression.

On the technological side, Africa had the fastest growing and cheapest cell phone networks in the world. You could be expected to be able to easily purchase a new cell phone prepaid line in developed Germany. But it was just as easy to be able to do the same in Zambia, Malawi, Somalia and in Senegal. New, legitimate SIM packs are available from tuck-shop vendors with no hassles whatsoever, at prices that are reasonable even in local terms. Paradoxically, Somalia had the cheapest cell phone call charges in the world by 2004, some of the cheapest IT products sourced from Dubai and had five functioning airlines that could have easily embarrassed more developed Zimbabwe's or Nigeria's national airlines on efficiency. However in comparatively more advanced Zimbabwe, the three cell phone networks had for years perpetuated the fiction that having a cell phone number was a complicated, expensive exercise "because we are upgrading our network." It was a political reality that the rulers did not want the population to be in touch as the opposition used SMS systems to campaign.

After their independence, Zimbabwe and Namibia governments formulated policies and issued legislation to promote sustainable tourism and involve all communities throughout the country in tourism and natural resource management, including wildlife conservation based on the very successful Zimbabwean CAMPFIRE project (Communal Areas Management Programme for Indigenous Resources). NACOBTA (The Namibian derivative) had 38 member enterprises, including conservancies, campsites, rest camps, traditional villages, craft centres, museums and indigenous tour guides. Community-based tourism is a viable option for generating economic opportunities, fostering environmental conservation and keeping alive traditional cultures and customs in rural or isolated areas of African countries and was catching on in many countries. Before Mugabe 'killed' tourism, CAMPFIRE had been a roaring success.

The informal sector of the Kenyan economy is known as *Jua Kali*, or "hot sun", referring to micro-business operations along streets and outdoor markets. The sheer number of women who worked on garments and the restrictions they face made them an obvious target group for assistance. They were confined to garment making and repairs, produce low-quality goods but had difficulties in obtaining credit, lacked technical and business skills. A newly created non-governmental organisation that took over the projects ensured that at least 100 entrepreneurs and 25 trainers would undergo training each year.

There are so many struggles for freedom in Africa. Very few Africans believe in capitalism. Africans believe in some form of feudal socialism and if there is any example and proof that socialism has nothing to contribute in this world, then the destruction of Zimbabwe is it. The main problem with the Zimbabwean ruler had been his near limitless capacity to hide dictatorial tendencies behind a facade of democracy. It had been his fear to share power and the ability to deploy doses of tyranny in brilliantly masterminded fashion and pace, leaving room enough to deny the act and claim sainthood.

But then Africa had NEPAD (New Partnership for Africa's Development) by 2002 to counter Mugabe and company's unilateralism and isolate them. Several African countries signed up to NEPAD, spearheaded by South Africa's President. This entailed a voluntary submission to peer review. NEPAD was not without its own problems but it was founded on noble principles and was a step in the right direction supported by the USA and the EU.

The dubious conflation of free markets and semi-free politics had become an Mbeki trademark. But still, Zimbabwe continued to be the core challenge to NEPAD's legitimacy, in no small part because the symbolism of property-rights violations against white farmers had become, for the West and for many whites in South Africa, the central question. Questions were still hanging on how credible the mechanism could be if leaders failed to openly condemn racist thugs like Zimbabwe's Mugabe, Dos Santos (Angola), Mswati (Swaziland), Nujoma (Namibia) and Kabila (DRC).

Uganda had its HIV/AIDS problem under control mainly due to the president's positive interference. Further, Uganda's education system had undergone radical changes since 2000 with donor funded free education and hospital treatment accorded to all children thanks to Bill Gates and the USA. Uganda had become a partner in the war against terrorism and was being well equipped militarily by the CIA, enabling it to attack its neighbours.

Mozambique on the East coast had one of the highest international economic growths in the late 1990s and early 2000s but that was reduced due to floods and drought. However the country continued to receive massive investment and aid from South Africa and the Western world. It successfully changed leaders in 2006 without any major incident and had some of the best examples of democratic electoral laws.

Development and poverty alleviation take discipline, honesty, openness and democracy in national political life. It takes hard work and commitment and the strict observance of the rule of law and the guarantee of investor rights and business contracts. If African leaders applied these principles to their own and their public lives they would bring prosperity and freedom to their countries.

African leaders have to learn that development has got nothing to do with race, or discrimination, or unfair trading practices or a shortage of resources, human and financial. If they fail to address the issue of leadership in their countries then they condemn both those countries and their millions of people to hardship and poverty and human deprivation that can only be overcome by war. Human migration on this basis simply makes things worse in the affected States via human resource depletion.

Marching towards democracy

"Man is man because he is free to operate within the framework of his destiny. He is free to deliberate, to make decisions, and to choose between alternatives. He is distinguished from animals by his freedom to do evil or to do good and to walk the high road of beauty or tread the low road of ugly degeneracy". Martin Luther King, Jr., the Measures of Man, 1959.

"If whites in Zimbabwe want to rear their ugly terrorist and racist head by collaborating with the Zimbabwe Unity Movement, we will chop that head off." Mugabe declared when challenged by Tekere during the 1990 presidential elections. Tekere, a founder member of Zanu and more senior than Mugabe, broke with Mugabe in October 1988, saying, "There is a very clear trend to repression, corruption and dictatorship".

If a place so vast can have a single characteristic, it is resilience. Africa has seen off the enslavers and the colonisers, its people have overthrown white-settler kingdoms in Zimbabwe, Namibia and South Africa, the cousins of those that still endure in the Americas, Canada, New Zealand and Australia. Africa is also slow to change. Drive an hour out of most big cities, and the way of life is largely unaltered since the advent of iron tools. Women carry firewood on their heads, boys herd cattle and villagers' lives rely on good rain, a witch doctor and luck.

Since the colonial era, the state has been a foreign, interfering power in these people's lives. There maybe plenty watching Wimbledon, but no one in Africa had even heard of Bob Geldof and most believed that pop music was for children. Few ordinary Africans are politicised to the extend of knowing the real implications of voting. The majority of Africans, educated or not, know nothing about mortgages or interest rates. Usually it's the outside world that talks of elections, not Africans.

If the U.N. Security Council fails to threaten strong action against Sudan, Sudan gets the message loud and clear that there is no cost to continuing its campaign of ethnic cleansing. African and Western leaders had also been reluctant to criticize other African leaders who were at first heralded as hopes for a new era of democratic rule but who had since shown signs of leaning toward autocracy, like Museveni of Uganda, Mugabe, Nujoma of Namibia, wa Mturika of Malawi and Paul Kagame of Rwanda.

In Blantyre, Malawi, 2004, the police halted a peaceful interdenominational prayer meeting organised by civil society in October 2004 to show solidarity with their brethren in Zimbabwe by appealing for divine intervention to avert a 'looming human rights catastrophe in Zimbabwe.' The police commissioner wished the prayer meeting cancelled or delayed until the President met the civic society leaders on the Zimbabwe issue. However, as the vigil organisers went to talk to the President, police officers were already dispersing participants. In a press statement the organisers said, "Malawi is still a police state under democratic camouflage!" The presidents of Malawi and the DRC were married to Zimbabweans and hence were considered in-laws.

The winner of Mozambique's election replaced Joaquim Chissano, a popular peacemaker and technocrat who had been president since 1986 when the country's first independent Marxist president, Samora Machel, died in a plane crash. When Chissano stepped down, only Zimbabwe and Angola in Southern

Africa were still governed by the liberation-era leaders, although tiny Swaziland continued to be ruled by Africa's last corrupt and eccentric absolute monarch. Joachim Chissano of Mozambique came to bid Mugabe farewell before he left office. Sam Nujoma of Namibia and Bikili Mluzi of Malawi did the same. The last was Benjamin Mkapa of Tanzania.

For the ordinary residents of Mozambique, a former Portuguese colony, the 2004 elections marked a decade of peace, stability, and economic growth after more than 16 years of brutal civil conflict. Although the country remained one of the world's poorest and most underdeveloped, it was a democratic success story. South Africa, Botswana, Namibia and Malawi all held presidential elections that, for the most part and by African terms, were peaceful and fair. The uneventful votes revealed a maturing of African democracy.

These leaders were subtly trying to convey a message, that there was life outside the presidency, that while they were younger in age and experience, they might just set an example for Mugabe. But apparently this was not seen in the same light. Anybody harbouring any such speedy romantic notions would probably be told politely not to "misdirect their efforts". Tanzania's young new president Jakaya Kikwete must have been surprised to hear Mugabe promising to work closely with him.

Still, if pushed far enough by a renegade regime, African leaders, particularly Nigeria, had shown a willingness to intervene on behalf of the oppressed Africans. Liberia's notorious drug addict President Charles Taylor was eventually forced into exile after fomenting a brutal civil war there, escorted on to a plane flanked by two regional leaders and ended up singing before a UN court. But such interventions remained rare elsewhere, and they usually came about as a result of sustained pressure from abroad as well.

In elections held in Liberia 2005, the first woman president on the continent of Africa appeared a welcome development indeed. There was silence in the corridors of African leaders as though to lament on the soon ending dominion by man in political authority over the continent. Thinking of Africa as a grave yard of torture and victimization because of the fear of those in power to be removed democratically by those more favoured by the populace, gives one hope that fresh elections of this lady Africa would inspire hope to an almost lost cause, freedom in Africa.

The recent changing of the guards, however, did not necessarily herald political change. In every election the governing parties won and in many cases the new president was a liberation-era politician handpicked by the outgoing leader.

Surprisingly and contrary to this trend, voters in poor and tiny Benin May 2001 renewed their unlikely, and so far successful, experiment in multiparty democracy, an experiment in which the West African country's non-official news media had taken important reinforcing roles. Print and broadcast outlets offered detailed coverage up to the eve of voting in the first round. The vote, which took place with few disruptions, marked the third time in 10 years that the Beninese had cast ballots for a president. Elections in 1991 and 1996 saw the incumbent president voted from office, outcomes exceedingly rare in sub-Saharan Africa.

Africa's longest serving head of state, Omar Bongo of Gabon, was still raring to go after almost 40 years in power. Bongo (69), who first assumed power via a coup in 1967, was sworn in for another seven-year term of office December 2005. By the time that term of office ends, Bongo would be 76 years old and will have been in power for 45 years, a record surpassed worldwide only by Cuba's Fidel Castro, who had so far clocked an incredible 46 years in office and Queen Elizabeth of the UK. Bongo is one of the wealthiest heads of state in the world.

This was not the first election Bongo had won whose results had been disputed by opposition groups. His re-election in 1993 sparked rioting after he was accused of rigging the polls. But Bongo's re-election by a wide margin after 38 years in power suggests that outright rigging was becoming old hat for Africa's life presidents who were only too aware of the international scrutiny elections were now subjected to. Vote buying, fed via corruption, was emerging as the new prestigious survival strategy and as it is almost impossible to prove, long-suffering opposition parties must accept they had a new kind of fight on their hands.

Other survival trick incumbent leaders were increasingly resorting to was the discredit-or-eliminate-your-strongest-rival-ahead-of-presidential-elections approach. South Africa's Thabo Mbeki had been accused of playing this new political game following his decision to dismiss his deputy, convict Jacob Zuma in June 2005. Allegations had been made that despite an earlier pledge to step down in 2009 in line with the provisions of the constitution, the South African leader had other ideas, such as remaining ANC president after 2009.

Nigerian President Olusegun Obasanjo was another incumbent to have caught the "I am-indispensable-and-I-won't-go bug". He was at loggerheads with his vice-president, Atiku Abubakar over whether or not to amend the constitution to pave the way for him to serve a third term. By adopting this approach, Obasanjo had embraced the dangerous delusion of indispensability that saddled Africa with leaders who are long past their sell-by dates.

Surely one man can only do so much after which he should step aside to let others have a go. Maniac Abacha could have killed Obasanjo in prison as he did his blue-blooded former second in command, General Shehu Musa Yar Adua, with impunity. Yet by a combination of local and international campaign and sheer luck or divine intervention he survived, not only escaping with his life but was parachuted to the Presidency for a second time and as his eight years drew closer, he could not remember the exit door again.

Uganda's Yoweri Museveni was another president who evidently believed that his country could not do without him at the helm. The first step he took in propagation of this strange belief was to force an amendment of the constitution 2004 to enable him to seek a third term of office. He had been in power for 20 years. The plot thickened following the arrest of opposition politician, Kizza Besigye, who had subsequently been charged with treason, an accusation that was apparently in vogue among long-serving incumbents because it was guaranteed to totally cripple a political rival as long as he had charges hanging over his head; a tactic one Matibili-Mugabe of Zimbabwe perfected and brought into fashion.

"Third term apologists" typically become legalistic on the issue arguing that "the people" have spoken through a referendum and there had been appropriate change to the constitution the President was not doing anything unconstitutional. They overstated their democratic credentials by stating the seemingly obvious: voters are supreme in what they say and whatever they decide is sacrosanct. It was a very charming democratic case even if democracy was the last thing on the minds of those pushing it. It was amusing why voters were not supreme on the key economic decisions of the government or the various wars these countries had been involved in.

It was obvious that African presidents compare notes on how to deceive their people and which manipulation methods work best. It was sad that, in spite of the new African Peer Review Mechanism (NEPAD), they did not compare notes on how to improve the lot of their people. But with incumbents rendering the two terms limit ineffective through constitutional amendments, changes were very unlikely through the ballot box. "This country will collapse if the Old man leaves", "Nobody can govern this country but him" and other apologetic justifications by self-serving, corrupt regime-worshipping apologists for status quo. Any country whose social, political and economic well being depends so much on one ruthless murderer probably does not deserve to survive.

The African Commission on Human and Peoples' Rights courageously led the way when, at the conclusion of its 38th ordinary session, it emerged that it had adopted a progressive resolution on the human rights situation in Zimbabwe and Sudan. Beyond these useful beginnings, however, the more systemic question of how protocols and other forms of regional treaty law were translated into the legal systems of African countries begs wider discussion. Without domestication, excellent regional agreements signed by African leaders are useless nationally, except as fashionable showpieces on the international good governance catwalk.

In some cases, SADC and African norms and standards were in any case framed in such a hide-and-seek way that countries could claim to have domesticated them without doing anything meaningful. Take, for instance, the SADC Principles and Guidelines Governing Democratic Elections, agreed in August 2004 in Mauritius. How is it that a country with an electoral system as creatively defective as Zimbabwe's was passed by the 'official' SADC observer team as having complied with these principles? Depending on which way each of the SADC leaders reads the document on SADC election principles, vastly different permutations of democratic growth in SADC countries may be the result.

Another problem with SADC and African norms and standards was that not all of them were framed as binding treaty law. In opposing Tsvangirai's application 2007, Justice Minister Patrick Chinamasa said: "They (SADC guidelines) are not a protocol. They are not enforceable or amenable to enforcement. The SADC Guidelines and Principles are a political document pegging out for the region a roadmap, which we must all follow towards a perfect democratic future." Ideally, the principles should have framed a clear and inviolable set of norms to be elevated as the electoral standard for the region, with the imperative that national constitutions, laws and processes must be aligned with this yardstick.

With such a normative base, auditing national constitutions and legislation for compliance becomes imperative. Such an exercise would easily show significant shortfalls in Zambia's public security legislation, Zimbabwe's repressive media legislation and so on. It could also show positive models such as the law enacted in Mozambique in June 2004 regulating the use of state resources during electoral campaigning. Otherwise the positivistic approach results in the SADC principles meant everything to every member country.

The positive areas, in Africa in general, though not everywhere, were the fairly good election administration and the freeness of the process in terms of freedom of expression, freedom of association, freedom of movement. But on the negative side, there was a trend that not much was being done in terms of fairness, in terms of access to resources, such as funding and the media. But then at least Africans were experimenting with democracy. From the evidence it would take a long time to get it right it seemed.

It even becomes difficult for Africans of goodwill to decide how to feel about the numerous transactional initiatives that often come up within the continent. What is to be the most constructive Africanist attitude that one should have? This credibility gap, the distance between policy rhetoric and action, remains the Achilles heel of African policy-making, particularly in relation to progressive policies such as those that would improve access to human rights and democracy.

I love to hate you relations

Many people, some of them not politicians and others not necessarily Marxist-Leninists or religious fanatics, don't like some things about the West: rock'n roll, Madonna, Bill Gates, jazz, Elvis Presley, Coca Cola, Soul and Rap music, fast food or George Bush. But for Chavez and Mugabe, the USA seemed to be the epitome of The Great Satan, as Iranians said of the country.

As Africans continued to mourn about why they were perceived lowly in the global development chain, it was important to note that they had not invested in communicating who they were to the global audience. Although some Africans had done exceptionally well as individuals, body corporates and nation states, they could not avoid being contaminated by the African image disease. The need for Africa and its global family to communicate, differentiate and symbolise itself to all the global audience of consumers and investors cannot be overstated.

It is important to underline that the audience is split into two major categories: African people and everyone else. In the case of Africa, the ruling elites were more concerned about improving the image of the continent to foreigners than invest in image building targeted at citizens. Ultimately, the hope of Africa and its global family lied in investing in a new identity of a functioning Africa than a selective approach where islands of hope were created in the midst of an ocean of hopelessness and misery.

Everything that was happening in Africa was not under the control of Africans. Africa did not control the prices of the commodities it sold on the global markets; it did not have any real say in the setting of the prices at which they bought from the developed world. Despite the endless propaganda trumpeted from the West about free markets, the reality for Africa was that most markets for the things, largely agricultural, which they could produce cheaply and easily, were closed to them. The European Union was the supreme case in point. What Africa faced were quotas, tariffs and cartels.

The minerals produced in abundance were controlled by Western capital from source of production of the raw materials, their sale, and destination of sale, with no value added at source. African economies were perpetually under siege through pernicious and unequal trade practices managed by corrupt black leaders, the West and the related BWIs. These latter institutions had become de facto parallel governments in many African states.

Even after independence, Kenyan and Zimbabwean courts (and most Commonwealth countries) followed British procedures and formalities. Judges and lawyers wore powdered wigs and long black robes, witnesses stood on their feet in a box and address judges as "my lord". In one instance in 1988, Kenya's chief justice, Cecil Miller, emerged from his chambers screaming nonsense and punching at shadows, threw a guard down and raced outside the court building, dancing to shout "Nyayo! Nyayo!" Moi's official slogan (peace, love, security). French West Africa was still heavily influenced and at times controlled by France both in traditions, military and language.

In their struggle for economic independence, African leaders realized they would need the aid of the former colonial masters but at what cost to their political independence? A few African leaders did not hesitate to put the welfare and well being of their people in the forefront of this new struggle. Samora Machel in Mozambique realized, a little late in his political life, that "Aluta Continua!" had to translate pretty quickly into food on the tables of the poorest Mozambican for it to have any meaning at all. It was left to Joachim Chissano to complete what Machel must have realized was the real politic of the objective of the struggle against the Portuguese. Even earlier than that, Mwalimu Julius Nyerere of Tanzania had stumbled upon that reality too. Ujamma, fashioned on the collective farming tragedy of the People's Republic, would not be the panacea of the hunger among his own people.

In Zimbabwe, it was Mugabe's concept of sovereignty that had gummed up the works of a return to the reality of the geopolitics of the world after the Cold War. Europe still had the wealth to help Zimbabwe; what Mugabe wanted Europe to forget was the horror of the land reform programme, Gukurahundi, Murambasvina and rigged elections. For him, it was a quarrel between Zimbabwe and Britain, which, to him, may be in Europe but is not the total of Europe. If Britain, the United States and the European Union had not acted against him on the aftermath of the land reform horror and the questionable conduct of the elections that followed, where would Zimbabwe be today? More importantly, where would Zimbabweans be today?

However, even with all these similarities and inequalities, there are many reasons that Africans and many others across the globe have a mixed, love-hate relationship with the Western world. It was not difficult for a lot of Africans who listened to Mugabe's racist and evil rhetoric from afar and did not have to live under his chaotic and barbaric rule and the world's down trodden to understand his emotional appeal.

Yet standards for leaders must be much higher than how well they articulate the much resentment at past and present, real and perceived mistreatment from the West. It might have been largely enough to rally Africans to support the continent's various liberation struggles many decades ago, but the challenges were quite different. Among them was unemployment, HIV/AIDS and many other chronic health issues, development of human capital and physical infrastructure, agricultural and industrial productivity, unfair trade terms and so on.

The solutions to these great challenges would continue to elude Africa as long as Africans allow ourselves to be mesmerized by rulers who appealed more to emotions than they do to what concrete plans they have to deal with those challenges. Years after the now very Westernised, comfortable and bourgeoisie Mugabe, Dos Santos and Bongo came into power as poor guerrilla leaders, they had rhetorically reverted to a role they no longer fitted to play. Africa had to show the moral high ground and take over leadership and the initiative from the West.

But would Africa see a Gorbachev to bring down this intricate system of patronage any time soon? Gorbachev recognised the need for a new relationship between Russia and its neighbours and also the need for loosening of the planning straightjacket that was stifling the country. The Russian economy was also in a perilous state, unable to provide for its citizens the same level of life style enjoyed by Western nations. Russian satellite states were draining the country of vital resources it could not replenish.

Can Africa's new breed of leaders ever come up with a perestroika (radical restructuring) and glasnost (openness)? It's doubtful as the new "enlightened" presidents of Botswana, South Africa, Kenya, Senegal, Tanzania, Malawi, Mozambique and Zambia all looked they did not have any ideology to speak of, let alone implement. African Renaissance looked doomed every time Mbeki opened his mouth.

Mugabe on a trip to Iran seemed to bellyache about the lack of solid African support for his nameless stance against the West. Exactly why he would choose Iran, a non-African country, to make this appeal was a little problematical. Perhaps, he hoped the Iranians, who had many friends among African leaders whose grudge against the West may never be dissipated even after billions of dollars in aid, would pass on the message on his behalf.

Mugabe sounded very pained that not too many African countries were as aggressive in their anti-West stance as he was. Yet Mugabe's cry in the wilderness suggested he was not getting his way as far as the continent was concerned. All Zimbabweans were praying that Africa and the nuke building mullahs would tell him in no uncertain terms: respect your people and everyone will respect you. Who knows even Britain, the European Union and the United States might have decided the old man had had enough of their stick, if he decided not to ape Mobutu and Idi Amin.

An eye for an eye will lead us nowhere. If the West is evil, that does not mean Africans should be too. Though this is not as simple, African leaders seemed too scared to take the argument and the fight to the Europeans more forcefully in pain of losing certain privileges like their fat Swiss bank accounts. The rhetoric that sounded so "radical" from outside Zimbabwe had cost the country incalculable goodwill way beyond the Western countries it was directed at. African leaders who cynically cheered Mugabe's populist rantings in public would never think of following his ruinous example and let their subjects suffer to the same extend.

The African nights: unbreakable Chinese lebensraum

The characters for 'Africa' in the Mandarin language mean 'wrong continent.' But the Chinese have often ignored this. Outwardly, China's 'Year of Africa' (2006) had been a striking success. President Hu Jintao, Prime Minister Wen Jiabao and Foreign Minister Li Zhaoxing had all travelled to Africa, visiting a total of 15 countries.

China knew what it wanted from Africa and probably how to get it. The converse wasn't true. In the 15th century the Ming emperor's emissaries sailed as far as Mozambique, carrying silk and spices and returning with a giraffe. In the cold war Maoists dotted Africa with hospitals, football stadiums and disastrous ideas.

The yarning gap left in Africa as a result of the end of colonialism and the cold war was to attract another power; China. China was accelerating its already spectacularly successful drive to tap the African natural resources it needed to fuel its rapid economic modernisation. When China, one of the world's most corrupt countries starts dishing out tens of billions of US dollars in aid and business contracts in Africa, the world's most corrupt continent, alarm bells had to go off.

The Chinese were increasingly acquiring control of African resources at source in a bid to sidestep high commodity prices. They were negotiating the prices of assets with corrupt local politicians and then locking them into 20-year deals; the strategy was to cut out the middleman, such as the London Metal Exchange in a bid to secure the resources required for Chinese industrialisation.

Moreover, the Chinese would set up their own parallel commodities market as they viewed existing markets as "a London and New York old boys' club". This Chinese market would eventually be bigger than existing institutions. The Chinese had already set up their own diamond exchange to rival the bourse in Antwerp to the delight of the Zimbabwean elites whose drawers were full of blood diamonds.

The USA invasion of Iraq and the Middle East had accelerated Chinese business interests in Africa as they had lost oil assets in that region. The USA had strategically "locked down" the Middle East, with the Chinese now having access to Iranian oil only. On top of this the Russians had purposefully excluded China as oil customers, preferring the Japanese. As a result, the Chinese had chosen Sudan as a strategic energy partner, with the 3,000 Chinese peacekeepers in that country acting as "energy asset protectors" and this explained the Sudanese government's reluctance to allow UN peacekeepers into Sudan.

Isolation from the West meant that Khartoum barely pumped a barrel of crude a decade ago. After intensive Chinese investment, it had the third largest oil business in sub-Saharan Africa. And to the gratification of Omar Bashir, Chinese deals came with few political strings. China shipped in thousands of workers to build the Heglig pipeline in record time, and a second pipeline was under construction. The Khartoum refinery, CNPC's first outside China, opened in late 1999, just in time for the 10th anniversary of the coup that brought military leader Omar al Bashir to power. The gamble had paid off handsomely. Sudan was expected to earn more than $1bn in oil revenues a year and its economy was one of the fastest growing in Africa. Meanwhile, China won a new loyal puppet to fuel its thirsty factories and exploding rate of car ownership.

But apart from demand for resources, the Chinese saw the 700 million sub-Saharan Africans as an important market for Chinese manufactured goods. The fact that Africans were poor, the Chinese had experience in their own country of producing goods for the bottom end of the market. On top of this, Chinese 'international' companies were interested in operating in Africa as part of a quest to learn how to become true 'multinationals' before expanding across the globe.

China's economic progress was cited by statists, protectionists and thugs alike to 'prove' that keeping the state's grip on companies, trade and political freedoms need not stop a country growing by 8%-plus a year. Sadly, China's success was an obstacle, as well as an inspiration. Its rise bid up the price of Africa's traditional raw commodities, and depressed the price of manufactured goods. Thus Africa's factories and assembly lines, such as they were, were losing out to its mines, quarries and oilfields in the competition for investment.

China's links with Zimbabwe went back to when it supported Mugabe's Zanu, whilst the Soviet Union backed rival Joshua Nkomo's ZAPU. Mugabe, who had been isolated by the West, stated that Zimbabwe was "returning to the days when our greatest friends were the Chinese." He also told supporters somewhat cryptically: "We look again to the East, where the sun rises, and no longer to the West, where it sets." This type of talk sort of embarrassed the Chinese but Mugabe was way beyond that by then.

The excessive generosity with which China assisted dictators of the world made them scoff at any appeals for human rights or democracy. Mugabe had the Chinese to thank for the blue-glazed tiles on the roof of his new presidential palace. The tiles came gratis, but the Chinese had also won contracts totalling hundreds of millions of dollars to provide hydroelectric generators for Zimbabwe's power authority (ZESA). In addition, China was supplying second hand prop-jets no one wanted to the perennially mismanaged Air Zimbabwe and buses, 1,000 of them, to the country's municipalities. Zimbabwe's air force had also been strengthened by China, to the tune of $200 million. The Chinese were even farming about 1,000 square kilometres of the land that had been seized from white farmers since 2000.

Ignoring human rights abuses, electoral fraud and Western sanctions, China presented Mugabe with an honorary degree in recognition of his 'remarkable contribution in the work of diplomacy and international relations'. In return China gained favoured access to Zimbabwe's gold and platinum resources and new markets for its manufactured exports.

Chinese diplomats featured at every African summit, flying the red flag of Third World friendship and offered to cancel some $1.3 billion in bilateral debt. Chinese businessmen snapped up commodities, while Chinese doctors treated Africa's sick under assistance programmes that won friends among people often forgotten by the rest of the world. China made and launched satellites into space for African countries, saving the continent over a billion dollars in hard currency.

In key countries, China was becoming the new IMF of Africa with strings that tied to Chinese national commercial interests. But China's influence in Africa extended beyond oil fields and financial markets, and was moving deeper into the continent by improving one of its 1960s era political gifts to Africa, the Zambia-Tanzania railway, which was now proving useful as a conduit for Zambian copper that China used to make telephone lines, electronics and construction material.

China extended a US$2 billion soft loan to Angola, which increased to $6 billion, in exchange for favourable oil contracts. The Chinese were offering the loan as an alternative to working with the IMF. The loan gave Angola the ability to ignore the IMF's demand for an agreement on accountability and to delay indefinitely an 'international' donors' conference.

Roads in Rwanda, a port in Gabon and a dam in Sudan had all been paid for with Chinese loans and built by Chinese contractors. Business with Nigeria and South Africa was booming in the billion dollar regions. China announced it would forgive debts owed to it by the poorest African countries and: a) More exports from Africa to China will receive tariff-free status (b) will train 15,000 African professionals (c) will build schools, hospitals and anti malaria clinics (d) will send experts and youth volunteers to Africa (e) double the number of scholarships to African students to 4,000 by 2009.

In Ethiopia, China offered to make good any shortfall in assistance following the suspension of European Union aid due to human rights abuses by Zanawi. In Equatorial Guinea, China gained influence in the US-dominated oil sector by providing military training and specialists to the country and the president described China as its main development partner. Equatorial Guinea has approximately 1.28 billion barrels of proven oil reserves.

China agreed a "strategic partnership" with Nigeria, a big oil exporter, and had oil interests in Angola, Chad and Gabon. Major trading relationships were developing with Egypt, while Chinese-financed infrastructure, telecoms and tourism projects were proliferating from Sierra Leone and Rwanda to Madagascar and Lesotho. In all, China-Africa trade doubled to more than $37bn within 5 years from 2000 and was projected to double again by 2009. At that rate, China would soon surpass the USA, whose trade with Africa in 2004 was valued at $50bn.

China not only saw Africa as a source of vital strategic resources but was also promoting multi-literalism to balance USA's Bush's unilateralism. China was not oblivious to Western concerns about rights and democracy but it put respect for national sovereignty first and an emphasis on what China called the Five Principles of Peaceful Co-existence, which enshrines mutual territorial respect, non-aggression and non-interference in each other's internal affairs. Beijing did insist however that its African stooges back its "one China" policy and shun Taiwan.

In Lesotho, an impoverished nation dependent on textiles for 90 percent of export earnings, the garment industry collapsed dramatically after the end of WTO restrictions on Chinese exports killed off Lesotho's USA orders. Chinese and Taiwanese investors set up factories there in 1999 to take advantage of Washington's Africa Growth and Opportunity Act, which gave textile exports from qualified African countries duty-free access to American markets. They simply closed shop and walked away when the USA orders dried up, leaving thousands of workers, mostly women, jobless in a country with a 40% unemployment rate.

Support for China in international forums was quietly encouraged. Senegal in October 2005 switched diplomatic recognition to China, reportedly with the curt reminder to Taipei that "states have no friends, they have interests only". But its political demands were limited. Beijing was "a strong supporter of south-south cooperation", and had set an example by agreeing to voluntary tariff exemptions.

All the same, and as usual, ordinary African complaints were growing about widening trade imbalances, damage to indigenous industries caused by the dumping of Chinese textiles and other products, poor labour conditions and Chinese arms sales in conflict zones.

The first load of Chinese-made trade had arrived in the Zimbabwean capital Harare in November 2004. Equipment for oppression and torture; riot gear, mobile water cannons and a consignment of sophisticated Internet monitoring technology. The order included 12 useless fighter planes that screamed overhead as the nation 'celebrated' its 25th anniversary of independence in a massive Chinese-built sports stadium and thousands of AK-47 assault rifles for the militia. The arms deal, worth $240 million, was concluded in defiance of international arms sanctions.

Also on the aging Zimbabwean dictator's Chinese shopping list were two Chinese-built aircraft for the broke national airline, Air Zimbabwe (He got three for the price of two!) and a number of combine harvesters and tractors to bolster the chaotic 'land reform programme'. Then of course there were the numerous Government construction project tenders "won" by the Chinese, not to mention the building materials, construction and fittings at the various presidential (but personal) mansions scattered around the country. And of course the thousands of Chinese computers dished out to schools by Mugabe during his election campaign. Even by the most conservative calculations the bill came to several trillions of Zimbabwe dollars.

Zimbabwe had often resorted to novel forms of payment. In 2000, it paid the Chinese using ivory from stockpiles gathered from its national parks. It had also bartered tobacco, but the tobacco sales floors were empty by 2005, the crop being a fraction of what it used to be. Mugabe had done this before, but with another sinister accomplice, the sly, wrinkly brotherly Libyans. Zimbabweans were not only fearful but also sceptical; the fear for their country, their sovereignty and children's future was being mortgaged to the Chinese and foreigners by another foreigner, Matibili-Mugabe.

Southern Africa is globally strategic in many terms. The main effect is with regard to strategic materials e.g. uranium, gold, diamonds and chrome and also the Cape sea route. The other thing to remember is that if the USA did not have a presence in Africa then someone else would. The Russians had played in Africa for a long time and still play many military and political games behind the scenes. But China was very keen on moving into Africa. The idea was to cut off supplies of raw materials to US industry in the event of a future war.

But why would Russia still support anti-freedom leaders of Communist nature if it were a "strategic partner of the West", and a free country? The fact was Russia was not democratic at all. The Communist Party was still the only true national party in Russia, and President Putin was just another product of the KGB. Russia was still armed to the teeth with nuclear weapons all pointed at the USA and was still openly communist. Russia and China helped each other constantly and in the UN they stood together hence nothing had changed except the perception in the minds of American leaders and that perception was false. The Russians were striking deals with the West in order to get money and buy time. Soon, they would retarget Europe with their nukes.

From Burma to Nepal to Zimbabwe, China was providing political, diplomatic and security support to failing dictatorships. Beijing gave just enough help for the dictator to survive sanctions and domestic popular revolts, while the PRC gained a dependent state. In repayment for reanimating these near-dead regimes, the PRC was demanding and getting obedience to its nationalistic policies of creating strategic space around China, isolating Taiwan, securing critical resources, and guaranteeing markets for Chinese products.

The Zimbabwean national assembly laid down laws to ensure that high priority be given to the Chinese enterprises. Although there were no Tibetan refugees to persecute in Zimbabwe, Mugabe did his best to please his new master by helping to isolate Taiwan and arrested and beat up African street vendors in Harare, Gweru and Bulawayo to pave and sustain the fledgling Chinese traders.

As a latecomer to Africa, China was prepared to enter regions and take risks that others would not. Like the West, China was not sniffy about dealing with despots. In Zimbabwe, Mugabe may have been admiring the free blue tiles on the roof of his palace, but ordinary citizens had coined a new phrase to describe Chinese goods; from buses that break down to clothing that falls apart; as "zhing-zhong". Zimbabweans had even started using this epithet to describe Chinese people.

Although China's Africa policy had won the hearts and minds of the continent's corrupt rulers, the people themselves appeared to lag behind. As usual, they were waiting to see whether the Chinese model of engagement with the continent was going to be any different than those of the exploitative colonial powers of the past. So far the formula seemed much the same, propping up unwanted juntas, corruption of the worst kind and resource pillaging with no local gain.

Case study: Zimbabwe

"Human rights and fundamental freedoms allow us fully to develop and use our human qualities, intelligence, talents and conscience to satisfy our spiritual and other needs. It follows, therefore, that the denial of human rights and fundamental freedoms is not only an individual and personal tragedy but also creates conditions of social and political unrest, sowing seeds of violence and conflict within and between societies and nations," President Robert Mugabe on April 20 1989.

In 1884 England, France and Germany held The Congress of Berlin to discuss how to divide Africa between them. Not surprisingly, there were no African representatives invited. France ended up with the biggest patch of Africa but the English, largely thanks to the ruthless Cecil John Rhodes, eventually captured a number of magnificent countries. The greatest prize of all was securing the Union of South Africa, where Rhodes and his friends found some of the world's largest deposits of gold and diamonds.

Rhodes was a man of racist vision and soon turned his imperial eyes northwards toward the rich lands ruled by Lobungula. A Charter Company was formed and in l890 the Pioneer Column marched through unknown territories to steal the country for Britain. Adventurers, miners and ambitious businessmen moved to populate the new country. Inevitably 'British black sheep'; murderers, rapists and thieves, sent by embarrassed titled families arrived, forcing the indigenous population into the mountains. In time the pioneer look faded and little Britain emerged; better roads were built, fine buildings constructed and eventually one of the finest and most efficient civil services in the world was established as Rhodesia was born. Soon an apartheid two-tier system was implemented; the whites were in command and the blacks, like children, were to be given limited health, education and the continuity of their tribal rule, provided they behaved themselves. This system was never discussed with the resident blacks; it was just imposed with everything neatly graded 'Blacks Only' and 'Whites Only'.

The first Chimurenga (rebellion) began when outspoken black leaders actively stood against the imposed British way of life. The Mashonaland Rebellion, when many innocent blacks were killed ended with the capture of the religious leader, Mbuya Nehanda. Nehanda and another religious leader, Kaguvi, were executed in Salisbury on 27 April 1898.

Zimbabwe has been the scene of much social and armed conflict, with firstly Zulus (1840), then white settlers (1890) dispossessing the Ndebele (Zulus) and resident population; nationalist 'black' armies forcing the minority supremacist white government to submit to elections, and the post-independence leadership committing atrocities in southern areas (ndebele) where it lacked local support and widely seen as revenge for earlier colonisation; to the chaotic and violent land redistribution also seen as revenge for past injustices.

While Zimbabwe, quite unlike many other countries in the region, has relatively few different ethnic groups, ethnicity has long dictated its politics, both in the ruling party and in the opposition, at the expense of rational policies and clear national concerns. During the campaign for general elections trivial slogans such as "Pasi naNkomo! [Down with Nkomo!]" and "Phansi loMgabe! [Down with Mugabe!]" were more visible than visions for the new nation were.

Zimbabweans are notoriously reluctant to discuss their political views, regardless of where they are on the political spectrum. Because of this lack of political maturity among Zimbabwean rulers and voters, Mugabe managed to retain the support he had gained at independence while he continued to butcher Ndebele civilians in Matabeleland and the Midlands for five years after independence. The problem with political systems that are deeply divided on ethnic lines is that conspiracies are easy to conjure up and politicians and ordinary people alike refuse to engage their minds in serious debate, opting to spend endless hours discussing phantoms.

The culture of using conspiracies as a scapegoat when tackling problems, dates back to colonial administrations. Rhodesian government ministers, just as Israelis do with the Palestinians, believed accusing nationalists of being communists and terrorist, instead of addressing their problems, was enough to dismiss them. Soon after independence Mugabe's ministers and apologists routinely accused Nkomo of trying to start an insurrection with the help of the apartheid South African government, killed more than 30,000 civilians on the basis of that, instead of owning up to the glaring fact that Zanu's blind desire for a one-party state had plunged the nation into a bloodbath.

Among the 1960 and 70s Zimbabweans, the debate regarding the broader post-colonial economic and ideological challenges to be addressed in order to provide hope and promise to the majority of the population was missing. For the crafty, crook Mugabe, the lack of this debate was convenient as it provided an avenue to hijack the post-colonial state using a populist agenda without affording the people an opportunity to debate the critical governance and economic issues.

What was striking was that the lack of debate became institutionalised and came to characterize the contemporary Zimbabwean political scene leading to the widely held view that while Zimbabweans are generally regarded as hard working and intelligent people, they appear helpless in the face of a humanly induced economic and political nightmare. The world had been surprised that a people who, twenty six years ago, were distinguished architects of their own liberation against an organized and economically, militarily strong regime, had now been transformed into a nation that now pinned its hope on the retirement or death of one old senile man.

Emmerson Mnangagwa, a chief Mugabe collaborator told a rally at the Victoria Falls "...the government is considering as one option the burning down of all villages infested with dissidents ...... are F**ng roaches....we have the 5th Brigade 'the DDT' brought in to eradicate them!" he continued, "Blessed are they who will follow the path of the Government laws, for their days on earth shall be increased. But woe to those who will chose the path of collaboration with dissidents for we will certainly shorten their stay on earth". Mnagagwa was in charge of the dreaded CIO at the time.

From the moment it was deployed in Matabeleland in 1983 under General Perence Shiri, the 5th Brigade waged a campaign of mass murder, beatings and arson deliberately targeted at the civilian population. "Villagers were forced to sing songs in the Shona language praising Zanu while dancing on the mass graves of their families and fellow villagers who had been killed and buried minutes earlier," wrote Martin Meredith.

Flash back: When Zimbabwe gained independence in 1980, some ZIPRA (Ndebele) guerrillas remained in the bush because of mistrust of ZANU (Shona). There followed a period of insurrection, lawlessness and outright warfare between Zanu and ZIPRA forces. Ndebele ZIPRA deserters were labelled 'dissidents' and were killed often brutally and in cold blood wherever they were found.

The 5th Brigade, an unconstitutional militia, was directly answerable to Mugabe, was variously deployed in Matabeleland over the period 1983 to 1984. By February 1983, some 16000 square kilometres of Southern Matabeleland and an area of the Midlands inhabited by mainly Ndebele people, was cordoned off and a 24-hour curfew was imposed. No food was allowed into the curfew area and 1000s of innocent rural people starved to death. The atrocities committed by the 5th Brigade are legendary and well documented especially by the Zimbabwe Catholic Commission of Justice and Peace. Following an international outcry, Mugabe in September 1983, set up a commission of inquiry headed by Mr Chihambakwe, to investigate the allegations. Although fearful of the repercussions, hundreds of eyewitnesses to the atrocities turned up to give evidence. When taken to court (December 1999) in an effort to force the release of the report Mugabe, through his legal representative, claimed that it was lost!

When Mzilikazi fled from the wrath of Shaka, 1840, he crossed the Limpopo River and made his new home at a place he called Gubulawayo, the 'place of slaughter'. He felt safe on the other side of Matopos hills and from this base, his Impi's (battalions) of the Ndebele traversed the central African region building an economy based on pillage, kidnapping and murder.

The extremely cruel yearly raids on the Shona by the Ndebele, only ceased in 1890 when Rhodes' pioneer column reached that part of the continent and put a stop to the practice. Because of the past tribal history, intense hatred still exists between the two ethnic groupings.

However what is clear is that if the Ndebele raided Shona girls in the mid 1800s, then these are the matriarchs of the majority of present day Ndebeles (vana vaTete; Auntie's kids). It is more logical to claim that Ndebele raids made the Shona and Ndebele more of blood relatives of each other. The Shona have been wrongly taught by the British and by the Malawian Mugabe, a foreigner, to despise their own blood, just because the Ndebele speak a different language from theirs. This fact should be taken seriously as a point for forging stronger Shona Ndebele unity.

At the beginning of the nationalist movement in Rhodesia Joshua Nkomo rose as a leader of all the people. Nkomo was a labour activist, and labour issues affect all people working regardless of their origins. Little mileage was made out of Shona-Ndebele rivalry in the early days of nationalism. Names like Chinamano, Sithole and Jasper Savanhu shared the same platform in these days. Mugabe introduced the tribalism as he entered the playground and coveted the cherished position of Father Zimbabwe held by Nkomo. Mugabe pushed the argument that in order for Nkomo to be acceptable as a National Leader, he had to appease the angered Shona spirits, aggrieved by Nkomo's ancestors. A name like Nkomo is not a 'true Ndebele'. Nkomo's ancestors were obviously Karangas who were co-opted into the Ndebele system. Nkomo was in fact a victim, whose family was raided, and stripped of their identity, and forced to assume a second-class status in the Ndebele Kingdom.

The new state of Zimbabwe was born out of a civil war. Since 1980 a new system ensued. The new system assumed an alien populist socialist ideology, packaged as communism that pretended on worker representation embraced trappings of foreign cultures and abandoned the ideals of the liberation struggle. The new system merely replaced the colonial administrator and adopted an agenda that was at variance with the expectations and aspirations of the Zimbabwe people. Party loyalists whose brief was to serve and save the party regardless of national needs staffed the state. It was, in short, a Western backed and funded corrupt state that was widely hailed as a model for post-colonial stability and racial reconciliation.

Ever since he took power in this Southern African country in 1980, Mugabe had tolerated little internal and external dissent, cowering SADC, the AU and at times causing impish mischief at the UN. Mugabe was concerned only about power and used race and tribes purely as a screen behind which he could crush and maintain his rule. Against every opposition party, from Ndabaningi Sithole's Zanu-Ndonga, Muzorewa's UANC, to Edgar Tekere's ZUM, Joshua Nkomo's ZAPU, Enoch Dumbutshena Forum Party to Tsvangirai's MDC, Mugabe had acted with such a single-minded viciousness. Against everyone; students, workers, whites, coloureds, squatters, African foreigners, traders, against everything, Mugabe had used brutal force. Rowdy, gullible and manipulatable youths were made agents of repression and were unleashed on the electorate where anyone perceived to be supporting contrary views was punished severely.

The use of youths in this way was not new. Muzorewa who was prime minister of the short-lived Zimbabwe-Rhodesia, introduced   Ziso revanhu. Bishop Abel Muzorewa began his political career as a courageous opponent of the racist regime of Ian Smith. In 1972, he rallied the black people to vote 'No' to any extension of racist rule on the Pearce commission. Later, for reasons perhaps related to his inherent pacifist philosophy as a man of God, he seemed to collaborate with the pathetic Smith regime, until he ended up as a puppet prime minister. Muzorewa's Ziso reVanhu youths became agents of terror as they invaded rural and urban communities, forcing people to join the unpopular UANC party and to support it without questioning. Many atrocities were committed by Ziso revanhu youths. Muzorewa and his cronies were ever charged for these atrocities.

Smith's acceptance of majority rule was momentous: It opened the way for an opportunity to peaceful transition. For years, Smith had tried to negotiate a settlement with several Black Nationalist leaders. Primary among them was Muzorewa, a small, American-educated pastor. He was a forthright critic of the government's racial discrimination and had supported civil disobedience and mass protest in the past. The United Nations had honoured him for Outstanding Achievement in Human Rights. The other black leaders with whom Smith pledged to work were the Rev. Ndabaningi Sithole, a Methodist founder of Zanu who had been imprisoned for 10 years for opposition activities, and Chief Jeremiah Chirau, a tribal elder who had long been amenable to white interests. Smith and his moderate black allies hoped that if a multiracial government could be cobbled together, black African states would withdraw their support for the guerrillas and make way for an anti-Communist black government.

By contrast, Mugabe and Nkomo made it clear that their Patriotic Front would not give up the fight and participate in elections unless they were assured of victory. In so doing, the guerrilla leaders removed any doubt that they had no interest in democracy. Presaging the edicts of Al Qaeda in Iraq, both guerrilla leaders pledged violence against any black Zimbabwean who dared take part in the April balloting.

Nkomo called for a "bloodbath." He said, "We mean to get that country by force, and we shall get it." Mugabe, not to be outdone, issued a public death list of 50 individuals associated with the internal settlement, including the three black leaders of the executive council. Zanu described these individuals as "Zimbabwean black bourgeoisie, traitors, fellow-travellers, and puppets of the Ian Smith regime, opportunistic running-dogs and other capitalist vultures." Mugabe also expressed his belief that "the multiparty system is a luxury" and said that if Zimbabwean blacks did not like Marxism, "then we will have to re-educate them."

This was the same Mugabe whom Young, in a 1978 interview with the Times of London, had called "a very gentle man," adding, "I can't imagine Joshua Nkomo, or Robert Mugabe, ever pulling the trigger on a gun to kill anyone. I doubt that they ever have." But as Muzorewa immediately discovered, to the Carter administration, no government without Robert Mugabe in charge was worth having. Muzorewa, spurned by the West, deemed illegitimate by the African dictatorships, and forced to contend with Communist-armed insurgents, would hold power for a mere matter of months. The betrayal of Muzorewa is one of the more pusillanimous episodes in American foreign policy.

Other religious leaders have not fared so badly in their brief sorties into politics. There was Rev Canaan Banana who became the first ceremonial president of the republic. Even if he ended his life in circumstances approximating the ignominy of someone quite unsavoury, he did make and left his violent and dark marks on the people of Zimbabwe. The culture of political hatred by these leaders engendered was going to take generations or dozens of years of determined efforts to wipe out. This was the reason why Mugabe, and all the retrogressive and repressive elements of the regime had sleepless nights.

Zimbabwe does not have many state secrets to worry its neighbours and the rest of the world. It was not about Mugabe building a uranium enrichment plant in Zvimba, or about the army testing some potent biological weapon*. The only secrets in Zimbabwe had to do with Mugabe's methods of surviving the political turbulence and the economic turmoil; the acts of violence against his perceived opponents, were some of the secrets that Mugabe wanted to keep within his little chicken chest kept safely and were giving him sleepless nights.

*In 2000 while Mugabe was supporting Kabila's army in the DRC he happened across the fact that the Congo has one of the two nuclear reactors and research centres in Africa, courtesy of the now defunct Mobuto and USA collaboration. As payment for his army, Mugabe negotiated with Kabila to loot the nuclear reactor and the research centre. At the same time he sent his troops to guard the Shinkolbwe Mine where uranium used in the first atomic bomb was mined (Sunday

Times Oct 1999). In September 1999, Zimbabwe organized a visit by a North Korean Delegation to the Shinkolbwe mine where they also visited the nuclear reactor and research centre about 30 km outside of Kinshasa. (Sunday Times September 1999 South Africa). A plan was made to export this capability to Zimbabwe for onward transfer to interested parties. This was done via 'importing' 40 tonnes of "copper ore" from the Congo to the Alaska Mine in Zimbabwe for processing. Enriched uranium as well as other nuclear hardware was part of the 40-ton consignment. Involved were General Vitalis Zvinavashe, Permanent secretary of Defence Job Whabira, Colonel Francis Zvinashe and Brigadier John Moyo and Osleg, a Zimbabwe Defence Force company. These were all close military friends of Mugabe. Libya in June 2000 suddenly provided three ex Soviet MIG 23 fighter jets to Zimbabwe plus 8 more on loan, as well as allowing 400 troops from Zimbabwe to be trained at Bhengazi in Libya. The payment for this was to be a nuclear trade. During 2000,mulas of Iran, who were also in the nuclear market, agreed that it would work with Mugabe in building his nuclear capability. Iran had a long-standing relationship with a company called Investigacioes Aplicades (Invap) from Argentina that was trying to build electricity nuclear reactors in Zimbabwe. Invap had willingly engaged in nuclear negotiations and transfers over the years with countries engaged in covert nuclear weapons programs. At this time the CIA was busy trying to keep up with what had happened to the enriched uranium and Congo's nuclear capability. Due to the fact that the USA had built the Congo nuclear plant in the first place it was rather difficult for them to admit that their nuclear material had gone missing. One of the fuel rods turned up in Italy sometime later, where it was being marketed by the Mafia.

One of the most important restraints on any state becoming a failed state is if a significant majority of a nation's population retain faith in democratic institutions and hope in the capacity of those institutions to provide a way out of the nightmare. It is important to remember that a collapsed economy per se does not automatically result in a failed state. If a nation, despite a collapsed economy, retains a cohesive society then a state will not fall apart. In the darkest hours of World War II, Britain was isolated and its economy devastated. However one could never argue that at that point in time Britain was a failed state.

By 2002 over 1,300 Zimbabwe opposition activists had been murdered, some in cold blood, some in broad daylight, and some by known perpetrators yet not a single successful investigation of any of these murders was conducted. During the same period numerous opposition leaders and activists were arrested by the police and detained on spurious charges. In some of the more high-profile cases, such as the Cain Nkala trial, the police were accused of deliberately investigating the wrong people.

Just as the police had failed to investigated, so too had the Attorney General's office failed to prosecute successfully. In some instances perpetrators had been identified by High Court judges and yet the Attorney General's office failed to bring these criminals to justice. In high-profile murders such as the murders of Chaminya and Mabikwa the alleged murderers identified by High Court judges had still not been prosecuted over six years after the murders were committed. In the unsuccessful prosecution of Fletcher Dulini Ncube and his colleagues in the Cain Nkala case, despite very strong findings having been made by the presiding judge that the police were responsible for torture, no further investigations or prosecutions were brought by the Attorney General's office either against the police involved or against the actual perpetrators of the crime.

Whether or not the allocation of land compromises a judge's integrity or independence the fact of the matter remains that a judge's effectiveness is compromised if a he or she tries to hold down two jobs at one time. No one can possibly argue in good faith against the fact that being a judge is a full-time profession. Likewise no one can possibly argue that running a large scale commercial farming enterprise is also a full-time job. Neither can be done competently together. Criminals were literally getting away with murder.

Parliament has never been a strong institution in Zimbabwe. It was not so during white minority rule and it had certainly not been so since independence. It had always suffered from the disability that it was not adequately representative of all points of view and always under funded. That was certainly the case when it only represented the views of the white minority and sadly no honest and objective commentator could say that Mugabe's Parliaments adequately represented the views of all sectors of the Zimbabwean society and as a result it had not become a forum for the resolution of Zimbabwe's grave problems.

How to create the African bourgeoisie classes

Franz Fanon 'The Wretched of the Earth' described the character of the class that inherited power from the colonialists. It is "....a sort of little greedy caste, avid and voracious, with the mind of a huckster, only too glad to accept the dividends that the former colonial powers hands out. This get-rich-quick middle class shows itself incapable of great ideas or of inventiveness. It remembers what it has read in European textbooks and imperceptibly it becomes not even the replica of Europe, but its caricature... This class is completely canalised into activities of the intermediary type. Its innermost vocation seems to be to keep in the running and to be part of the racket. The psychology of the national bourgeoisie is that of a businessman, not that of a captain of industry."

Up until 1939, most Africans were educated at missionary schools as they were no access for Africans in most, if not all, government schools. Kutama and Waddilove mission schools were about some of the earliest church schools commissioned in or around 1893 in the Zvimba area populated by the Gushungo clan of the shona people.

The 'Gushungo' are not Zezuru or shona per se, but ironically have roots either in Swaziland or Lesotho. They came to Zimbabwe together with white men as scotch-cart drivers (chemutengures) in the 1880s-90s and then settled in the Buhera/Wedza area where the totem Gushungo was coined.

The Zvimba area proved to be resistant missionary teachings especially after the murder by the white BSA Police of seven chiefs during a church sermon. The chiefs were arrested, tried, flogged then shot and killed for resisting "arrest". From thence (1894), the area lacked respect and disbelief in white men and never again accepted without question a white man's statement. Nevertheless, some of the children in the area eventually converted, went to school and went on to work and hence encountered Western literacy and exposure. Thompson Samkange was one of the earliest mission educated sons of the area and of the Gushungo clan who went on to become a teacher and eventually an evangelist.

By 1928 the first missionary conference of Christian natives was held and saw Thompson Sankange elected as secretary, a post he retained for the next 20 years. By 1930 Bulawayo was also the centre of African politics in Zimbabwe. There, Martha Ngano was already running the Bantu Voters League; Masotsha Ndlovu the Industrial and Commercial Workers Union. The city also hosted the only black newspaper; Jasper Zengeza Savanhu's The Bantu Mirror.

Thompson was important to the elites in Zimbabwe then because of his association and recognition by the Methodist Church as a leader and shared this sense of centrality of Christianity and hence of the importance of the black clergy. For him and many others to follow him, black advancement was spiritual and it required repentance and submission to the judgement of God and this would eventually lead to the earthly kingdom promised by the white preachers. This inferiority complex is a cultural and central trite in Zimbabwean society.

Because of the frictions and racism within the church, Thompson soon realised that Europeans were educating Africans but would not give them political, social and economic equality. He also realised that Africans were not calling for equality with whites but for respect for their own values too. By 1938 the Native conference had became a political platform at which different black church ministers and politicians congregated to further the struggle for black emancipation. Distinguished ministers like Hlabangana, Rusike and Khumalo were active participants in the conferences.

There were complicating factors such as language affecting early black Christian politicians of the 1930s, especially the use of Ndebele and Zulu. The Christians of that time were using Zulu text bibles and were influenced by their white compatriots to favour the introduction of Zulu in Zimbabwean schools. Though to Thompson, it was a white inspired debate that did not require his time or effort, but then, since it was not resolved at that time, it still influences politics in present day Zimbabwe sometimes with catastrophic results as the debate has been expanded.

Besides Thompson Samkange, others were also advancing black aspiration via the Methodist church. The Zvimba brothers, Meshek Kamcheta and Matthew Chigaga all sons of Chief Chigaga went on to form break away White Bird churches, drove away the white Methodist preachers at their father's palace and assumed control of Zvimba Christianity. The new church had intense local sentimentalisms and colonial resentments and celebrated as saints Zvimba men and women who had died fighting whites. Matthew then went on to challenge the government in Zvimba by declaring ".... In Zvimba I am the Government official and Administrator" claiming back pay and expenses. For his efforts he was sentenced to corporal punishment for tax evasion.

The children of these early African elites had better education and life styles and went on to attend South African Universities like Fort Hare were they mixed with a more advanced African, the ANC. Usually it entailed a lot of sacrifice for the parents as missionary work was not paying very well. It was usually after graduation of one of these siblings from university that faster progress was made.

However the Native Congress continued to be the rallying point for any aspiring politician and it made greater impact in 1938 under the presidentship of Solomon Chavunduka. This was the first most political charged Native meeting and was attended by firebrands like Aaron Jacha, J. Maganya and Sigauke of Gweru. The congress also furthered the political aspirations of many regional leaders and brought out some into the limelight; e.g. D. C Dhliwayo, Z. M Magkatho, R.B Sibindwane, B. Manyanda, J.Z Savanhu and others.

Hence in the early 1940s there was need for the Native Congress to become a national movement and bring out plausible leaders. Again this role was filled in by the church, which had the resources and the numbers and the educated membership. Thompson became the President of the new umbrella body but by 1944 the organisation was riddled by tribal differences, jealousy and differences of opinion. Later presidents, Enoch Dumbutshena and Joshua Nkomo, called it weak and ineffectual. Further, rival organisations, like Benjamin Burombo's African Voice Association and Mzingeli's Reformed Industrial and Commercial Worker's Union, were equally dismissive of the Congress especially after the effective 1945 and 1948 Railways strike.

These strikes made the unions powerful and weakened Congress as the unions pulled out when the president of Congress disagreed with the strike due to pressure from the colonial government. Further Congress critically depended on the existence of clusters of enthusiasts. It was strong in Bulawayo, and Gweru but ineffective in Harare were there was a feud between Jacha and Munyanda. In actual fact congress was too moderate and hence weak as it was allegedly partly finance or encouraged by the white government.

Following the end of World War 2 in 1945, there was increased industrialisation in Rhodesia. Poor working and living conditions provided the first set of complaints that unionists campaigned against. By the 1940s, Jasper Savanhu was tripling up as trade unionist, journalist and politician. The pool of the first nationalists cut their teeth in the trade union movement. Experiences within the church and nationalist movement showed that the white regime was not willing to surrender power.

This changed however in 1945 when Aaron Jacha resigned from Congress and was replaced by the more combative Bulawayo Journalist Savanhu. Savanhu was convinced that strong trade unions were needed and his paper "Organisation – trade unionism" saw unionism as the only way to obtain better wages. He was deeply involved in the 1945 railway workers strike as secretary general of Congress. His speech at Congress then is often cited as the dawn of proletarian consciousness in Zimbabwe. Though it sounded like a socialist speech as it combined invocations of capitalism as the enemy, it seems Jasper Savanhu was operating within some favourable ideological ambiguity as "depravation of opportunity to work our way up the ladder of success..." evoked emotions of socialism. Thus for Savanhu the aftermath of the strike was the creation of a Federation of African Workers was natural and progressive, advising the workers to stick to their graduate African leaders whom he thought would not mislead the masses. He had fallen ill in 1946 and exited union politics.

Enter Sipambaniso who was even more militant than Savanhu and blamed the Europeans who did not consider the African to be human beings. Hlabangana followed him in this line of thought that eventually led to the 1948 workers' strike. By then Bulawayo was red hot as a rift had developed between the leaders and the led.

The 1948 strike eventually led to the creation of new educated leadership headed by Enoch Dumbutshena, Sipambaniso, Benjamin Burombo and Masotsha Ndlovu. Enoch was fairly anti-communist and the general people in the unions did not understand what communism was. However among the new leadership were communist influences from Fort Hare University in South Africa who were advocating for workers committees, which eventually led to Enoch's resignation. This was very damaging and led to the introduction of Graduate politicisation of the Zimbabwean political arena with Stanlake Samkange (the son of Thompson) and Enoch 'intellectual' public debates.

The federation of Rhodesia, Zambia and Nyasaland was however to take central ground though the masses showed no signs of appreciating these intellectual debates calling for passive resistance against whites. Hence a rift again appeared mainly on the issue of tactics. Once Federation was a forgone conclusion, Samkanage put himself forward to contest the election supported by his Zvimba roots and Isaac Samuriwo, Chief Zvimba and the Southern African Association. Nkomo bid for the Matebeleland seat. The Federal Party chose neither of them instead opting for the recovered Jasper Savanhu and Hove. Hence Stanlake and Nkomo stood as the Nationalist and were roundly defeated by Savanhu and Hove whom in turn where unable to advance the masses grievances due to party discipline.

In reality, Jasper Savanhu had attempted during the 1940s and 1950s to build bridges between privileged white worlds and those of the disadvantaged black majority but had failed due to the emergence of radicals in both black and white camps. Between 1958 and 1962, youthful elites, like Savanhu's son Godfree Sonono, embraced Pan-Africanism, not the paternalistic, dreams of earlier generations. The ultimate fate of Jasper Savanhu's multiracialism was that Europeans rejected it for the Rhodesia Front's intransigence in 1962 general elections. Especially on its own terms, multiracialism was fairly successful as Mugabe would try to resuscitate in the early 1980s. Before its electoral demise black elites expected, in ever-small numbers after 1958, colonial assimilation. Recognizing the importance of encouraging, acculturating and assimilating them, some white Rhodesians campaigned for such black elite 'privilege'. About 50,000 (5%) of them were allowed to vote.

The National Democratic Party was formed on 1 January 1960. The days of the NDP marked the turning point or transition from political or nationalist activism to the humble beginnings of the armed liberation struggle. There was no way the white regime could be dislodged without recourse to violent means and the seeds for a military confrontation were sawn, leading to a 15 year civil war headed by the nationalist movement.

Angry at foreign financiers, fearing winds of change and nervous about the African nationalist mobilization that was currently underway, the Rhodesian white electorate's fascists ensured the ascent of a new Rhodesian Front government headed by Ian Smith in 1962. The new government responded to pressure for racial reform by declaring an illegal "Unilateral Declaration of Independence" (UDI) in November 1965. International sanctions followed, but with the state intervening extensively through central planning and strategic investments, support from South Africa and Portuguese-ruled Mozambique, a default on Rhodesia's foreign debt, and prohibitions on capital outflow, saw one of the world's fastest growth rates at 9.5% p.a, from 1966-1974. This, however, only resulted in over capitalisation.

If white capital suffered throughout from uneven development and periodic crisis tendencies, so did black resistance under the nationalists. The only time black workers openly and effectively revolted was the Burombo/Savanhu led 1948 general strike. Leaders of emergent trade unions were detained by the repressive Rhodesian security apparatus together with their fellow nationalist friends. The black petit-bourgeoisie was systematically stifled, usually through classical colonial racial constraints, restrictions on commercial activities, and unworkable informal financial markets.

Within a decade, the peasant-based guerrilla war began having an impact, and white fears mounted as Marxist-Leninist rhetoric drew nearer and louder. The two Patriotic Front liberation movements were countered by the Rhodesian army's intensified violence, which was primarily responsible for the war's 140,000 civilian deaths during the 1970s.

The war of liberation was fought from so many fronts and many people were involved than the world is made to believe by selfish people with selective and chronic memory lapses. It would appear now as if only a handful of people risked their lives during the war, yet villages upon villages of masses risked their lives, parting with hard earned property and livestock to give logistical support to freedom fighters, some of whom turned into national traitors and copters after independence. There was untold suffering in the villages where people would be shot dead in front of children and relatives, or battered and left for dead simply because they were proven or even suspected to be aiding the freedom fighters. In some areas like most parts of Mashonaland people were herded into protected compounds (conscription camps), the so-called 'keeps' that were initiated by the Rhodesian regime as a way of cutting them off from any ties with the 'terrorists'.

The psychological trauma of being so close to the struggle and witnessing all the harrowing scenes of death and survival still live with most of the ordinary people some, if not all, of whom had not been compensated in any way. This was against a backdrop of massive rewards that had been given to "..war veterans" who were not in office while those in government office simply helped themselves to the national pot.

After South Africa withdrew explicit military support to Smith in 1976, half the white population fled the country and economic depression cut production by 40 percent between 1976 and 1979. The Rhodesians finally surrendered at the 1979 Lancaster House peace talks in London, yet Zanu-ZAPU's indecisive military victory, as well as nationalist infighting leading up to negotiations, left various kinds of residual economic and political power in white hands. White Rhodesians and the West were stunned at how much black voter support Mugabe garnered in the April 1980 election (62 percent, with ZAPU getting 24 percent, and the collaborating black party, UANC, just 8 percent, with turnout at 95 percent). Similarly, black voters were surprised by how immediately Mugabe was willing to compromise with white-owned capital in the name of racial reconciliation by resuscitating Jasper Savanhu's 1940-60s multiracialism theory. Tsvangirai of the MDC would also try this in the early 2000s.

Vorster, Henry Kissinger and ultimately the British managers of Zimbabwe's transition together hoped for a typical neo-colonial solution, in which property rights would be the foundation of a new constitution, willing-seller/willing-buyer land policy would allow rural social relations to be undisturbed, and nationalization of productive economic activity would be kept to a minimum. A black government would, moreover, have greater capacity to quell labour unrest, strikes, and other challenges to law and order. If a new black consuming class were to be built, this was to occur primarily through an expanded civil service rather than via an assault on those who retained economic power. Traditional modes of patriarchy would remain intact, in no small part to ensure the ongoing reproduction of labour at a very low cost. A foreign debt load would soon crush any hopes for future economic autonomy. Intensification of the inherited export-led-import-substitution bias would ensure the steady supply of raw materials at ever-lower prices. This was to be implemented in South Africa as well 14 years later.

Once the question of capitalist accumulation had been raised, then the question that followed, almost trivially, was that of the capitalist class that was to drive the process of capital accumulation. One thing that emerges clearly from the Asian experience was the significance of the dependence of the state on the activities of the private sector for its development strategy. The culture of capitalist accumulation in a specific country ultimately depends on national characteristics (class formation and resource base) and policies towards both foreign and domestic capital. Historically, this class was referred to as a 'national bourgeoisie'. If capitalist accumulation were to take place, private domestic capital would serve as a catalyst.

Africa is unlikely to constitute an attractive place for foreign capital for some time to come. It is clear that capital does not flow from the developed to the developing countries on the scale implied by the relative factor endowments doctrine (Eatwell, 1996; Krugman, 1993). There is growing theoretical and empirical material suggesting that the segmentation in global markets is such that sub-Saharan Africa regions may not benefit from capital movements. The point here is that capitalist accumulation will be largely national for much of Africa and dependent on black entrepreneurs. Indeed, given Africa's very tarnished image, confidence by Africans in the continent's future will be of prime value in resuscitating future investment.

It is generally presumed that African capitalists are wasteful. However, compared to similar classes in the successful Asian countries, African capitalists are not big spenders. The problem with African capitalists is lack of faith in their own countries as investment sites and the consequent tendency to expatriate capital abroad. One should stress here that funds held by Africans abroad count in hundreds of billions.

If capitalism is to be politically viable in Africa, it will have to have some national anchoring based partly on the capacity of the indigenous capitalist classes to direct state policy toward their gaining access to labour, land and capital, toward limiting the role of foreign capital, and toward nurturing indigenous capitalist investment by facilitating institutions of stabilising capital-labour relations and supplying technical services and physical infrastructure. For political legitimacy the capitalist class will have to convince critical sections of the nation that its 'project' of capital accumulation is in the national interest.

It breaks many people's heart to see that the freedom all fought for so hard and for so long had been privatised by the few in leadership positions. The "combatants and comrades" were now a special breed of Zimbabweans with special privileges ahead of those that "did not fight the war". The duty of the rest was to vote these privileged few into positions of power over and over again. An old senile President now ring-fenced from the people by psychophants was an institution that had to be held in awe and fear. Why citizens were not told this was going to be the situation when "fighting for freedom" is anybody's guess. Capital accumulation and the developmental agenda by this lot was a wet dream.

The totem struggle:

Zimbabwean people can roughly be grouped as the Shona and Ndebele with a sprinkling of indigenous whites and Indians (1%). The Shona people (the major Bantu tribe) share a mutually intelligible language and customs. But ethnically they are not homogenous. In real terms there is no shona; rather the so-called shona tribes are more related by totems than language. The term shona is a Ndebele references to the disappearing tactics of these people (eshonele). Between the clans there is a diversity of dialects, religious beliefs and customs.

The five principal shona clans are the Karanga (reference for "from the East",) 35%, Zezuru (The term 'Zezuru', first used by 18th-century Portuguese traders, means 'people who live in a high area', not inappropriate for a people who occupied all the higher echelons of power in Zimbabwe.) 30%, Manyika, Ndau and Korekore are all related by totem. Of these, the biggest and most powerful clans are the Karanga and the Zezuru. The Ndebele are an off-shoot of the Zulus of South Africa, having migrated to this south western part of Zimbabwe in the early 1800s. Today they comprise about 12% of the Zimbabwe population and generally migrate back to South Africa on reaching puberty.

Largely unperceived by outsiders, an almighty struggle was always going on between Karangas and Zezurus inside Mugabe's ruling ZANU party and between the Ndebele and Shonas inside the MDC that at some point was destined to explode and completely reshape Zimbabwean politics. The Karanga provided the bulk of the fighting forces and military leaders who fought the 1972-79 chimurenga (struggle for independence). Nevertheless, the Zanu movement was led by a Malawian intellectual, albeit outsider, with several degrees named Mataibili-Mugabe, who did not do any fighting himself. The ethnic differences at that time seemed to matter little since Zanu proclaimed unity as one of its ideals. Mugabe's predecessors as leaders were Ndabaningi Sithole, a Ndau, and Herbert Chitepo, a Manyika, assassinated in mysterious circumstances in 1975.

The take-over:

The Zezuru hegemony had crept up and become a fact of life in Zimbabwean politics, although for many years there was intense debate as to the authenticity of Mugabe's origins. What is more certain is that in 1963, when Zanu was formed, Mugabe was appointed to the powerful position of secretary general after being nominated by a simpleton named Nolan Makombe, a leading Karanga who had convinced his co-tribesmen in the movement that Mugabe was a fellow Karanga of the influential Mugabe dynasty of chiefs from the area of the Great Zimbabwe ruins near Masvingo. Mugabe cleverly encouraged this belief until he was well entrenched in power.

Although at its inception Zanu was led by Sithole, the party was dominated by the Karanga's that included Leopold Takawira, Nelson and Michael Mawema, Simon Muzenda and Eddison Zvobgo. The tribal composition replicated itself in the armed wing of with the Karangas, led by Josiah Tongogara, forming the backbone of the liberation struggle. Other prominent Karangas were Emmerson Mnangagwa, Josiah Tungamirai and Vitalis Zvinavashe.

Tribalism played a part in the death of the chairperson of Zanu's supreme war council (Dare reChimurenga). A 1976 report initiated by the Zambian government, The Special International Commission on the Assassination of Herbert Wiltshire Chitepo, found. He died in exile in 1975 when a bomb planted under the seat of his VW Beetle exploded. In a letter to his wife, Chitepo, a Manyika, told of a list of men "the Karangas intended to eliminate". Once the report on the death had been published the idea that Zanu's power struggles were based on ethnic factionalism took hold in many circles. Indeed, by the time the letter was placed in evidence, the commission had heard many versions of ethnic strife in Zanu. The report also cites complaints of ethnicity as the reason behind the Nhari Rebellion, a mutiny by Zanla cadres due to frontline shortages.

By 2005, the Zezurus had finally steam-rolled themselves into power. Mugabe had selected 6,000 families that would eventually be permanently at the feeding trough. About 75% of them would be Zezuru. The two vice presidents; Joseph Msika and Joyce Mujuru were 'Zezurus'. Defence Minister Sydney Sekeramayi, who was also Mugabe's spymaster, was a Zezuru, as were the chiefs of the three main security forces. Army chief General Constantine Chiwenga, whose wife Jocelyn threatened to eat a white farmer at the height of the 2000-2004 farm invasions, replaced a veteran Karanga fighter, General Vitalis Zvinavashe. The air force chief was Air Marshal Perence Shiri, former commander of the notorious North Korea-trained Fifth Brigade, which in 1983 swept through Matabeleland destroying entire Ndebele villages and allegedly murdering more than 20,000 civilians, and was rewarded with three confiscated farms was Zezuru. The national police chief, who claimed 100% disability compensation, was Augustine Chihuri, a Zezuru ex-combatant loyalist. Mugabe had placed control of the electoral process since 1985 in the hands of his fellow Zezuru, Tobaiwa Mudede and rewarded him with two former white-owned commercial farms. Godfrey Chidyausiku, a Zezuru, was appointed chief justice in 2001 after Mugabe toppled his predecessor, Anthony Gubbay. With Chidyausiku's appointment came the gift of the 895-hectare Estees Park farm, north of Harare.

The takeover included the Church as well as any influential power had to be crushed or assimilated to the Zezuru hegemony. The Anglican Church had succumbed. Mugabe read The Marxist-Leninist ideology which is contemptuous of religion, which Karl Marx called 'the opium of the masses', presumably because it sends them into such a narcotic stupor they are deprived of the will to assert their rights. The Marxist-Leninists taught Mugabe to blame all failures on saboteurs of one kind or the other.

Another problem came from NGOs that had failed to live by the principles that they espoused all over Africa. First, they were prone to the charge of being elitist because they tended to concentrate their activities in urban areas and even then, their meetings and conferences are often held at posh hotels and conference centres, far away from the general citizens they served. The leadership was also often drawn from the elite educated middle class Zezurus.

People, genuine Zimbabwean citizens were by 1995 referred to by the elites as Svina (dirty) that had to be swept away; tukiti (little kittens) that could be swathed; "vasina mutupo" (totemless) and hence not fit to be citizens etc. Personal derogatory words were being spat out against those perceived to harbour different views. The highly respected leader of the opposition was not spared either. The Diaspora was not saved, frequently referred to as "English bottom wipers" by none other than the president himself who was supposed to be the father of the nation. Words like "...we'll kill..." and "don't forget the war" were now often used to scare people into submission, and the stick and carrot options were blatantly used for years to cower an already scared hungry nation, as the elites were sure they had won the "minds and soles" of the ruled.

Zanu

"Don't cry if your relatives get killed in the process. Where men and women provide food for the dissidents when we get there we eradicate them. We do not differentiate who we fight because we can't tell who is a dissident and who is not."
Robert Mugabe (1983)

Zimbabwe African National Union - Patriotic Front a.k.a. Zanu-PF (Zanu), the party that held Zimbabwe captive since independence from Britain in 1980, was born after the 1963 rebellion against the Zimbabwe African People's Union (Zapu), the main party that was led by the late Joshua Nkomo, who was Mugabe's second vice-president at the time of his death. Besides his many weaknesses, Nkomo lost the plot largely because he belonged to the minority Ndebele tribe.

Under a unity accord signed in 1987, Zanu was formed from the merger of the two liberation movements that had fought the war for independence against white minority rule in the 1970s. Both liberation movements operated mainly in rural areas, which explains why Zanu combined party had its main support base in rural areas. Zanu was dominated at the top by Shonas and shona loyalist and controlled by the Zezuru clans.

Zanu at its moment of glory was never able to command as wholesale support as the opposition MDC did 2000-05. Zanu's quest for hegemony just after independence was never successful. The Matabeleland provinces were always beholden to the Joshua Nkomo-led Zapu and later to the MDC. This uneasy political balance was seen in all the serious formations after the Unity Accord of 1987. All had variously been seen as tribal, regional or a home for intellectuals.

Zanu's version of history ignored scores of foreign supporters. It ignored churches and it downplayed states ranging from neighbours such as Zambia, Tanzania and Mozambique where freedom fighters were domiciled and trained, to the Swedes, Chinese, Soviets and even the many guises of Britain and the United States. It sidelined big NGOs such as Amnesty International. However Zanu also used history, race and the land issue every time it felt its popularity in Africa was going down.

Politically, the state and the ruling Zanu party were indistinguishable, as a lower-middle class was built quickly through the bureaucracy and corruption and patronage systems emerged parallel to the growth of a comprador faction. Mugabe had set the terms and conditions of such behaviour as the management of the large companies, TA Holdings, Lonrho, Rio-Tinto and Anglo American seemed to be impressed by and satisfied with Zanu's management and the increased level of understanding in government of commercial considerations.

Zanu members knew what Mugabe wanted to hear in terms of the party's ideology and the role of business in transformation. Mugabe believed that the state could manage businesses better than the private sector and no market system could address the developmental challenges of a postcolonial state. There were some within Zanu that shared his approach to development although in practice may not have subscribed to socialist policies. The nationalisation threat by Zanu was not new but was shared by many African governments. In such an environment, any profitable enterprise is easily seen as a negation of the struggle.

A left-wing Zanu member of parliament, Lazarus Nzareybani, concluded in 1989, "The socialist agenda has been adjourned indefinitely. You don't talk about socialism in a party that is led by people who own large tracts of land and employ a lot of cheap labour. When the freedom fighters were fighting in the bush they were fighting not to disturb the system but to dismantle it."

But then Zanu was past caring what the rest of the world thought of its actions because the party was no longer faithful to the principles that underpinned the struggle; to give the people their unfettered freedom and restore their dignity as human beings. To Zanu, dissent was not always the hallmark of democracy, but a sign of disrespect. The rule of one man was law. He was an aging dictator surrounded by a corrupt coterie who had seized private property in the name of land reform and turned choice farms and factories over to themselves.

When the Zanu provincial chairmen went to the Tsholotsho meeting, they thought they were exercising their democratic right to participate in the process of electing a vice president for the party. And by suspending the provincial leaders for voting for other vice presidency candidates, Mugabe wanted to send a clear message that dissent and negotiation were not allowed in Zanu and for that matter within Zimbabwe.

There were many intelligent, far-sighted, and judicious women in Zanu. Why Zanu did not allow these women's names to be put forward for the post of vice president in a fair contest in popularity? Vice President Mujuru had not up to then particularly distinguished herself in any of the various cabinet portfolios she had held since 1980. Mugabe personalized state power and sought to monopolize the liberation struggle. The crisis of governance in Zimbabwe assumed critical proportions and its resolution could not be located within the ruling party.

However Zanu was meeting resistance from unexpected quarters in a very unusual way. Women with flowers for love were harassed, arrested and tortured for calling for the elites to love their subjects. With its street action and frequent visit to police cells, the WOZA was slowly chalking up victories. While in cells, the women sung and danced for the arresting officers to realise that they too were victims of the socio-political environment with the result that some officers were refusing to arrest these women in the first place and magistrates setting them free all the time.

Another interesting development was the Free Zim youths, based in London, who gave Africa's ruling elites a hard time when they heckled them while trying to convince Londoners about their solidarity with other struggling Africans. The struggle was broadening but needed more of these forms of resistance from all sections of the society.

Hence to Zanu, those who were competent would be competent in serving the president directly in his machinations and not in setting a positive national agenda. Another interesting aspect of the composition of Zanu's 2005 cabinet was the appointment of die-hard and totally sterile psychopaths such as Security Minister Didymus Mutasa, governor David Karimanzira, Joseph Made, Hebert Murerwa, Gideon Gono and Flora Buka.

The making of a Mug Tyrant?

A fired up Tsvangirai (responding to Mugabe's "you are dicing with death" threat) said: "I am prepared to die in order to liberate the people of Zimbabwe from Zanu PF's misrule. Who are you Mugabe to talk about the death or life of an individual, are you God? Even if I am killed, one thing is certain, all dictators, just like other people, will die. If I die first, I will be waiting for you in heaven and I will ask you if you managed to improve the lives of Zimbabweans."

A 'dictator' or 'tyrant' is a head of state who exercises arbitrary authority over the lives of his citizens and who cannot be removed from power through legal means. The Top-10 world list was headed by Omar al-Bashir of Sudan, followed by Kim Jong-II of North Korea, Than Shwe of Burma, Robert Matibili-Mugabe of Zimbabwe, the presidents of Uzbekistan, China, Saudi Arabia, Turkmenistan, Iran and Teodoro Obiang Nguema of Equatorial Guinea. Other dictators include Biere of Cameroon, Qadaffi of Libya, Museveni of Uganda, Mswati of Swaziland and presidents of Rwanda, Togo and Dos Santos of Angola. Infect, by 2008 half the African leaders were still dictators according to the definition given earlier.

Tyranny is rule by fear. Tyrannies lack legitimacy and popular consent, relying rather on the abuse of state power to remain in office. Tyrannies deftly and crudely manipulate the discourse and institutions of democracy while simultaneously occupying its space. Under tyrannies, sycophantic parliaments pass immoral legislation; partisan jurists preside over its application and a corrupt unprincipled police enforce its adherence. For their duration, tyrannies are in control, but lack authority, particularly moral authority. Tyrannies rely on structural violence, state repression and privatised intimidation, such as hit squads, vigilantes and youth militia, to ensure tranquillity. Democrats are repulsed by such regimes, thugs are drawn to them.

Furthermore, tyrannies construct proto-ideologies and justificatory discourses that simultaneously create or recreate perceived external threats. Nazism used Zionism, Stalinism used Fascism and apartheid used both African nationalism and communism. Mugabe's Zanu tyranny had used white racism, Gayism, neo-colonialism, capitalism, farmers, Britain, British Prime Minister Tony Blair, the church, the opposition Movement for Democratic Change (MDC), UANC, ZUM, Forum Party, his own fellow citizens, International Monetary Fund (IMF), tribalism and World Bank structural adjustment programmes, to name but a few, to blame for the economic and political crisis.

Absent the death of its leader, key characteristics signify the fall of tyranny. The first is the appearance of fissures, then factions and then fractures in the ruling oligarchy. This is often preceded by inconsistencies and oscillations in governmental language and sloganeering.

Abel Muzorewa warned what would happen if Mugabe won: "Any talk of democracy, freedom, and independence will be turned into an impossible dream. This country will find itself wallowing in the dust of poverty, misery, and starvation." To Mugabe's Western enablers, particularly Andrew Young, this must have seemed like the jealous sniping of a man who had been turned out of office. Yet from the vantage point of 2007, Muzorewa's prescience is plain for all to see.

Matibili-Mugabe, a Malawian tyrant, had always wanted to turn Zimbabwe into a one party state and make himself a life president but then one of the clauses of the 1987 Zanu unity accord required the merged party (Zanu and Zapu) not to legislate for a one-party Marxist-Leninist state. But in the 1990s an increasingly confident civil society and growing middle class began to clamour for a new constitution that would help loosen Zanu hold on de facto absolute power. This was happening at a time when democratic movements undermined and toppled dictatorships in neighbouring Malawi and Zambia and a fierce political fight was on going in Kenya.

By 1996, a fusillade of optimistic moments in the country's biggest cities and in disparate rural sites of protest had signalled that poor and working people were poised for a period of mass democratic struggle. It is paradoxical, perhaps, how far Zanu had fallen from popular grace, for this strategic Southern African nation's independence was, of course, greeted as a major breakthrough against apartheid and imperialism in 1980. Mugabe, after all, had hunkered down in an extremely defensive mode, replete with the fierce tools of repression he inherited from white Rhodesia and his own brand of opposition-bashing, in which radical rhetoric, regular, paranoid accusations of counterrevolution, and even a promise in late 1998 to resurrect "socialism", featured but no longer confusing quite so much.

Paranoia and facts on the ground were now dictating the pace as an old inexperienced, corrupt and lazy Mugabe tried to get on top of the situation, posing grandly as the father of the nation, the champion of Africanism, the grand statesman of African politics. With inflation still above 20 percent and public sector wage offers in the low single digits, unprecedented civil service militancy emerged, signalling the great gap between Zanu and subjects.

For nearly a fortnight in mid-1996, a strike of more than two-thirds of the civil service paralysed the government and the nation. Daily demonstrations in downtown Harare attracted the support of trade union leadership, who had struggled unsuccessfully for several years to incorporate the civil servants' organization into the trade union movement. Just back from a honeymoon after a lavish wedding to his secretary, Mugabe revealed his lack of comprehension of peasantry and middle class grievances. Workers reacted by ratcheting up the pressure, and government quickly folded to their demands. Following this example, 100,000 private sector workers were involved in strike action in mid-1997, even extending to poorly-organized agricultural plantations. Again real wage increases finally won, the hard way.

These labour victories meant that when the series of economic catastrophes began in late 1997, the ZCTU (Workers' Union) easily stepped in to assume national oppositional leadership. Well-organized general strikes and demonstrations in December 1997 and March and November 1998 won nearly universal worker support, and were punctuated by a minor rebellion within the ruling party at a December 1997 conference and, via a few leading renegades, throughout 1998.

In the township communities, days of rioting over food and gasoline price hikes left several people dead at the hands of the police in both January and October 1998. Similar "IMF riots" had occurred in 1993 and 1995, but were far smaller and more rapidly extinguished. Emblematic of the growing conflict, Tsvangirai (ZCTU leader) was badly beaten by war veterans after the 1993 stunningly successful national strike. A few months later 'arsonists' razed the second most important ZCTU office in Bulawayo. While not yet paramilitary in character, the defence of Mugabe's regime was getting serious.

In October 1997, refusing strident advice and monetary arm-twisting from international financial institutions, Mugabe silenced nearly 50,000 liberation "war veterans" who challenged his legitimacy by granting them each US$2,800 at the time, plus a pension of Zw$2,000 per month. The ex-combatants were successful essentially because their demonstrations in Harare caused Mugabe acute embarrassment. After the payout, however, intense popular civilian resentment against the "war vets" emerged, as sales taxes, income tax and petrol tax increases were imposed to help cover the costs and the economy imploded.

The following year, without consulting even his politburo, much less parliament and again unconstitutionally and with virtually no popular civilian or business support, Mugabe sent 12,000 troops to the Democratic Republic of the Congo (DRC) in defence of discredited and playboy leader Lawrence Kabila. By year's end, dozens of soldiers had returned in body bags, amid reports of Zimbabwean troop participation in gross violations of human rights. The rationale for the intervention, joined mainly by the Angolan and Namibian armies but rebuffed by South Africa, was to include ruling party economic interests. The war was costing US$1.5 million per day, money Mugabe or Zimbabwe didn't have.

Ongoing and increasingly vociferous demands came from an indigenous business lobby still shut out of white-controlled markets and financial institutions. Although they were regularly cleared off by authorities, land-starved peasants and farm workers invaded a few white-owned commercial farms during 1998, egged on by the uproar over the land designation exercise. In February 1998, university students inspired by their Indonesian counterparts also took to the streets, prematurely predicting a Suharto-style endgame for Mugabe.

More general popular alienation from government intensified with each new revelation of political and civil service corruption, rigged official tenders, shady and incongruous international investment partnerships (especially with Malaysian firms), and conspicuous consumption by political elites. There was also the danger of socio-cultural de-legitimisation of the Catholic Mugabe, who had sired two children out of wedlock during the 1980s, or former president Canaan Banana who, in late 1998, was accused of sodomizing and raping members of his security staff and soccer team and temporarily fled the country in disgrace. Mugabe evidently had covered matters up during Banana's early 1980s tenure in the then-ceremonial presidential post.

In one emblematic scandal, Roger Boka, a vocal black-empowerment entrepreneur with close ties to Mugabe, brought down his own large merchant bank and a massive debt-laden tobacco processing-based empire when he faced bankruptcy in the wake of the 1997-1998 interest rate hikes. After resorting to selling US$50 million in counterfeit government bonds to other naive black bankers, he eventually skipped the country. Until the very end of Boka's antics, Mugabe searched for a bailout mechanism as his estate revealed the entire Zanu politburo owed Boka trillions of dollars. With Zimbabwe at its most politicised level in two decades, occasional but quite vicious police clampdowns had not deterred public dissent.

Finally, after realising that strong arm tactics were failing, Mugabe suddenly announced that, at long last, the government would begin implementing the disastrous 1993 Land Designation Act. The damage to the commercial agricultural sector and related industries would be heightened by the reality that the recipients of the farms would include wealthy politicians ahead of land-starved peasants. This patronage route was important, as other state-based options for embourgeoisement were closing. Mugabe apparently was not serious about redistribution, which would require vastly greater resources, support structures, and administrative staff than were budgeted and planned not to mention a shift in class power, away from the emergent bureaucratic bourgeoisie and the residually powerful white farming elite.

By February 2000, Mugabe had suffered his first-ever national electoral defeat over a proposed new constitution. A decade of economic decline, characteristic of the imposition of structural adjustment across Africa, preceded the rise of the opposition Movement for Democratic Change (MDC). Standards of living had crashed during the 1990s, the state withdrew many social services, and the economy de-industrialized. State and private sector corruption were rife. In response, various urban labour and social movements, trade unions, human rights advocates, ghetto residents' groups, militant students, church and women's organizations, community health workers and many others began to offer opposition. They came together in the streets during mass protests (1996–1999), then through a National Working People's Convention (February 1999), the National Constitutional Assembly (1999–2006), and the launch of the MDC (September 1999). Mugabe was caught flat-footed and was not pleased and the tyrant in him woke up.

The African Capo di tutti Capi

"If yesterday you hated me, today you cannot avoid the love that binds you to me and me to you. Is it not folly, therefore, that in these circumstances anybody should seek to revive the wounds and grievances of the past?" Mugabe 1980, repeating a speech made by Jasper Savanhu 40 years earlier.

"Mugabe go? Go where? He should rule even if it means he is walking with the aid of a walking stick. He is the father of our nation; he is entitled to rule us forever." Vice-President Joseph Msika 2004.

"Essentially Robert Mugabe is a racist thug. He has been killing the Matabele people for 20 years; he is a murderous fuck and one of the grotesque tyrants on the planet. The sooner he goes the better...... They should be doing whatever it takes to get rid of him....What we are seeing at the moment is a mutual dance of the ancient Africans." Singer and LiveAid front man Bob Geldof.

On a controversial visit to Malawi to open a road named after him, 2005, Mugabe, said: "Do you really know who I am?" Well we can only try and figure that one out.

Mugabe's father was a Malawian of the Tumbuka tribe named Masuzyo Matibili but the white settler Native Commissioner renamed him Gabriel Matibili. Matibili met Bona in Norton on the outskites of Harare and the two got married and had five children; Amon, Robert, Sabina, Albert and Bridget before he went to Bulawayo in search of work and never returned to see his family. Mugabe was 10 years old when his father left them.

Bona and her five Malawian children (Zimbabwean law did not allow dual citizenship) left the Norton farm where Matibili had left her for rural Zvimba where one of her uncles, Karigamombe, was staying. In Bulawayo, Matibili met another woman, MaTchuma, with whom he had several children, among them a Stanley Matibiri (a magistrate who always favoured Mugabe's cases) and Ntombana the wife of Tony Gata who later compared Mugabe to Jesus. Because of this connection Mugabe became cousins with notable Ndebeles like John Nkomo.

Masuzyo died later and was buried in Bulawayo. During this time Mugabe rarely saw his father and they were not on speaking terms for neglecting his family. Robert and his siblings were assisted in their day-to-day life by a Mugabe, who worked for the Jesuits at Kutama, hence the adoption of the name Mugabe. It is also very common for Malawians to adopt shona names and to abandon foreign kids.

Mugabe's upbringing was troubled. He blamed Ndebeles for his miserable, fatherless childhood. In Tumbuka culture the children belong to the woman and in some case take up her name. Mugabe could speak in Ndebele fluently but he never spoke the language in public except at Joshua Nkomo's funeral. As a head of state, Mugabe's hatred of the Ndebele people was never a secret that penetrated deep into the social fabric of the Zimbabwe society.

In 2000, Mugabe enacted a law that stripped Zimbabweans of foreign descent their nationality unless they renounced their claim to any foreign citizenship. He did not strip himself of Zimbabwean nationality or his relatives who clearly had Malawian blood. That was meant to deny many their right to vote in general elections because Mugabe feared they were going to vote for the opposition MDC.

Mugabe had on several occasions derogatorily described Zimbabweans of foreign descent as "totemless" and *vabva kure* (those who come from far away lands). Ironically, he topped the list of "totemless" Zimbabweans.

Mugabe grew up to be a spiteful teacher by profession, attained his first degree at Fort Hare University, South Africa. He returned to Zimbabwe and taught briefly before going on to Ghana where he took a teaching post under Nkrumah's government and married his first wife, Sally. He abandoned his four-year teaching contract in Ghana while on holiday in Zimbabwe in 1960 to join the nationalist movement in Zimbabwe.

But perhaps the unhappiness of the struggle in Rhodesia embittered Mugabe when the National Democratic Party (NDP), of which he was the publicity secretary, was outlawed in 1961. The same fate was met the following year by the NDP's successor organisation, the Zimbabwe African People's Union (Zapu), and Mugabe was forced into exile in Dar es Salaam. Disputes within Zapu led to the formation of the rival, more confrontational Zimbabwe African National Union (Zanu). Mugabe, by then a staunch advocate of full equality between white and black, joined the tearaways. He studied for his law and administration degrees from the University of London while he languished for a decade in a Rhodesian jail. The skills gained produced a talent for deviousness that proved more than a match for Ian Smith's duplicity in declaring unilateral independence so as to entrench white dominance.

In prison Mugabe learnt that white power bent only when met by force of arms, so he escaped prison and crossed into Mozambique where Samora Machel placed him under house arrest for a further two years, as he was not sure who Mugabe was.

For the record; Mugabe was part of the liberation war effort. He was involved in the nationalist struggle. However, in that war he was a coward who could not even fire a pistol or never knew how to return a soldier's salute. He even went into military camps with dozens of bodyguards because he never had hegemony over the entire Zanla (Zimbabwe African National Liberation Army). ZANLA was led by the nationalist leader Herbert Chitepo, followed by Josiah Tongogara from 1973 until his death in 1979. With the war drawing to a close, command fell to Mugabe, previously Zanu's number two leader after Tongogara.

On gaining the leadership of Zanu, Mugabe immediately visited communist led countries. The significance of Mugabe's close relationship with the political leadership of countries that were in effect under one-party, militaristic rule should never be under-estimated. Not only was he exposed to the rhetoric of communist ideology; he was also provided with a unique opportunity to study closely how authoritarian regimes like the DPRK and Cuba maintained their hold on power and was able to understudy them and learn from them some valuable lessons on dealing with any popular opposition.

Hence soon after independence there were signs of a trend towards a one-party state. The Zimbabwe Broadcasting Corporation started sedulously referring to "the prime minister, Comrade Robert Mugabe" and announcing in one breath "the government and the party", although Mugabe had initially formed a post-war government of national unity.

Mugabe was something of a political enigma. Ideologically, he belonged to the African liberationist tradition of the 1960s; corrupt, strong and ruthless leadership, anti-Western, suspicious of capitalism and deeply intolerant of dissent and opposition. Like all African Big Man his economic policies were geared to short-term political expediency and the maintenance of power for himself.

It was former American president John Adams who said that, "….it has been the political career of this man to begin with hypocrisy, proceed with arrogance and finish with contempt". Those words could have been targeted at a totally different individual. When Mugabe came to Zimbabwe in 1980 it is estimated that half a million people, then the biggest ever crowd on African soil, met him at the airport, mainly because very few of them knew him or had ever heard of him until then, thanks to Rhodesian propaganda. He won a resounding victory at the 1980 elections. Zimbabweans and Africans gave Mugabe their full support (and the big head he had) and respect in anticipation that he would do something to improve their lives and restore their basic democratic rights. At first, Mugabe appeared conciliatory and determined to meet people's aspirations.

In the right light, even the aged Mugabe didn't seem so wicked. He was smart, agile, yoga-exercising and he cracked crude and at times vulgar jokes (Australians are "genetically modified criminals"; Tony Blair is a "boy in shorts" who leads a "government of gay gangsters"). Yet he was a twisted charmer with a forked tongue and fingers dipped in blood. In March 2007 his militia fractured the skull of the opposition leader, Morgan Tsvangirai and murdered an opposition activist. Mugabe went on to boast about it to other African leaders who applauded him.

But for all his UK/Western phobia, Mugabe was a real Anglophile, who wore Seville Row suits and shirts and ties made in England and who initially practiced reconciliation, moderate but mediocre economic policies and reasonable, if slightly a corrupt Western funded administration. Mugabe condemned "….arrogant flamboyance and wastefulness: a dozen Mercedes-Benz cars to one life, hideously huge residences, strange appetites that can only be appeased by foreign dishes; runaway taste for foreign lifestyles, including sporting fixtures, add to it high immorality and lust." Mugabe clearly talked about himself.

Driving past Mugabe's official residence in bright sunlight you were struck by the extraordinary contrast between his world and that of his people. There were no potholes on that stretch of road and the traffic lights at that intersection surprisingly worked. Banks of shrubs and neatly clipped lawns edged the high walls and a series of boreholes powered by a generator (there were frequent power cuts) kept the sprinklers twitching merrily in the mid-day heat, as thin, abusive, bored but alert young soldiers patrolled the perimeter. By the main entrance, two colourfully dressed, white-gloved guardsmen, similar to those at Burkingharm palace, stood at attention all day whether Mugabe was in or not. Maybe Mugabe didn't see the decay through the tinted windows of his armour-plated stretched Mercedes 600L limo protected by one kilometre long convoy of bodyguards, ambulance, fire brigade and helicopter escort, but just 200 metres away, the real Harare and Zimbabwe started.

Ian Smith and the West had always defined Mugabe as a terrorist. Zimbabweans had always viewed him as a hero of the Zimbabwean freedom. But Mugabe's dictatorial acts against Zimbabweans created a crisis of credibility of Mugabe's credentials. People asked: How can a hero who fought to liberate the country from Ian Smith and settler colonialism end up behaving like this?

The fulminations by intellectuals about foreign countries reflect their own preoccupations rather than a true concern for the unfortunate people who live in those places. Controversies that seem to be about what happens abroad are often really to do with home-grown ideological disputes. Ian Smith, a wartime pilot in the RAF was rightly represented as a white racist thug and became the focus of swirling hatreds. As a former freedom fighter and Marxist, the infinitely nastier Mugabe did not fit into the Left's hall of infamy however many outrages he committed.

Mugabe's reputation as an African statesman started fading after the country, once the region's breadbasket and greatest hope and pride, slid into economic decline. Unconstitutional imperial wars in Mozambique and the DRC and patronage awards to former guerrillas had drained the fiscus. Violent land reforms, which had been left unresolved for 20 years were jump-started with the violent occupation of white-owned farms. This, after all, was a man who once boasted that he had "many degrees in violence" and warned his main opponent, Tsvangirai, "Does he know where we come from? If he comes that way we will blow him away like a fly."

Anglican bishop Norbert Kunonga seemed to know where Mugabe came from and had shocked the world when he said Mugabe was 'actually more merciful than God Himself.' Madzibaba Godfrey Nzira (head of a very influential church sect) said Mugabe was a "divinely appointed king of Zimbabwe and no man should dare challenge his office". Godfree was eventually imprisoned for raping young girls and married women.

In the history of the world, both rightwing and leftwing politicians have tried to use religion to boost their ideological positions. The extreme leftist position is that of the communists, that there is no God, that religion is the opium of the masses, that it is the direct antithesis of the dictatorship of the proletariat. Mugabe was an avowed Marxist-Leninist and was no way apologetic about his being a devout Catholic into the bargain. It was an Anglican clergyman who called him a caricature of the typical, boorish, tin pot African dictator, in the mould of Idi Amin, Jean Bedel-Bokassa and Macias Nguema. Archbishop Desmond Tutu never withdrew that characterization of Mugabe.

Since 1980 the Zimbabwean leader's penchant for outlandish rhetoric could elicit a giggle and a bemused headshake from anyone everywhere. Ever the great orator, Mugabe would respond to criticism by unleashing torrents of anti-colonial, anti-Western and vitriol everything, bile spiced with some vulgarities in the process to embarrass and disrespect. He would tell Tony Blair and "your gay gangsters" to "....keep your Britain and I will keep my Zimbabwe", and accuse Western nations of wanting to re-colonise 'his' country. He would rant about how self-sufficient Zimbabwe was and how it did not need a leg-up from anybody, yet behind the scenes accept British aid. It stopped being funny as Mugabe intensified his destruction of the very country whose birth he had midwifed and people began to starve and be fed by those so-called 'imperialist' and "gay gangsters".

By 2000, Mugabe had completed his metamorphosis and had become Rhodesia's Ian Smith. He was now tyrant of Zimbabwe, 'Butcher Bob' Mugabe, a criminally insane savage who thought that half-killing his political opponents was a perfectly reasonable way to conduct political discourse. He attacked the Church, just as Smith attacked the Church. He used Smith's legislation to imprison and torture his opponents. Mugabe had developed a siege psychosis, turgid paranoia and neo-fascist mentality which made him to see all opponents whether within his party, the government or in the country as traitors. He believed he was Zimbabwe and Zimbabwe was his. Having been in power for 25 years, Mugabe could not imagine himself ever losing power. Brazen bribery, manipulation and whatever tricks in the books of electoral brigandage were deployed to ensure only one outcome: Mugabe and Zanu victory.

When some Zimbabweans and blacks started calling Mugabe a terrorist it signalled this paradigm shift in the public perception of Mugabe. What Zimbabweans were now seeing in Mugabe was a self-proclaimed liberation hero whose objectives were not to liberate Zimbabwe so Zimbabweans could enjoy their basic human rights, but to install a black dictatorship with token freedoms for the Zimbabweans. It was these terrorist objectives of denying people their basic human rights that had led to a redefinition of Mugabe in the context of once a terrorist always a terrorist.

A number of 'cultural reforms' had been undertaken to 'Africanise' Zimbabwe's parliament, which had resembled metre for metre the British Parliament, turning it into an African safari lodge. A stuffed leopard and two antelope heads hang on the walls and a leopard skin adorned the ceremonial chair used by Mugabe. Two enormous elephant tusks framed the Presidential chair and it was between these two great teeth that 'King Matibili-Mugabe' stood to address the House in 2006. Near him sat Mrs Mugabe, the 'reluctant' Queen, on a high backed green leather chair that had been carefully placed on a striking zebra skin. The lavishly decorated safari parliament was about as far away from the reality of life in Zimbabwe as could possibly imagine.

He lived well in his Chinese pagoda sanctuary with his young family, poles apart from the maddening crowds of the resettlement districts, where kids were dying of hunger and the infrastructure was in tatters. Mugabe's second wife, Grace Marufu was known as 'The First Shopper' of Zimbabwe. While the nation's economy skid into morbid decline and ever more of the population faced hunger, Grace spent millions of US dollars visiting the haute couture boutiques of Paris and London. Marufu, who had a fondness for gold Christian Dior sunglasses and Ferragamo shoes, was derided as the 'Imelda Marcos' of Zimbabwe and exerted a pernicious influence over her husband's political failures and had become a symbol of his corrupt and nepotistic regime. On more than one occasion, Air Zimbabwe planes had been commandeered by Grace, for shopping and vacation trips abroad, leaving hundreds of paying passengers and tourists stranded at Harare's airport.

Mugabe celebrated his birthdays in style. Targets of at least US$1 - 2 million was set for his birthday celebrations every year were School children and Zanu youth brigades would hold parades to mark the occasion in military-style operation dubbed the 21st February Movement to "..mark our president's birthday with dignity".

Zimbabwe was not, prima facie, a fully-fledged military dictatorship in-so-far-as the political power was vested in an elected civilian president. Amid escalating authoritarian rule, the uniformed services, however, wielded an inordinate amount of power and influence outside their own ranks. This was facilitated by a network of former high-ranking officers who held positions of power in government and were largely loyal to their former commander, one Mujuru. While living in blissful and prosperous retirement, the former army commander emerged as, perhaps, the most politically dominant single individual in Zimbabwe, wielding more power than the ageing and anachronistic President.

By 2006 Mugabe was one of the world's wealthiest and longest serving head of state; in fact, it would be more realistic to call him a life President. The veteran Zanu leader, the grandmaster of African politics, had rode high above any pretenders to his throne for over 50 years. The history of Zanu had shown that it is one who stays longest on the course who emerged the winner. When Mugabe was sworn in as the first prime minister of Zimbabwe on 18 April 1980, a cousin and fellow freedom fighter James Chikerema said Mugabe would never leave State House of his own free will. "Robert will have to be carried out feet first," he told a group of disbelieving foreign journalists. Mugabe's mentality was based on hatred, on seeking and vanquishing enemies, real and imagined, on total control and a strong distaste for other or contrary opinion, James said.

Mugabe's power-crazed sixth sense drove him to calling "Father of Zimbabwe" Joshua Nkomo (respected opposition leader) with nasty names during the early 80s. He swore on his mother to shake and bring Nkomo to his knees. He made the ZAPU leader suffer a barrage of idiotic remarks than any other opposition leader in the history of the country, including racist Ian Smith. Mugabe was quoted in the 80s saying, "When all people carried Zanu PF cards, the present I.D registration cards would be abolished, because they would serve no purpose. It would be easier to identify the **enemy**." Zanu I.D cards had a picture of a younger looking Mugabe wearing a stupid self-satisfactory grin and Nkomo would never have carried one. Nkomo spent the next 12 years of his life in obscurity.

The country's black leaders who dared to oppose Mugabe received the same treatment inevitably meted out by a paranoid tyrant. In 1983 Mugabe jailed Muzorewa for 10 months, accusing him of plotting with South Africa and Israel to overthrow his regime. Also in 1987, rightly fearing for his safety, Sithole sought political asylum in the United States. He later returned to Zimbabwe and was elected to parliament. But in 1997, Sithole was convicted of attempting to assassinate Mugabe and was barred from returning to office. Other political opponents either fell into line or were imprisoned or killed.

Mugabe was furious when the bishops who produced the "Zimbabwe We Want" document said the Zimbabwe Lancaster House constitution was not home-grown. They said the constitution did not represent the consent of the people. Their reasoning was that those who participated in the Lancaster House negotiations did so on behalf of 'the people' but they were not elected representatives. But Mugabe was there and he believed he was 'our people'. Mugabe's claim that a "home-grown constitution" was cobbled together in the musty halls of Lancaster House in England is to stretch the metaphor of representation beyond belief. Is it democratic that a few intolerant individuals fighting an independence war outside the country can thereafter return to foist a constitution on the nation without putting it to a referendum, and then declare it non-negotiable?

That up to 18 amendments had to be made to that document since 1980 bore testimony to the inadequacies of the negotiation process, and those defects reflect the power imbalances between those involved and the compromises that had to be made for the sake of progress and to hasten majority rule. More fundamentally, to say the Lancaster House constitution was home-grown was to suggest that government sometimes played frivolous games like setting up the 1999 Constitutional Commission and conducting a costly referendum in February 2000. The truth about Mugabe's indignation was that a new constitution would trim his powers or even reduce his office to a ceremonial one in favour of an elected executive prime minister.

It is accepted in Zanu that without Solomon Mujuru (former gorilla leader, retired commander of ZDF) and Edgar Tekere's active support, Mugabe would have been a nobody. Under the war name of Rex Nhongo, Mujuru led Mugabe's guerrilla army during war of independence. Mujuru was far from an eloquent or engaging speaker, even in his native Shona language. Mujuru was uneducated and had a pronounced stammer. After the former Zanla supremo, Josiah Magama Tongogara perished in a questionable car accident in the dying moments of the war; Mujuru emerged in 1980 as the new commander of Zanu's military wing.

The legendary and reasonable Josia Tongogara, who was the commander of Zanla, the armed wing of Zanu, died on 25 December in 1979. The view among the freedom fighters was that he was senior to Mugabe and expected to be the first President of Zimbabwe with Mugabe as Prime Minister. No autopsy results or photos of the body were ever released though part of the CIO that viewed pictures of the dead Tongogara said he had bullet wounds on his chest and head.

Hence it was left for Solomon Mujuru, who implored the guerrillas, Nyerere and Samora Machel, who had never met Mugabe, to accept him as the new leader. As a result Mugabe owed Mujuru an eternal favour.

Mugabe dreamed of marching into Harare at the head of his forces, as Fidel Castro marched into Havana; he felt humiliated to be sitting at a round table at Lancaster House, London, with Ian Smith, the enemy, under duress from Presidents Machel (Mozambique) and Nyarere (Tanzania). He admired and envied Togogara's standing within the army. Mugabe's political make-up was never one to accommodate real consensus. Mugabe's political plans were always to establish a one-party state under the comfortable cloak of his allies in the Eastern bloc. Zapu leader Nkomo, Zanu leaders Chitepo and Tongogara stood in his way. They had to die.

Until the mid 1990s it had been assumed that Mugabe himself had not been corrupt but the size of his suburban Chinese Pagoda mansion suggested otherwise. By 2005, Mugabe's annual salary was ZW$83,8 million or US$79 a month excluding allowances and other perks. Among Mugabe's publicly known assets were two farms, a mansion in Harare and a plush thatched cottage in his rural Zvimba.

In 1980 Nigeria had donated US$6 million for Zanu to buy a controlling shareholding in Zimpapers, a propaganda news group. Mugabe confisticated the shareholding by force and pocketed the money. Even though travel sanctions were slapped on him in 2002, the European Union (EU) had provided at least £115m

2000-4. But while the money was meant to be spent on Aids and helping the poor, a 2004 EU audit found that 89% of the total had ended up in the pockets of allies of Mugabe. To get around the sanctions issue, Zanu had registered an assortment of NGOs to pilfer foreign donations targeted directly at the poor.

Mugabe's hatred for Blair started when the UK government asked the Mugabe regime to account for money (£35 Million) that had been advanced to the government of Zimbabwe for land resettlement. Mugabe could not account for the money. Edgar Tekere had warned Mugabe about the sharks that surrounded him, but Tekere was fired from Zanu as a result.

As his foreign currency reserves ran low and the economy crumbled around him, Mugabe turned to his long forgotten friends. China, which had provided buses, malfunctioning passenger planes, ammunition and fighter jets, but they gave him only $6m in 2005 after it received warning telephone calls from the presidents of Nigeria and South Africa not to give him the US$160m he wanted to hand over to the IMF. Some companies had been forced to make 'donations' to the ruling Zanu party to continue operating. Those that failed to do so were well aware of their likely fate. In the past years seven private banks had been 'specified' - closed down and their assets seized. Mutumwa Mawere, one of Zimbabwe's richest tycoons, had his flagship conglomerate, Shabanie Mashaba Mines, along with finance and insurance companies and supermarkets seized by presidential decree and he was forced to flee the country for his own safety.

Mugabe was willing to downsize the whole economy just to feed the political elite, a few thousand at most. During his 28 years in power Mugabe had become extremely skilled at drawing people from all sectors into his web of patronage and deceit. Among those handed farms that had been seized were High Court judges, police chiefs, military officers and the Anglican bishop of Harare. However, Mugabe was running out of the means to do this. The Central Bank had no more foreign exchange available. Mugabe's lieutenants were increasingly resorting to criminality in the scramble for the country's remaining assets. Apart from extortion, many had launched get-rich-quick schemes.

Mugabe had done everything in his power to ensure that less than half the eligible population was allowed to vote, that the conditions under which they voted were neither fair nor free and that the information reaching the average voter and the international community was completely distorted by propaganda and lies. It would seem as if he rigged all the elections since 1980 to a greater or lesser degree. The spectre of helicopters flying full ballot boxes to polling stations in 2002 is still fresh in people's minds.

Mugabe continued to be surrounded by ministers, relatives, advisors and others who grossly misinform him as to the political, social and economic realties of the country that he led. From the beginning, addresses by him revealed major misconceptions of the causes of Zimbabwe's ills. Even as the president's opponents and critics acknowledged his "renowned intellect", the greatly erroneous perceptions and perspectives that characterised his addresses can only be credibly attributed to his being the victim of extensive, ongoing, misinformation and disinformation or a senile mind. The misrepresentations by him of facts and their causes were pronounced and very wide-ranging. Mugabe was so renowned for his diplomatic skills that he convinced Zimbabweans and foreigners for a long time that he himself was a reasonable democratic fellow let down by his ministers.

So many things had gone wrong, become worse, failed or fallen apart, and so few things had improved that all knew which group would form the longer list. Worse than that, the few things that a few people might say are improvements would be disputed, if not rejected outright by almost everybody else. In other words, narrowly subjective opinions apply to most of the claimed benefits, but broadly objective facts describe the horrendous costs that had been inflicted on all but a privileged few.

One of his undoubted achievements was a brief expansion of education and primary health care in the early 80s. The education system in Zimbabwe, though mainly donor funded, used to be Africa's finest. The fine tuned agricultural sector he inherited from Rhodesia drove the economy so fast it was almost breathtaking. According to the United Nations, Zimbabwe achieved 85% literacy within 15 years of independence, and health care was up there too. Even by the mid 2000s, when the country was mired in staggering domestic and foreign debt and a collapsing infrastructure, there was still zeal and dedication among many public health workers struggling to alleviate the suffering of those affected by HIV/Aids.

But by 1996, schools were in crisis: by expanding education, Mugabe dug his own grave, as the young beneficiaries were now able to analyse Zimbabwe's problems for themselves and blame him of corruption and mismanagement and for the lack of jobs and rising prices. Having realised his political mistake, Mugabe was trying to disenfranchise these young, who generally wanted political change and jobs. The man who fought for one-man-one-vote now wanted potential voters to prove their residence with utility bills, which the young and unemployed, were unlikely to have.

Mugabe's tactic had been to suppress the opposition, AU and SADC and bid for time, a strategy that had been mostly successful. One source of pressure to which Mugabe did respond to was that he craved legitimacy. Mugabe recognised that he could not become a Mandela in the twilight of his life. His dilemma was how to buy the people's loyalty without giving them the political freedom to go with it. So, despite the MDC's gains, Zimbabwe remained almost as much in Mugabe's thrall as it was in 1980. To separate Mugabe and Zanu from the state was impossible. They were now as one. Kumbirai Kangai, a former agriculture minister, told the huge civil service in 1995 that none of them should claim: "I work for the government and not for the party. If you hear any civil servant saying that, please let me know so that I may approach the minister he works for, so that he is removed."

Mugabe seemed to have successfully deployed a (literal) black and white divide to the African debate. In Mugabe's rhetorical world, the contest was between progressive blacks, black stooges of imperialism and white Anglo-Saxons. The first are the good guys, the second the bad and the latter the ugly guys. He led the good guys and British Prime Minister Tony Blair led the bad and ugly guys. In his warped mind, Tsvangirai and the MDC gained relevance in this scheme only as Blair's foot soldiers. In this context, such "trivialities" in Mugabe's world, as human rights were necessary evils to achieve the greater good; Africanisation.

This type of Pan Africanism brings upon itself the criticism of apathy and ineptness. Its emphasis on the sentimental or emotional confers no intellectual tools with which to confront present and future challenges. It feasted on rhetoric to evoke the inevitable sentimental responses connected to dark chapters in collective black history as a way of deriving political capital for a purely hegemonic domestic political programme. For his imperial entry into DRC, Mugabe's family-owned companies were awarded a US$200 million contract and various mining rights. In exchange, Mugabe lent mercenary troops and support to a war that claimed nearly 4 million black lives.

Mugabe's Pan-Africanism embraced all identities beyond particular national identities as defined in the narrow sense of ethnicities that are indigenous to the sovereign state. The reason for this was because sovereign Zimbabwe itself is not an indigenous form of political community but merely the product of the very colonialism that Pan Africanism is a response to. Mugabe treated the hundreds of thousands of Malawian (his kith and kin), Mozambican and other Africans that had for generations resided in Zimbabwe and for generations contributed to the economic development of the country through their supply of cheap labour to the commercial agricultural sector as mere footnote in the entire 'land redistribution scheme'. Mugabe also branded Zimbabweans in the towns and cities as 'traitors and stooges of imperialism' simply because they voted for the opposition, which, truth be told, was a legitimate participant in an electoral process that was provided for by the country's constitution. He haunted them out of their slums and chased them into neighbouring countries.

Internally the primary purpose of Mugabe's land distribution strategy against neo-colonialism fell outside of any emancipatory agenda, whether economic, cultural or political. The real spontaneous land demonstrations around 1997/1998 in communal areas like Svosve were met with the full wrath of Mugabe's security apparatus. Anti-riot police armed to the teeth were sent in to forcibly remove the hapless but daring villagers from the white owned farms.

To further expose this Pan African subterfuge for what it was, an ironical consequence to the land invasions was the internal monopolisation of political space by the state and its virtual suspension of civil liberties in the manner of the colonial government. Ian Smith's Law and Order (Maintenance) Act was dusted up and expeditiously passed as the now infamous POSA.

"We must make the white man tremble," Mugabe thundered before loin wagging women out to greet him at the airport from his numerous luxurious foreign trips. Yet all those women's children and Mugabe's own were abroad learning at whitemen's schools in a whitemen's language. Note that the comment was directed at "white men", not the "racist Rhodesian white farmer", not the "racist Tony Blair", but "the white men" in general. It was a comment that was certainly ill advised and it did more to damage Mugabe's image than anything else he had done since then. He forged further by calling gays worse than dogs and pigs and criticized Blair's government as gay gangsters.

If Blair was to make a comment asking his supporters to "make the black man tremble", he would be out of office faster than he could blink. He would be reviled by every black man. The same scope presumably applied to Mugabe seen through the whitemen's eyes and that's why he was so hated in the West. For his troubles, most of the Western world forbade the Zimbabwean strongman and 127of his cronies entering any EU, USA, Canada, New Zealand and Australian territory. Zimbabwe was also suspended and eventually opted out of the Commonwealth.

The whites then failed to understand it when Mugabe was elected into power by the people of Zimbabwe. It had now become a case of "..if you can support such a nakedly racist man, then you do not deserve our help and support. If you got cheated at elections and accept it without protest, without marching in the streets, then you are no better than the racist who wants all whites to tremble simply because of their skin colour. If, on the other (unthinkable) hand, you were actually voting for this man, then you are all racists as well, for you supported his call to make whites suffer."

For the average right thinking black Zimbabwean it was a no win situation. Mugabe invested a lot of bad blood in that one statement. Despite all the talk about the world "feeling for the oppressed people of Zimbabwe", one thing was certain: should the people of Zimbabwe actually vote for Mugabe freely and fairly, they would still not get any Western support. The West would still be urging each other to boycott holidays in Zimbabwe because they were considered "immoral".

In light of Mugabe's revolutionary teaching that lacked the democratic tinge, his Pan-African raving which camouflaged the reality behind the kind of Jacobin-verbiage that promises much and delivers remarkably nothing, one concludes that no positive lessons would be imparted to the young generation of leaders in Africa. Mugabe's untimely outbursts left a lot to be desired. History had already judged Mugabe and his party. The world, in 2006, was exploring possibilities of offering him amnesty if he agreed to step down. The question was what happens to the sins committed in the 1980s, and the deaths incurred during the struggle for democracy in Zimbabwe?

The referendum of February 2000 which showed the strength of the opposition, set back Mugabe's retirement by several years. That defeat stirred him into action, making him desperate to remain at any cost, even willing to destroy the country and party he had fought to liberate. The Zanu National Congresses at which this succession matter should be deliberated had been manipulated to ensure that the people simply rubber-stamped what Mugabe and his select inner circle decided. And this was an inner circle that was both scared of and beholden to Mugabe. At Goromonzi 2006, Mugabe was to test defeat again, this time at the hands of Zanu.

The experience of the abortive Tsholotsho challenge and Goromonzi had shown that Mugabe was not prepared to countenance the renewal of the party and had treated this as a personal threat instead. Indeed, Mugabe's response to Tsholotsho confirms that he was only comfortable when surrounded by subservient personalities. The appointment of Joyce Mujuru as the second Vice-president had little to do with a principled gender agenda, but all to do with a strategy to sideline a potent political threat from the young Turks in the party. The challengers were Mnangagwa, Jonathan Moyo and the six provincial chair-persons: July Moyo, Daniel Shumba, Jacob Mudenda, Lloyd Siyoka, Themba Ncube and Mike Madiro. Other minor players included Chinamasa and the shabby Joseph Chinotimba.

Outside Zanu, and unlike Mugabe, Tsvangirai of the MDC was able to travel without restriction to Europe and America and was able to strengthen his international position. As a consequence the status of Morgan Tsvangirai was rising while Mugabe's own star begun to set. There was a significant improvement in African understanding of the struggle in Zimbabwe. There was less criticism of the West's position that Mugabe was a tyrant and had destroyed his country and more understanding of the suffering of ordinary Zimbabweans.

This was demonstrated by a number of shifts on the African continent; the AU demand that Mugabe explain a negative report on human rights in Zimbabwe and the effects of Murambasvina. Mugabe had thought that he had the full support of Mbeki only to discover that in fact Mbeki wanted change, not only in Zimbabwe, but in Zanu too.

Then came George Bush's victory in the States, Blair's election to head the G8 and the EU Presidency. Mauritius and Botswana to the Chairmanship of the SADC, the exit of Chissano's (Mozambique) followed that of Malawi's Muluzi and that of Namibia's Nujoma, Kaunda, Chiluba, Nyerere, Banda, Moi, Mandela, Mwinyi, Rawlings, Masire, Mkapa; all having peaceful retirement and some even enjoying international respect than they did when in office. South Africa's President Mbeki and Botswana's Festus Mogae were firmly on their way out of public office. The final straw was the nomination of the American Ms. Rice, to the post of Secretary of State. Mugabe could well remember a time in the late 90's when Ms. Rice came to Harare to see him and was given a very rude reception and dismissal. He must have squirmed at the thought.

Do not for one-minute think Mugabe did not understand what he was doing. He was intelligent and astute albeit in a weird way. He was also a totally ruthless catholic, but then so are the Mafia in modern Europe. The great difference was that he claimed to be a Marxist, a modern socialist and a Pan African humanist. Kaunda used to cry into his white handkerchief for these ideals.

These ideals encouraged people to think of themselves as permanent victims of seemingly everything and everybody, from the weather, monkeys, to the past, but especially of Europe and the West in general. According to Mugabe, all escalating problems could in some way be traced to colonialism and its aftermath. Not only that, but Mugabe effectively painted Africans as being utterly and helplessly at the mercy of that past. Africans were expected to spend more time and energy in feeling sorry for themselves over the past than on working to ensure a better future.

He attacked the church regularly and blacklisted the church as one of many societal institutions without a place in national politics. Mugabe had also proclaimed that non-governmental organisations, diplomats, teachers and numerous other organisations and individuals, in actual fact the whole country, should stay away from the politics of the nation.

At law, there are various legal instruments that grant citizens the right to participate in politics. Under the Universal Declaration of Human Rights, the International Covenant on Economic, Social and Cultural Rights, the International Covenant on Civil and Political Rights, and the Constitution of Zimbabwe, among numerous instruments, citizens are entitled to take part in the politics of the nation.

As stated earlier, Mugabe subscribed to the "no politics for the church" movement. Because he worshipped in the Catholic Church, the dogmatic justification for the involvement of the church in politics is drawn from the teaching of that Catholic Church. In its social teaching, the Catholic Church describes politics as an "honourable" or "noble" profession.

Diaspora Zimbabweans had a true picture of the difference between illusionary impressions and reality. Their fellow Africans could not afford living in Zimbabwe, and for that matter in Africa, due to harsh political crimes of the ruling parties, compounded by hard economic realities. Having no choice should not be counted for a choice which Mugabe could brag on before the UN august assembly, as "....my people can eat potatoes instead of corn their staple food...." Leadership is not given to insulting her people, but Mugabe insulted both the citizens of Zimbabwe and those of the world generally, without remorse.

Mugabe had been called upon to take measured, reasonable, and responsible steps to end the humanitarian crisis caused by Operation Murambatsvina; he refused. He was offered humanitarian support if only he agreed to allow independent, international aid agencies to distribute assistance to those in the most dire straits, free from the corrupt influence of Zanu and its self-serving functionaries; he refused. Mugabe had been offered a desperately needed influx of foreign exchange credits, if only he agreed to enter into talks with the MDC; he refused. Mugabe had even gone so far as to deny that these victims existed, commenting to reporters on the subject in Libya for the African Union 2005 summit: "Where are they? We don't know about those. It's just nonsense."

Like Pharaoh, Mugabe was hardening his position even as Zimbabwe sunk to new depths every day. The strange thing, and this had to do with his mental state, was Mugabe was desperately trying to engage in what he called building bridges with the West even as he "bashed" his imagined enemies. The late Edison Zvobgo, founder member of Zanu, once described Mugabe as "...a madman from Ngomahuru hospital for the mental patients, who had been given a baton in a relay race to pass on to the next runner. Instead", argued Zvobgo, "..the madman decided to run away with the baton and was still running wild in the bushes and mountains!"

A humble Mandela, resigning from politics said: "I will count myself as amongst the aged of our society; as one of the rural population; as one concerned for the children and youth of our country; and as a citizen of the world, committed, as long as I have the strength, to work for a better life for all people everywhere. The long walk continues." It was unlikely this would be the case with Mugabe.

But Mugabe had different plans too; "In peacetime, these aircraft should enable air-force personnel to perfect their skills through more systematic training and preparation for the war," he said after receiving 6 J8 fighter aircraft from China. Which war he was preparing for, Mugabe described Britain as "this enemy country" and said he was continuing to wage what he called a chimurenga, or civil war, against the remaining 20,000 white Zimbabweans for control of natural resources, particularly land. There were no more whites on the farms.

Zimbabweans were being held hostage while Mugabe and his vipers' nest of robbers, extortionists, killers, rapists took liberties with the country. They had reduced Zimbabwe to a vassal state in which they felt they could do practically anything they want; some commandeering fire brigade trucks to fill up their swimming pools as the city water systems crumbled. Women in Zimbabwe were taking to the streets and crying for love, but police arrested 1000s of them for their attempts; some spending months detained in filthy police cells, sometimes with babies on their backs. Some had even gone into labour while in police detention.

For the torture and murders since independence, Mugabe was prosecutable and chargeable with systematic violations of economic, social and cultural rights under international law as understood by the Princeton Principles of Universal Jurisdiction, interpreted in light of Article 7 of the Rome Statute of the International Criminal Court. In addition, Mugabe's regime could be pursued under the 1986 Limburg Principles on the Implementation of the International Covenant on Economics, Social, and cultural Rights, the 1997 Maastricht Guidelines on Violations of Economic, Social and Cultural Rights and the evolving General Comments of the UN Committee on Economic, Social and Cultural Rights. Such principles, guidelines and comments were all essential elements of the emerging normative framework of international poverty law.

There was a world of a difference between Ian Smith and Mugabe. Smith at least tolerated democracy among the white Rhodesians. When Ian Smith's Rhodesia Front was in power there were other white parties, like the Centre Party, that did not fully support Ian Smith. They campaigned and participated in the then whites-only elections without being harassed, tortured or threatened. Except for white radicals like Bishop Lamont, Garfield Todd, Judith Todd and Guy Clutton-Brock who opposed him, Smith was, by and large, very tolerant of white opposition to his rule. He never dispossessed whites of land or property, nor forced them into exile. He never demolished their houses enmass.

Within just two years of Zimbabwe's independence Mugabe had shown far less tolerance of black opposition than Smith had shown among white opposition parties. Ironically, while Smith was intolerant of black political opposition, Mugabe was more conciliatory to the whites at the very same time he was intolerant of black opposition.

The speeches that Mugabe made had become too predictable, a pain, a shame and utterly inconsequential in terms of defending or promoting Zimbabwe's national interest. In 2007 Mugabe was increasingly finding himself in exactly the same political predicament that surrounded Bishop Abel Muzorewa in 1979. The essence of the political mood in 1979 was a national consensus in which everyone had gotten fed up with the war and the economic sanctions associated with it.

Come the general election in 1980, an overwhelming majority who had supported Muzorewa ditched him not really because they disliked him but mainly because he simply could not stop the war and economic sanctions. The principles and values of the armed struggle included democracy, freedom, liberty, equality, universal suffrage, justice and prosperity. By 2008 the question was: Had Mugabe achieved these aspirations? The unequivocal response was a big NO.

Mugabe's private life was breaking apart too. His marriage to Grace had been an unhappy one. In 2005, Mugabe personally led intelligence officials on a sweep of businessman James Makamba's Johannesburg home after hearing claims that he was secretly seeing his wife. Before Makamba came on the scene, Grace had also enjoyed secret trysts with another businessman, who sired a child. The businessman died in a bizarre car crash in what his family believed was murder. And even before that, Mugabe's brother, Albert, died in mysterious circumstances after he had been rumoured to be close with Sally, Mugabe's Ghanaian first wife.

Oppah Muchinguri, a Minister in Mugabe's cabinet, was tall, energetic, well built and attractive. She had excellent wartime credentials and considerable charm. Mugabe, while cheating on his first wife, Sally, with his second wife Grace, apparently found the time for a relationship with the stunning Muchinguri. This friendship, despite noisy objections from Grace, continued, up to were Mugabe saw Muchinguri as his successor, because she would let him set policy, make money and enjoy immunity in his retirement.

He continued to make guarantees he couldn't keep. Grace Marufu stormed off as she no longer seemed to like the idea of her husband continued reign and cheating. Mugabe and 20 cronies bundled out tourist from an Air Zimbabwe jet to chase her to Malaysia were they dined and wined for £250,000 at the five-star Nikko Hotel in Kuala Lumpur for five days before the 2007 Grand Prix race. Grace Marufu had left Zimbabwe with their three children, Bona, Robert Jnr and Chatunga, just days after the couple returned from Ghana's 50th independence celebrations where she was publicly humiliated by relatives of Mugabe's late wife, Sally.

Making threats against Zimbabweans was now his major pastime. Looting national resources was a major pre-occupation. Mistrust amongst his cabinet was rife. Workmen placed bombproof underground shelters and concrete posts around his retirement mansion in Borrowdale Brooke. He repeatedly claimed that he faced a 'terrorist threat' from local opposition forces on British pay. His growing security paranoia made him thoroughly frisk politburo members and cabinet ministers before going into meetings apparently fearing that people could bring charms and weapons into meetings. He suspected his lieutenants were approaching traditional healers for good-luck charms to help them oust him.

Like his countryman, one Kamuzu Banda of Malawi, denying responsibility for the mess and human skeletons around him flooded his whole consciousness. Old and paranoid Mugabe constantly looked over his shoulders in fear of what could happen to him if the rage in the land broke free and found expression. He no longer had enough confidence in his arguments and mental abilities to want to honestly and robustly debate issues with those who disagreed with him.

Instead, like the easily threatened bully that he was, he sought to clamp down on dissent by bludgeoning those opponents. The Malawian Mugabe came to the helm of leadership through the blood of many Zimbabwean people. So through the loss of blood of his faithful ones he would also go out. On April 28, 1945, the fascist dictator of Italy, Mussolini, was found hanged upside down on meat hooks in a public square. Mugabe was very much aware of what happens to dictators once they lose power.

Tsvangirai and the MDC

"On the one occasion we were granted an audience with Mugabe, he informed us to go and form our own political party if we were serious about achieving our objectives. Well, on 11 September 1999, we did just that. The Movement for Democratic Change (MDC) was formed in September, 1999." Tsvangirai, President of the MDC.

"The new beginning desired by the MDC and the people of Zimbabwe can only be achieved through peaceful, democratic and constitutional means. Violence and chaos will not lead to job creation and food security," Paul Themba Nyathi, MDC secretary for information and publicity.

There are two political personalities that shaped Zimbabwe's polity, Robert Matibili-Mugabe and Morgan Tsvangirai. Tsvangirai was leading in the 'numbers game' but seemed to have failed to capitalise on this popularity. Various factors contributed to this failure. These included the mere presence of a third counter power; the threat of the manipulated state killing machinery. Power lied in the elite coercive apparatus, the military, and this coercive apparatus was controlled by the ruling Zanu elite. Tsvangirai's challenge therefore was how to unlock this coercive power, the military without a war.

The Movement for Democratic Change (MDC) was Zimbabwe's and indeed Africa's strongest opposition political party so far since independence. It derived its strength primarily from its roots in the labour movement into a political party. The MDC was a social democratic party that rallied the workers, students, peasants and the poor to attain political, economic and social justice in Zimbabwe after years of political and economic plunder.

Although it had a firm foundation in the labour movement, the MDC was backed by big business, commercial farmers, church and women's organisations as well as student leaders, human rights and civic groups, and representatives of the impoverished rural and urban population. Here was a party that for the first time in the history of Zimbabwe able to unite under one roof capitalists and socialists, the workers, the unemployed, peasants, intellectuals and students. In a phrase: everyone. The leadership of the MDC was derived largely from four organisations; the Unions, students, intellectuals and the NGOs.

Over the 1990s, unrest and dissatisfaction over the deteriorating state of the economy and government corruption brought the workers and students unions into direct conflict with Zanu. The unions (ZCTU), under the leadership of Morgan Tsvangirai organised a series of national strikes by large sections of the labour force. These were an attempt to force the government to take steps to halt the economic decline and instil discipline and accountability amongst the political elite. The government however failed to respond to the strikes and continued on its course and by 1995 it was obvious that what was needed was an organisation to directly confront Zanu in Government and in the political arena.

Morgan Tsvangirai was a self-made person, a solid and charismatic leader and a family man. He initially became branch chairman of the Associated Mine Workers Union and was later elected into the executive of the National Mine Workers Union before becoming Secretary General of the ZCTU in 1988. He had held several high-ranking positions in many regional labour movements. He was a multi-talented person and displayed an amazing amount of energy.

It was Tsvangirai's team who led the ZCTU away from its alliance with the ruling Zanu in the late 1980s. As his power grew, his relationship with the Government deteriorated. He had been imprisoned on charges of being a South African spy; had been a victim of government inspired harassment and violence and there had been three assassination attempts on his life, which include the attempt to throw him out of a city centre sky scrapper tenth story window, and was once saved by his armoured car when a policeman opened fire on him.

By 1995 the crisis in Zimbabwe had quickly and considerably became rooted in the social reality of the dominant class in the leadership of Zanu. This elite class was a bureaucratic capitalist class reliant on its monopoly of the state and financial machinery for its own social reproduction. This class was unable to provide a coherent and hegemonic strategic leadership capable of beginning to address Zimbabwe's political, moral, economic and social crisis. Indeed, in many respects, it thrived on conditions of crisis, using its access to state power for land and currency grabs and other speculative activities. It was able to use state power as insulation against the terrible impact the crisis was having on most other classes. It was also incapable of surrendering direct control over state power. This double-bind, an inability to constructively and strategically use political leadership on the one hand, and an inability to cede some bureaucratic dominance, on the other, lied at the heart of the Zimbabwe crisis.

But very quickly, what had begun as a working-class party resisting Mugabe's nationalism, corruption, mal-governance and repressive state control was hijacked by international geopolitical forces, domestic (white) business and farming interests, and the black petite bourgeoisie. Fundraising from these sources became crucial to the MDC's ability to contest the June 2000 parliamentary elections. The presence of eloquent worker representatives in the MDC leadership, including, incongruously, an International Socialist Organization of Zimbabwe member of parliament, had failed to pull the program back to the left.

Soon after its formation in 1999, according to evidence led in legal challenges to both elections, the MDC went on to win well over 55 percent in the disputed parliamentary poll in March 2000. During the disputed 2002 presidential election, Tsvangirai surely trounced the veteran leader by a wide margin. The rigging was massive and even then Mugabe only managed to win by a slim margin. The opposition challenge to the outcome of the presidential election result in 2002 had yet to be heard up to the 2008 elections, rendering them academic. The plain truth was that no bench of judges could be trusted to adjudicate on such matters without seriously embarrassing the State and its regional defenders, especially South Africa. The evidence was overwhelming.

By 2003, the MDC were in charge of 12 major towns and cities after the local government elections. In essence the result meant the MDC controlled a constituency that generated 70% of the country's Gross Domestic Product and a large percentage of the electorate. Politically, the result meant they drove the national agenda and in a free society should have been invited to form part of the government.

Tsvangirai's earthy style, focusing on basic economic problems, made Mugabe's lofty and combative oratory appear abstract and remote for ordinary Zimbabweans. Although he missed some opportunities and was cheated in the presidential elections, Tsvangirai was seen as a hero by many progressive, conservative Africans for standing up to the violent bully, Mugabe. The MDC had continually played its strength trump card. These strengths included sound, youthful and pragmatic leadership, a culture of non-violence, broad-based party support, and sensible policies. More than anything, the MDC offered a reasonable, sensible alternative to the eccentric, and costly behaviour of Mugabe's party.

Tsvangirai was one of the best-known opposition politicians in the world and yet he had not been seen or heard on radio or TV in Zimbabwe up to 2008. All references to him in local government media were simply negative propaganda cleared through the offices of Zanu. The State controlled media would not even generally accept paid advertisements by the MDC. The star, however, continued to shine for the MDC leader who over the years had greatly matured and become world-wise. No one underestimated the enormity of the challenge the MDC leader faced. Every aspect of the political landscape, the media, military, militia, judiciary, law enforcement and legislation was heavily tilted in favour of the incumbent.

Tsvangirai had come to symbolise the struggle for freedom in Zimbabwe and Africa more than those who sought to perpetually feed off the liberation war mantra. Those from the opposite side could shout all they want about puppetry, re-colonisation and sovereignty but the truth was stark naked to most Zimbabweans.

By 2005 all was not roses and wine however. The MDC had serious internal tribal, managerial, financial and logistical problems; its morale and resilience had been shattered by five years of persecution; there were internal squabbles and insufficient funds to pay even the telephone bills at its headquarters, let alone run an election campaign which inevitably entails not only the usual costs but also huge amounts of money to hire lawyers to free campaigners after arrests. An insider and opposition member of Parliament remarked "......only God could save the party from itself".

Even those who looked at the mass base, especially organised black working class, urban poor and progressive middle class, were also wary of the MDC's ambiguity on a number of key issues about the economy and reconstruction of Zimbabwe after Mugabe. There were fears that an MDC government, led by Tsvangirai would just be an imitation of the tragedy of yet another populist trade unionist, the little man with an even smaller brain, one President Fredrick Chiluba of neighbouring Zambia.

The trade unionists within MDC were claiming the party as their own and marginalizing other factions such as allied civil society, the student movement and intellectuals. There were also forces ranged against what was perceived as Ndebele influence in the MDC, which had wreaked havoc and paralysed it and eventually led to a spiteful split.

The MDC held itself out as a social democratic party and claimed to be a party for the poor people, implying therefore that the agenda of social justice was at the core of its programme. However, there were signals that the MDC needed to build cosy relationships with the likes of the BWIs implying that it would not escape the force of neo-liberal policies. The MDC was therefore likely to face the same conundrum, having to meet the demands of free market economics, which is largely pro-corporate power and at the same time having to meet the demands of social justice, especially for people who had suffered so much and were expecting a lot.

Party activists spoke about these issues and supporters and analysts were reluctant to discuss them openly for fear of further weakening the party. By 2004 the facts on the ground showed an ineffective opposition party that lacked vision and strategy. To be fair, years of violence and intimidation, a slew of repressive legislations had all conspired to undermine the party's effectiveness. Tsvangirai's treason trial had further reduced its finances and effectiveness.

Zanu had realised that the MDC had lost the political clout and were now in disarray. Africa in general was indifferent to the MDC's plight. Mbeki revealed some of the answers when he reportedly said that only 13 percent of Zimbabwean voters supported the MDC, lowering the ANC's earlier estimate at about 24 percent. Yet at that time and without doubt the MDC could win any free and fair election that allowed all Zimbabweans to vote.

While Zanu and Mbeki had forwarded the argument that Tsvangirai's simple background reflected a lack of sophistication to deal with the intricate demands of running a country, they opted to forget this was exactly what endeared him to the majority of people in Zimbabwe. People do not want leaders who are complicated, aloof and stubborn since the ability to get representation rides on the simplicity and approachability of their leader.

Many had drawn unwarranted attention on Morgan Tsvangirai's educational qualifications. So do the millions of Zimbabweans and Africans who don't have degrees represent the unelectable community? Whose standard is it that all world leaders should hold degrees? Further, ordinary people knew that academic prowess does not always translate into fine political acumen, as well as socio-economic benefits for the people.

It is the educated that had relegated Zimbabwe, once the prosperous breadbasket of southern Africa, to a basket case and banana republic. The educated unleashed Gukurahundi on Matabeleland and peasants of limited education suffered the dire consequences. The uneducated may have physically planted the bombs that destroyed The Daily News printing press, but they were assigned by an educated Professor. It is not the unschooled that amended the constitution to create a de facto life-presidency before enacting the draconian AIPPA and POSA. It is the educated that printed useless money, sent troops on imperialist escapeades in the DRC, looted farms and industries; it was the uneducated that tortured defenceless prisoners but they were led by the so-called educated.

Despite his shortcomings, especially in articulating national issues and taking crucial decisions, Tsvangirai had been the glue holding the various voices of better governance together. But he had to be more than just an adhesive. His leadership was under scrutiny and for grabs. MDC leaders had in the past failed to agree on how to engage Zanu in dialogue. There was also no homogeneity among them on whether to participate in the 2005 and 2008 elections. This fragmentation threatened any prospects of successful dialogue between Zanu and the opposition. With it, Mbeki's diplomacy, geared to achieving a government of national unity, was in jeopardy.

The MDC had failed to respond effectively to "trivialities" in Mugabe's and Mbeki's warped world that human rights abuses and famine are necessary evils to achieve the greater good. It had focused on harping on the wrongs of Zanu. This was as pointless as it was counter productive. First, no one needed to be convinced that Mugabe's was not a democratic regime. The media was doing a better job at this than the MDC. Second, by focusing on the wrongs of Zanu, the MDC allowed the party to hog media coverage. In politics, any publicity is good publicity. Most disturbing was that by focusing on the sins of the Mugabe regime, in the same language as the international media, the MDC vindicated Mugabe's contention that it was a puppet of an external enemy.

Not that the 2005 electoral defeat was unexpected. What was painfully unexpected was the absence of Plan B on the part of Tsvangirai in particular and the MDC in general. Notable leaders have long-term vision. Vision as in the ability to look through the mud of the future, and be able to read the terrain as accurately as possible, and work out how to navigate the terrain once the mud settles. Those who can only plan their strategy when the mud settles, history has always judged cruelly.

The real losers however were the people of Zimbabwe. They lost a chance to get jobs, they lost a chance to be able to feed their children, get treatment for HIV/Aids. They lost a chance of attracting investment, lowering inflation, getting mortgages and having a better life. As the Zanu supporters celebrated their "win" the price of soft drinks, cigarettes, buses, fuel (shortages) and beer went up. Inflation hovered at over 5,500% and rising and the black market was running away with all the foreign currency and goods. For Mugabe to insist that the MDC and Tsvangirai had 'lost' showed that he had lost his soul to Satan.

When opposing a regime that has few qualms about using strong-arm tactics to get its way, it was naive for the opposition to expect electoral victory. In such circumstances, the thing to do was to try to change the rules of the game, or entirely refuse to play. And here lies the chicken-and-egg impasse. To change the constitution, the opposition needed to control a majority in parliament; to get a majority in parliament, the constitution had to be changed. The safest and most plausible route would have been civil disobedience. For civil disobedience to work, it should be well organised, overwhelming and cataclysmic enough to bring the functioning of government to a standstill.

The MDC leadership, however, did not come out as radical and bold enough to plan for, and accept responsibility for ugly outcomes such as violence and dead people in the streets. It was striking that after its electoral loss in 2002, Tsvangirai actually accepted being bogged down in drawn-out court battles. This not only sapped the MDC's energy and resources, but exposed its weakness. If it had had the wherewithal, the MDC could have easily prevailed on its leader to ignore court summons, and used his arrest to precipitate civil disobedience. Unfortunately for the MDC, Zanu was already leading its own bizarre form of state-sponsored civil disobedience (jambaja) in the form of farm invasions.

The MDC chose to play the nice guy. This was, of course, a good strategy as it gave the MDC the moral high ground among international constituencies. But, along the way, the MDC seemed to have taken the strategy for the truth, a highly nebulous thing in politics. The MDC lost political initiative and became captured by external actors with interests in Zimbabwe; it allowed itself to be hijacked by corporate business and theorists leaving it sometimes indistinguishable from Zanu. Even knowledgeable Zimbabweans who thought that Zanu was the worst thing after colonialism started to doubt the MDC's credibility.

However, Tsvangirai, who seemed to have remained well anchored in trade union political thinking, did not seem to need the presidency as desperately as Mugabe needed to keep hanging on to it. It was hard to think of Mugabe outside the presidency since he had lost much of the respect people had for him. Through ruling like a dictator, besieged by imaginary forces while in power, he would just be another has-been outside it. Zanu would never mention how in the presidential election a "puppet" garnered over 2,5 million votes, half of the electorate and then went on to beat Mugabe.

The MDC leader clearly stated his party's policy on the land issue was to see an equitable, fair and transparent reform programme championed and funded by the UN. However, those opposed to this applied selective comprehension and told the electorate the opposition wanted to give land back to the British. Though this could have been mentioned early on in 2000 by an over zealous MDC official, this was not official party policy. But then the majority of Zanu supporters were easily swayed by delivery than by content.

The other issue why the average Zimbabwean might seem so "intellectually barren" is the lack of freedom in the communication platform. The Daily News launched in March 1999 was soon selling more than 400,000 copies a day, far more than any other paper in Zimbabwe and Africa, and three times that of the state's flagship, The Herald. Later it was bombed twice, its journalists arrested and tortured, before being shut down by the government. The Daily News had arrived in the same year the MDC was set up and the fortunes of the two had been closely linked. Without a daily paper willing to give it space, the MDC struggled to get its message across. It did succeed in mobilising people during the election campaign but in between polls it struggled to remain visible and fight off Zanu's crude misinformation machine.

The MDC, which had been seen by South Africa's ANC as being too pro-western, as well as having ties to the predominantly white South African opposition parties developed a more pro-African nuance approach by mid-2003. The MDC had also attempted to improve its relationship with the ANC, which had helped to an extend. The problem was Mbeki wanted a government of national unity between Zanu and the MDC. Mugabe and Tsvangirai would never work together so Mbeki's only option was to split the MDC along tribal lines and Zanu along ideological lines and let the willing parts work together.

The critical issue that was faced by the MDC and South Africa was to see that the MDC power to bring Zimbabwe to a point of real crisis increased with the number of parliamentary seats that they won rather than the converse. The MDC entered the election late January 2005 and won; tried hard but it was no good. The election field was uneven and Zanu rigging was too extensive leaving the opposition not only bewildered but with no plan B. South Africa stood by Mugabe and it emerged the ANC had in actual fact financed Zanu's election campaign. It left a lot of bitterness not only to the opposition but also to most people in Zimbabwe and beyond.

The row between South Africa and the MDC over the Zimbabwe crisis deepened as the opposition accused Mbeki of propping up Mugabe's embattled regime. "...For some strange reason South Africans seem to think we are all morons and we can't see what they are doing," Welshman Ncube said. "But we can see they are engaged in a game of pretence. ....We won't talk to the South Africans as if they are mediators because we have realised they are funding Zanu and engaged it in strategies on how to win a two-thirds majority. ...... It's public knowledge they gave Zanu PF some money....... Zanu also printed election material for the ANC before last year's general election in South Africa that secured Mbeki a second term in office." He continued. "We spoke to other SADC observers and their governments and leaders and they all confirmed South African observers intimidated them to support their views," he said. "Observers with dissenting views suffered severe intimidation. So why should we treat such kind of people as impartial?"

Many opposition political parties in Africa choose to boycott elections out of pique, but the MDC had participated in two parliamentary elections and a presidential election despite tremendous pressure. Despite the laws limiting meetings and publicity, the MDC had not only survived, but grown, building a grassroots movement capable of bringing tens of thousands to its rallies and forcing the Zimbabwean Government, SADC and the AU to reluctantly recognize it as a significant political player. Zimbabweans were putting too much emphasis on the MDC defeats because they were not thinking about Africa but about the West or developed countries. In the Western world those defeated step down. In Africa, incumbency is long, so the opposition has to stick it out longer.

It is near impossible to unseat an incumbent by conventional political means. But by comparison, the MDC seems to have fared better than any other opposition party in Zimbabwe's history. Joshua Nkomo's ZAPU was "swallowed" by Zanu following the 1987 unity accord after losing two elections. Even in Rhodesia, Ian Smith used elections to weed out the opposition or right-wingers who had broken away from his Rhodesian Front. By comparison the MDC beat the government in the constitutional referendum of 2000, had 62 parliamentarians in 2000, beat Mugabe in presidential elections of 2002 and had 41 parliament seats by 2005 elections.

But the election story took a bitter twist soon afterwards. When Mugabe first mooted the idea of resurrecting the Senate, which his party had abolished long ago as a "...useless colonial relic", he never dreamt that he was in fact aiming a body blow at his archenemy. For him the Senate idea was just part of his life presidency strategy, the more of his old cronies he ensconced in power the better for him.

There was a very heated and acrimonious debate about whether the MDC should participate in the Senate elections. The debate was not about participation in the Senate per se but rather reflected a fundamental disagreement over the way in which the struggle for democracy was going to be fought in the future. There was disturbing intolerance displayed by people on both sides of the debate albeit to say that the Senate elections were an irrelevance and whether the MDC was in or out of the elections would not have greatly affected the tide of events in Zimbabwe. Zanu had no mandate to reintroduce the Senate and to that extent what it had done was illegitimate in the minds of the people of Zimbabwe.

The pro-Senate group, though made of intellectual democrats, was misleading the populace. Their strategies included the removal of those in the MDC leadership considered by Zanu and the ANC to be stumbling blocks, alter the central focus and policies of the MDC to resonate with those of Zanu and pave the way for a second Unity Accord and Mbeki's government of national unity. This is why Arthur Mutambara, 'president' of the break away faction, talked about re-branding the MDC.

Tsvangirai breached the party constitution by trying unilaterally to bar the party from the elections. However, this does not mean he breached the democratic process. He rightly decided to obey the spirit of the constitution rather than the letter. Tsvangirai knew that his political survival had little to do with whether he did right or abide by the authority of his party. He knew that, ultimately, his tribe would play a big role in his political future, as the long-held suspicions between Zimbabwe's two major ethnic groups would come to the fore in the event of any dispute.

On the other hand, supporters of the pro-Senate faction had also not taken time to ask themselves if there was anything to gain in risking the existence of the party to a project that was clearly designed for Zanu succession programme. The splinter pro-senate group led by Welshman Ncube and Gibson Sibanda opted for the politics of accommodation. Yet Mutambara, at his inauguration said, "My position was that the MDC should have boycotted those Senate elections. I guess then that makes me the anti-Senate leader of the pro-Senate MDC faction. How ridiculous can we get? That debate is now in the past, let us move on and unite our people."

The MDC had not budgeted on having to campaign in another general election within a year of the 2005 Parliamentary general election. Aside from draining financial resources many of the party's members, staff and supporters were mentally, socially and physically exhausted as 90% of them had been arrested and tortured during the 2005 elections. Most civic organisations strongly opposed the Senate elections and it was argued that the MDC should not jeopardise its relationship with its sponsors by participating in the elections. Indeed the logical progression of a boycott of the Senate elections would be to pull out from Parliament and to boycott all corrupted institutions such as the courts.

The grave consequence of pulling out of these institutions such as Parliament and the courts was that the MDC would be left with little other than the streets as an arena to confront the regime. When left with that then civil war and bloodshed could well become a reality no matter what the original intentions of opposition civic and political leaders were.

If people in Zimbabwe were happy amidst economic plenty it would be reasonable to expect that they would turn out to vote in order to sustain what they had and enjoy. And if the pro-senate faction did not want to concede political space to Zanu all they had to remember was you didn't give anything to Zanu, let alone political space. They took it whether you like it or not. If you look at what happened to the democratically elected mayor of Harare, Elias Mudzuri, the mayor of Mutare, Misheck Kagurabadza and Misheck Shoko, the mayor of Chitungwiza you realise elections meant nothing to Zanu; all were fired and replaced by corrupt Zanu cronies. Fewer than 15% of the electorate turned up to vote for the senators endorsing the people's will that they did not want to be involved with Mugabe's tricks.

The senate debate came as a grand opportunity for both Mugabe and Tsvangirai; it enabled the former to deliver a coup de grace to an MDC already wrecked by internal leadership convulsions while the latter took it as a chance to get rid of those challenging his leadership style.

Apart from dealing with internal dissent, Tsvangirai also had to work hard to restore the confidence of donors and diplomats who had supported the party over the years. Key financial backers had been alarmed by the disclosure by St. Mary's MP, Job Sikhala that party leaders were squabbling over US$ 2.5 million allegedly donated by Nigeria, Ghana and Taiwan. Although Sikhala made a u-turn and said he was out to test the gullibility of journalists from the State media, his pronouncements damaged the opposition party. In the long term it's sad to say the Big Man of Africa prevailed over the status quo and unless the MDC did a complete u-turn and engaged Zanu violently, then it was doubtful they would ever taste power of any form.

When Mutambara came from South Africa to lead the break-away pro-senate faction of the MDC argued that the MDC did not have an ideological underpinning and needed one and then started to preach and coin the pro-Zanu nationalism mantra as his faction's rallying ideology. The crisis in Zimbabwe was a crisis of legitimacy and governance not an ideological crisis as Mutambara would have wanted to believe. This kind of political naiveté would further alienate Mutambara from the generality of victims of state violence and the Diaspora. The MDC was not in power because they lacked an ideological crisis but because the incumbent regime used extra-legal means to hang on to power.

This was further proved as thrice as many voters in the Harare suburb of Budiriro preferred to be governed by a "foreign party" as Mugabe liked to call the MDC than by Mugabe. Mugabe was in Budiriro attempting to drum up support for his dysfunctional party, claimed that the MDC was a "foreign creation" whose aspirations were "at variance with the aspirations of Zimbabweans". By a three-to-one margin, voters either declined to believe Mugabe's claims or alternatively said they didn't care.

What became crystal clear about the senate debate was all about the strategies to employ in the future to bring democracy to Zimbabwe. The electoral route was dead and there was no point in using that route any longer. It was futile to use the courts and there had to be a total withdrawal from all institutions, including Parliament and confrontation was the only means by which this evil regime would be removed. Indeed the elections were a complete irrelevance, they would not solve hype-inflation, the collapse of the economy, starvation and crimes against humanity. Tsvangirai's and the anti-senate MDC's flank was again left wide open. This gave Mugabe a chance to use some of his degrees.

The feeble independence and Murambasvina

"We want our society to be characterised by vigorous debate and dissent where to disagree is part and parcel of a vibrant community, that we should play the ball not the person and not think that those who disagree, who express dissent, are disloyal or unpatriotic." Desmond Tutu

"To set up something nice you have to first remove the litter and that is why the police did what they have done." Chombo, Government minister on Murambasvina, the forced removal of squatters, (2005).

Operation Murambatsvina (destroying people's homes) has been, "...a long cherished desire." Robert Mugabe, Executive President of Zimbabwe, June 2005

The difficulty with analysing the Zimbabwe situation through the lens of Western political values is that Africa, despite its rule by a Western power, has never been governed by the best principles of Western governance. Beginning in the 1840s, Zimbabwe has been ruled in an autocratic fashion. The country never developed a system of property rights and protection because neither Mzilikazi, Lobengula, Rhodes, Smith, Muzorewa or Mugabe governed in a way consistent with these principles. Rhodes was granted some mineral rights concessions, but then simply took the rest of the land for the colonial settlers. Smith snubbed his nose at British insistence that Africans have political rights, and Mugabe did not understand the meaning of the word 'freedom'.

Under colonial rule the rule of law applied only to white settlers. The rule of law was exercised only as it accelerated Rhodes' conquest of the land. This also explains why Smith abandoned the rule of law as it applied to his diminished role as leader and rejected the British government's demand to construct a plan returning power to the demographic majority.

Having never ruled over a village, Mugabe continuing in the tradition established by his predecessors, ignored numerous legitimate trans-national and international authorities and secured absolute political rule for himself. The once-oppressed had now become the oppressor. Mugabe had furthered his rule in the very same fashion and using the very same strategies as did the tribal and colonial elites he so derided. There seems to be an inability among African politicians to distinguish between the rights and obligations of a government and those of the governed.

Those who spent long years in exile fighting for liberation had to deal with their anger to accept a contrary view. Robust and open debate in the bush could only be allowed up to a point and unlike dissidents inside the cities, fighters did not have the pleasure or satisfaction to tell Ian Smith to his face what they thought of him. They therefore missed out on the opportunity to work the anger out of their system. The anger lingered on and Zanu was still caught up in the language of Radio Mozambique, where cheering your side and hurling insults at the enemy passed for political discourse or commentary.

Zimbabwe had passed Bills that embody the most fascist legislation the country or SADC has ever known; far worse than the most draconian laws passed by the Smith regime continued to be passed by parliament. Criminal laws being rushed through Parliament made it virtually impossible to criticise the Mugabe regime in any meaningful way inside or outside the country.

These laws were made to protect the ruling elites and their subordinates from litigation over torture and other human rights violations. For example Shumba, together with opposition Member of Parliament Job Sikhala, and three other opposition youths were arrested and charged under the Public Order and Security Act. All the five were tortured while in police custody as subsequent medical examinations proved. Sikhala and Shumba had electric shocks applied to their genitals, mouth and feet and were also forced to drink their own urine in front of jeering policemen.

According to Shumba, one of the officers confiscated his Lawyer's Practicing Certificate and informed him that there was "no place for human rights lawyers in Zimbabwe". From then on Shumba and later Tswangirai, President of the opposition, claimed that they were subjected to various inhuman treatments that included beatings and blindfoldings. Although a report was later lodged with the police over the alleged torture, no action was ever taken in both cases.

Instead of attracting investment, Zimbabweans saw their government exerting more energy in destroying their investments and mortgages. They saw a calculated assault on property rights and a further curtailment of civil and political rights. While Kenyans took offence at the offer of dog food for hungry children, Zimbabweans were queuing up at butcheries and abattoirs to buy pet food. Not only was pet food popular among poor families, but pigskin, tripe, intestines, cow feet and heads, chicken tripe and heads, meat sawdust and discarded fat from beef also sold well in the country's teeming working class suburbs. Dignity was a luxury few could afford in a country that until 2000 was the breadbasket of southern Africa. As a heartless leadership grappled with the seemingly huge political challenges facing the country, nutrition was not on the agenda. Both consumers and their government were paying little heed to the long-term implications of a poor diet, particularly among children.

Africa Day, 2005, and the regime decided to treat its poor to one of its most callously and brutal menus since the 1980s genocide in Matebeleland-Midlands. The rulers went into over drive in front of the United Nations World Food Programme chief James Morris (remember Rwanda) who was in Zimbabwe. For one hour talking to Mugabe about his refusing to receive food aid for the starving masses, Morris made no comment on the ongoing blitz that had put over 750,000 people on the move. If, when he left, he had looked out of the window of his personal jet, he could have not missed the columns of destitute people and black smoke billowing from burning houses. And if he had his ears and nostrils open he could have smelled the unmistakeable stench and the hopeless cries of the hungry, tired, tortured and maimed, crying for his help.

This was the so-called 'Operation Restore Hope and 'Operation Marambatsvina' (a Shona word meaning "to drive out rubbish") on its long-suffering docile, hungry and defenceless people.

The day arrived under the dark and heavy clouds of doubt and uncertainty about the nation's future hopes. One had to pinch himself to be reminded that this was the people's government and not some foreign invasion which certainly was what it looked like. Then the new Chinese jets and Russian helicopter gunships flew over and made the illusion that they were under attack by some foreign force complete.

116

A housing shortage mixed with grinding poverty, unemployment and black market trading had led to the common practice of home owners renting out unplanned overcrowded illegal shacks, built in their backyards, to families scrambling to make a living in the city. In an operation that was initially started by Gideon Gono (Reserve Bank Governor) as an attempt to rid Harare of illegal foreign currency dealers, criminals and illegal immigrants it then expanded to target illegal street vendors, whose wares were confiscated. Subsequently the campaign moved into working class areas in urban centres, where illegal structures were demolished selectively.

Informal settlements (squatter camps), which had mushroomed around Harare as the country's economic crisis worsened, were not spared either. Overnight, Zimbabwe had been turned into a massive internal refugee centre, with between 1 million and 1.5 million people displaced in Harare alone. As the mass of people moved through the cold winter, relentlessly chased by police and army with dogs, water cannons, helicopters and tear gas, with no clean water, no shelter, no food supplies, no health centres and no fuel or logistics, many succumbed to diseases, fatigue and nutritional deficiencies. Many NGOs were unable to help immediately as they had already relocated to neighbouring countries.

The former inhabitants of Harare's shanties were labelled "economic saboteurs" and "miscreants" by senior government officers and ministers. Mugabe, who had a history of accusing Tony Blair and George Bush for his country's woes, had now turned onto his fellow countrymen. All over the City, homes were destroyed, goods stolen or destroyed and people threatened with loaded weapons and live ammunition. They were tear gassed with gases supplied by none other than the masters of oppression Israel that stuns its victims. Officers in charge of this mindless destruction said that they had orders to shoot to kill anyone resisting.

Glen View, Mabvuku, St. Mary's, Mbare, High Fields and other townships initially fought back weakly. Some residents tried to make their way to the rural areas but Zimbabwe's crippling fuel shortages ensured that not a single bus was available. Mbare bus terminus began to resemble a refugee camp as more and more families arrived. Impassive gestures belied the frightened eyes and simmering anger of the Bulawayo traders, who had been collectively murmuring the word of their darkest horrors, "gukurahundi".

As Murambasvina progressed, Mugabe directed Treasury to release an unbudgeted Z$100 billion to train more police guards for himself and his top officials. The money, enough to feed more than 50,000 hungry families for a month, was used to hire specialist trainers from South African and Israeli private security firms and training equipment. The new guards were recruited from graduates of Mugabe's controversial national youth training service, blamed of hunting down, torturing and murdering opposition supporters across the country.

No matter the reasons for the clean-up one thing was clear: it was a costly move in terms of legitimacy and history will eventually judge murambasvina as heavy handed if not all together without justification and illegal. Outside the possible reasons that either wanted to exonerate or blame the government, what was alarming was the ease with which the government destroyed places people called home. In an Africa where collective memory includes constantly being up-rooted and forced into Bantustans (conscription camps) such careless action recalls this painful history. It recalled forced colonial migration and dispersal. By forcefully moving an African people, collective memory and the legacies of colonialism make it such that only an injustice came out of it.

When the apartheid government in South Africa deployed similar tactics in the 1970s in defence of white "group areas", the civilised world quite understandably reacted with revulsion and supported the ANC's demand for sanctions against Pretoria. A generation later, the ANC, AU and American black governments were spookily silent about these grotesque activities north of the Limpopo.

Zimbabwe becomes a best case study for compromise of efficiency with an institution of corrupt people named a political party. The AU representative on human rights was unilaterally shown the door out by the Zimbabwean authorities who knew very well that humanitarian rapporteur would have discovered awesome abuse in human and people rights during the operation. The UN discovered, much to the horror of all dictators and tyrants of Africa that Zimbabweans had suffered a worst humiliation from one masquerading as messiah for the black race, the Malawian Robert Matibili-Mugabe and his Zanu party.

With barely 8% of adult Zimbabweans in formal sector employment, the wholesale destruction of these small family businesses was a betrayal of the principles of the liberation struggle. The use of armed police and soldiers to carry out this exercise and to intimidate those affected and the refusal of letting SADC or the AU to investigate revealed the true character of the exercise.

The Government was acting in blatant violation of civil, political, economic and social rights of the poor guaranteed under the African Charter on Human and Peoples' Rights and the AU was noticeable by its silence even though its emissary had been embarrassed and chucked out unceremoniously. "The vast majority are homeless in the streets," AU's Kothari said. "This kind of a mass eviction drive is a classic case where the intention appears to be that Harare become a city for the rich, for the middle class, for those that are well-off ... and the poor are to be pushed away." In fact Mugabe was in the middle of a "ruralisation" program with clear echoes of the Cambodian genocide.

The psychological trauma for the Zimbabwe Republic Police (ZRP) and army details was in cases worse than that suffered by the people whose homes they were destroying. In some cases they were destroying their own houses. They had to act against their own people and conscience. If they didn't, they faced dismissal. Some had been made to commit atrocities and knew they would be jailed if dismissed. This was a clever plan to divide the community. Those in power had long been unsure of the loyalty of the police and youthful army.

For a long time Mugabe refused to allow the United Nations to launch an international appeal to help the poor, starving and homeless Zimbabweans he had made homeless. When Mugabe eventually agreed to the offer to build homes for the homeless, his vice president, Joyce Mujuru, had seized a brick-making company. What kind of cruelty and evil had possessed Mugabe's senile mind to deny homeless people the right to be sheltered in tents? The reason is purely economic. Mugabe knew he could not generate a viable business from prefabricated tents. None of his companies had foreign exchange to start manufacturing the tents.

The government had not become a doyen of transparency and was not acting responsibly as the first recipients of the two roomed, toilet-less houses, were police and army personnel. The government had never been known to possess this virtue when it comes to the allocation of scarce national resources. All its actions had been steeped in the mire of political patronage. The government in its clientelist mode had built a complex system of power largely based on its ability to co-opt interest groups in society through a patronage system in which they exchange support for the regime for material benefits. The new houses were no different.

As it were, in June 2005, in the mid of the clean up, Mugabe arrived for the early state opening of parliament in a black Rolls-Royce, fake medals pinned to his chest, inspected a guard of honour of mounted police lancers, bowed to a picture of himself albeit looking young, then delivered a 35-minute speech condemning lawlessness and demanding "greater cohesion and unity" from his countrymen!

Mugabe had watched the world to see if there was going to be action after rigging the 2000 elections, and the world was divided between strong action and another chance. In 2002 the world saw that Mugabe was a cheat and so was the basis on which Zanu premised its stance for democracy. The commonwealth took action to boot Zimbabwe out of the club. Unfortunately nations like the USA played a monopoly of trusting South Africa and it equally revealed the crude policy of America on Africa since the 1960s.

This however was not the first time Zanu had done this. Gukurahundi, Matebeleland, 1984, ground zero and thousands were massacred, thousands more tortured and hundreds of thousands put on the move with no medical facilities, food or logistics, edged on by the North Korean trained and armed 5th Brigade led by Perence Shiri and presided over by Mugabe, Mnangagwa and Enos Nkala. After the 1985 elections when Zanu mobs, reacting to comments by Mugabe, forced thousands of families suspected of supporting the opposition from their township homes until they could produce ruling party cards. An unknown number of people were killed while police refused to intervene. The world stood by and watched. From 2000, hundreds of thousands of farm workers were once again on the move, 100s murdered and 1,000s maimed, as farms were illegally occupied without any assistance being provided by the government to those negatively affected by the occupations.

September 2004 Zanu attempted to evict thousands of people from Porta Farm, an informal settlement on the outskirts of Harare, during which police misused tear gas against residents. The police were acting in defiance of a court order prohibiting the eviction. The police fired tear gas directly into the homes of the Porta Farm residents and at least 11 people died but no investigation is known to have been carried out. The world watched and did nothing.

December 2005 and the government attack on the Diaspora began: confiscating travel documents belonging to independent newspaper publisher Trevor Ncube and opposition politician Paul Themba Nyathi, indicating how personal liberties had come under siege from the authorities who had virtually put the country under a state of emergency. The state had sort to proscribe persons movement in "the national interest or in the interests of defence, public safety, public order, public morality". Public morality!

A couple of years later The African Commission on Human and People's Rights (ACPHR) eventually condemned Murambasvina and the decisions of the commission were a significant indicator that the judiciary and the justice delivery system in Zimbabwe no longer guaranteed enjoyment of universally recognised human rights and fundamental freedoms. The indictment of the Zimbabwe government was a reflection of a paradigm shift permeating some AU institutions, which was that good governance, the rule of law and responsible governing can not be shelved as Africa writhes from the periphery of the global economy.

Despite attempts at censorship, films of the bulldozers at work filled the screens of Europe and America, the very countries being asked to provide more aid to Africa. Aid agencies had already reported a fall in donations and funds for Africa partly because of a perception that aid would be stolen, embezzled, misused or simply disappear in a maze of bureaucratic incompetence. And there was to be little enthusiasm in Washington to support Tony Blair's call for more money for Africa unless the continent gave clear proof of good governance. That included a halt to the atrocities in Zimbabwe, a moderately developed country gone to pieces.

Raiders of the last farms and the land question

December 1, 2000: "What I think the Zimbabwean government should do is to strictly follow the law that is already in place for the resolution of the land problem," Mr Obasanjo said as Mugabe sat to the side. It was a rare occasion when two African leaders publicly criticise a fellow head of state. "The issue of land reform in Zimbabwe is an issue that is not only current but it affects almost everybody's life in this country and the lives of others beyond this country," he said. "We do know that there is a law that stipulates what needs to be done and how it should be done so that this problem can be resolved."

The challenge of fairly distributing land that, for historical or political reasons, has been concentrated in the hands of a few wealthy owners has been around for centuries. Land reform dates back to Roman times and the agrarian laws passed by the Senate around 133 BC, which indirectly led to the undoing of the Roman Republic and presaged the emergence of feudalism.

In its essence, land reform is about redistributing arable land, whether previously collectivised by the state or held by rich farmers. The distribution usually proposes to take from the rich and give to the poor. The process sometimes involves compensation schemes, but in many places, farmers are forced by the government to give up their land at prices the owners regard as unfair.

The goals of land reform are multi-fold: reducing poverty, expanding rural development, or returning land to its previous owners. In more recent times, land reform is a consequence of post-colonial or post-communist economic and social needs. Other times it is driven more by ethnic and racial divisions, or an interest in manipulating political sentiment, than by any desire to redistribute land equitably. Most rich landowners in southern Africa, for example, are white, while most landless people are black.

Across southern Africa, where agriculture often remains the only viable occupation, land retains enormous economic, political, traditional and psychological value yet it is African agriculture itself that is in crisis. What appear as isolated disasters brought about by drought or conflict in countries like Somalia, Malawi, Niger, Kenya and Zimbabwe are, in reality, systemic problems.

Most poor people in Africa have no title to their land, which is communal and overseen by corrupt, ruthless and humourless traditional chiefs, a legacy of the British colonial system. Most southern African states are also young democracies and over the past decade, their governments have vowed to promote land reform; the process of handing over land to the 'landless' Africans. But, faced with numerous challenges, from corruption, holding on to power, holding unfree elections, to combating HIV, most countries stalled on land reform.

Decades of under investment in rural areas, Africa's elites response to political pressure, compounded by corruption, mismanagement and poor governance are major issues that have serious repercussions for long-term food security and land redistribution. Southern Africa had the world's highest HIV prevalence rate, and as a result of the virus the farming workforce had been dramatically weakened, which had a devastating impact on food production. Farmers need political, legal and economic stability and certainty before they can succeed in producing the food their families and societies need.

Populations have been growing drastically all over Africa and this forced farming families to subdivide their land, leading to tiny plots or families moving onto unsuitable, overworked land. This problem is compounded by the state of Africa's soils. In sub-Saharan Africa soil quality is classified as degraded in about 72% of arable land and 31% of pastureland. In addition to natural nutrient deficiencies in the soil, soil fertility is declining by the year through "nutrient mining", whereby nutrients are removed over the harvest period and lost through leaching, erosion or other means.

The Zimbabwe land situation was predicated in colonial land theft and an agreement signed in Lancaster house in the UK in 1979. Rhodes and his cronies simply designated land they had no right to, forcing the indigenous blacks into mountains with no compensation.

In 1979, no provision was made in the Lancaster House Agreement for a specific fund to support land reform after independence. But a Zimbabwe Donors Conference in March 1981 raised £17-million for development in Zimbabwe, including land reform. Between 1980 and 1985, the UK provided £47-million for land reform: £20-million as a specific Land Resettlement Grant and £27-million in the form of budgetary support to help the Zimbabwean government's own contribution to the programme.

By 1988, the Land Settlement Grant had been largely spent. The then UK Overseas Development Agency fully endorsed the resettlement, which had taken place and suggested measures for further improving the UK-funded programme. The Zimbabwean government did not respond to these proposals and the grant was closed in 1996 with £3-million unspent.

The fact that most of the international media attention had focused on the issue of white farm invasions, had fed the misperception that the state violence was part of a black-white struggle for land ownership. Without doubt, many human rights violations occurred in the context of the land invasions: but very few of these violations involve white farmers, with poor rural Zimbabweans being the victims in more than 95% of cases.

Mugabe's famous land reforms ensured that 1.5 million black farm workers and their dependants were deprived of their jobs and homes and poured into squatter camps throughout Zimbabwe only to be attacked there two years later by police and the Army under 'Operation Murambasvina'. Mugabe's justification for sowing this violence and misery was that Zimbabwe would be rid of the white farmers and totemless foreigners from Malawi and Mozambique. These "racist oppressors" would be driven out of the country yet its the blacks who suffered most, as the white farmers were quickly embraced by other African countries.

Stevens was the first white farmer to be murdered at the outset of Mugabe's land reform in April 2000. During the next 18 months, another ten white landowners, one of them abducted from a police station and shot, and 139 of their workers would die at the hands of the president's mobs. There was much talk of the "war veterans" who supplied the muscle. The label was misleading in many cases as these were uneducated teenager losers led by another illiterate loser named Joseph Chinotimba. They were cheap to find and easy to bend to the government's will. Scores of farms were looted and burned to the ground, armed gangs were unleashed across Zimbabwe and law and order collapsed.

122

At the time Police Assistant Commissioner Loveness Ndanga, was the head of a task force that went on the rampage, seizing farming equipment worth trillions of dollars. Zanu had established the task force in a bid to seize everything from the white farmers who had kept their equipment in warehouses in the hope of leasing the equipment to new farmers, and hoping that one-day they would be allowed to farm again. The task force included members of the Police, army, prison services and officials of the Zimbabwe National Water Authority(ZINWA), Zanu politicians and war veterans. The looted farm equipment included tractors, ploughs, cultivators, disc harrows, harvesters, graders, irrigation pipes, pumps and grass cutters. All these were shared between police officers and top Zanu politicians and left to rust.

Members occupying BIPPA-protected farms included Higher Education minister Stan Mudenge who moved into Chikore Farm in Masvingo protected under a Dutch BIPPA, displacing the Buchan family. President Robert Mugabe ratified the Dutch agreement in 1996. Zanu MP for Mudzi West, Joseph Christopher Musa invaded a multi-trillion dollar Danish-operated Zengea Farm, housing Red Dane Dairy which was protected from acquisition under a BIPPA signed in 1996. Italy signed a BIPPA in 1996, protecting up to 30 farmers and a host of other investments in different fields. The move to redress violations of 100s of BIPPAs was to be met with stiff resistance by Zanu members including cabinet ministers who occupied most of the best properties.

Edged on by the IMF and Mbeki's threat of cutting off of electricity and fuel lines, Mugabe finally woke up from his murdering slumber and posing as a magnanimous leader inviting back his former enemies in the interests of national recovery, decided to 'lease' some of the grabbed land back to the white farmers. Behind closed doors, the International Monetary Fund told Zimbabwe's finance minister, who had helped himself to a white-owned farm, that land seizures had to halt immediately and that without increased agricultural production there was no chance of halting Zimbabwe's slide.

Under severe pressure, with soldiers resigning enmass and to get some 'breathing space' from the serpent he knew, Mugabe accepted that some of those white farmers must be allowed to return on their land under new leases and revive his chances on holding on to power. The murders and beatings, the poverty caused by destroying the backbone of Zimbabwe's economy, were entirely pointless.

He personally granted 125 leases to a handful of whites and Zanu cabinet ministers, cronies and MPs. This was Fifteen years after enacting the Land Acquisition Act, more than six years after declared intents of redistribution of the expropriated lands, 20 years after much land vested in the government as a result of purchases funded by the United Kingdom and five years after enunciating its 99-year lease policy. This encompassed an aggregate of less than 1% of the land supposedly to be redistributed and resettled. At that rate, all the land would have been leased to farmers by about the year 2500!

Section 20 of those leases Mugabe issued out under pomp and ceremony said government could cancel the lease at any time under conditions it deems necessary! "The lessor may, at any time and in such manner and under such conditions as it may deem fit, repossess the leasehold or any portion if the possession is reasonably necessary in the interest of defence, public safety, public morality (that word again), public health, town and country planning or the utilisation of that or any other property for purposes beneficial generally or to any section of the public."

Lets give Matibili-Mugabe and other like minded Africans a crush course on leases: Leasehold arrangements first evolved from the earlier feudal systems in Europe, as landlords and tenants tried to find means of unlocking the capital value of land. When new areas of settlement and investment were being established in the Americas, the feudal systems of Spain and Portugal were transplanted into South and Central America. However, in North America, the evolving freehold land tenure systems were adopted. Today, hundreds of years later, South and Central America remains a collection of developing countries, but North America has become the most prosperous area in the world.

The essential difference between these two vast areas and the essential difference between the former communal and commercial areas of Zimbabwe is that, where they had individual title, the owners of the land used its capital value as leverage to raise the funds required to develop the land's potential as well as their own. With access to the capital they needed and the confidence that came from security of tenure over their property, they achieved remarkable successes. Their ability to make long-term plans and their eagerness to repay their loans to preserve their ownership rights drew from them exceptional levels of resourcefulness, ingenuity and determination to succeed.

Unfortunately, the conditions the Government of Zimbabwe had entrenched in the leases made them distinctly different from conditions that apply in Western countries. In the countries concerned, the leased land in question was not owned by the State; a property-owning individual, family or company owns it, each lease is on an identifiable piece of land, each lease had a market value and therefore marketable. Because of the marketability of the lease, it can be offered as collateral in support of a loan. This protects the lessor, as a bank that is owed money that the lessee cannot repay has the legal right to place the lease on the market. When a new lessee pays for the remaining years covered by the lease, the bank will recover the funds owing. Laws governing tenant rights also protect lessees, but in exchange they are required to meet these fully acceptable obligations or forfeit their rights.

In the event of a lessee deciding to relinquish a lease, the market value of the remaining years will be established in the market. Other than collecting transfer duties and registering the new lessee, the State plays no part in the procedures. These features make all such lease agreements bankable in other countries, but the leases being issued by Mugabe were not bankable, simply because no mechanism existed that could be used to establish a market price. Government's right to approve or reject any applicant wishing to take over an existing lease further distanced the arrangements from the open market requirements of genuine, bankable collateral.

Another case to note is The Zimbabwe State-Indebted Insolvent Companies Bill; under this law, the state would take over private firms as and when it deems that a company is no longer able to repay money owed to the government. The state would not require the courts to authorise the seizures but will only need a certificate signed by the justice minister authorising the seizures. And the rights of shareholders and management of targeted companies automatically fall away once the ministerial certificate is issued. To deny shareholder right to their companies, in the absence of a court order amounts to an unjustifiable interference with their right of freedom of property enshrined in the Constitution and it scares away investors plus this Act was a copy of the Agricultural laws that had brought down the country.

As the conditions created by land reform in Zimbabwe had effectively eliminated the collateral value of farmland, they had made development funding entirely the responsibility of the State and each individual farmer's performance dependent on State subsidies and support. Personal progress within such a system, therefore, become dependent upon political patronage, rather than upon resourcefulness, good management and hard work.

Although fixed assets of some value could be built with money loaned by an insane bank manager, the separation of land from the improvements on that land made the recovery of the debt almost impossible if the borrower defaults. This was because the farmer's right to remain on the land was conferred, not by business procedures supported by market forces, but by a political act that the bank could not challenge.

But how do you rebuild something that had been smashed into a thousand pieces? When a mob of Mugabe's fanatical supporters dragged a David Stevens from his farm, they subjected the father of four to hours of torment and torture before finally killing him with shots to the head and chest. How do you rebuild that when the known murderers were still out and about free?

Entirely predictably, Mugabe's violent land grab had failed and caused an economic and social catastrophe. Few serious international investors would take up the leases; only insane bankers would respect them. Mugabe's decision to revert to feudal State-ownership of land was proving to be a massively retrogressive step.

Commercial agriculture was the pillar of Zimbabwe's economy. Recovery was impossible unless production of tobacco for export and maize for domestic consumption revived dramatically. Farming paid for the electricity and fuel that ensured everyone was happy. A week after South Africa's Eskom power utility cut off electricity and fuels supplies to Zimbabwe, residents in Harare and other cities suddenly found themselves back in the Stone Age, forced to cook meals over open fires and to grow vegetables in their back yard. So the officials with the unenviable task of rebuilding Zimbabwe's economy had reached the unavoidable conclusion: some of those hated white farmers must be allowed to return.

Wealth redistribution and politics of sadza

Tito Mboweni, the governor South Africa's Reserve Bank, warned, "The wheels have come off there [in Zimbabwe]. I am saying this as forcefully as I am because the developments in Zimbabwe are affecting us and stressing us unnecessarily.......The situation has become untenable when it is seen that the highest office in that land seems to support illegal means of land reform, land invasions, beating up of people, blood flowing everywhere."

Maize is what the Americans call corn and feed to their pigs and cows. Mealie meal or cornmeal is used to prepare 'bota', a porridge made by mixing the cornmeal, water and heat, to produce a thick paste. This is usually flavoured with peanut butter, bread, milk, butter or sugar. Bota is usually eaten for breakfast. Cornmeal is also used to make 'sadza'. The process of making sadza is similar to bota, however after the paste has been cooking for several minutes, more cornmeal is added to thicken the paste until it is hard. This meal is usually served with spinach, rape, beans or meat that is stewed, grilled or roasted, curdled milk known as lacto (mukaka wakakora), or a small dried fish called kapenta. On special occasions rice and chicken with cabbage salad is often served as the main meal. Most poor families would have cold sadza for breakfast (left over from the last evening meal) and then at least one large meal at lunch or in the evening with hot sadza as the main course.

Zimbabweans eat 115 kilograms of vitamin 'A' spiced maize meal per capita per annum. It is therefore a very important component of daily social, political and economic life and the key to the tenuous stability of Zimbabwe lies in the fact that it is cheap and reasonably available. The problem arises when issues of how to grow the maize to feed this great appetite, the means to pound it into flower and the distribution politics kick in. A shortage of 'sadza' is called 'food shortages' in Zimbabwe even though there is a surplus of rice, macaroni, potatoes, oranges, pumpkins and spaghetti. Maize was mainly grown on white commercial farms.

Agriculture is probably the most commonly known source of production power. Marxists long argued that power reposes in those in control of the means of production. The ones that decide the mode of production and control production levels have the power over those with an interest in accessing the means and items of production. They seek to strengthen and defend their position and establish rules and institutions to create enclosures that others cannot challenge.

It is within this context that we can see Mugabe's strategy in relation to land reform and other areas of production such as industry and the mining sector. Zanu knew that in an agro-based economy, it lacked sufficient control of the production structure. Instead, the commercial farmers with greater control of the production structure appeared to favour the new opposition party, the MDC. It therefore became necessary to break this pattern to avoid having the power from the production structure residing with the opposition.

Some of the Zimbabwean white farms were so huge and demanded such a large labour force that in addition to a run-down township and a rudimentary school, some of them had a clinic, a small shopping centre and a bar, all for use by the black workers courtesy of the owner. Admittedly African farms are far away from any town so that for the families whatever lacks in store literally lacks in their lives.

The store is eager to give credit to the workers to keep them ensnared in a vicious cycle of credit and debt. The clinic patched up injured workers just well enough to see them working the following day. The primary school ensured that the black child learns just enough maths to count and enough English to take instructions from the owner. In short, it was slavery and was most likely to be resisted in the end.

After the murders and the occupations, Mugabe initially used the drought to 'explain' the precipitous drop in agricultural output and economic activity. Then there was AIDS, then the British and the Americans, the internal saboteurs, then the poor street vendors, the Diaspora, a monkey, imperialists etc.

Let's give some semblance of respect to drought and AIDS. Zimbabwe's next-door neighbour is Botswana. Botswana had the world's second-highest rate of AIDS infection and if there's drought in Zimbabwe, there's likely a drought in Botswana, whose major geographic feature is the Kalahari Desert. However, Botswana had one of the world's highest per capita GDP growth rates. The World Forum rated Botswana as one of Africa's two most economically competitive nations and one of the best investment opportunities in the developing world. Botswana shares a Bantu heritage with Zimbabwe, for it, too, was a British colony. What it doesn't share with Zimbabwe explains its success: the rule of law, minimal corruption and, most of all, respect for private property rights. No amount of Western foreign aid can bring about the political and socio-economic climate necessary for economic growth. Instead, foreign aid allows vicious dictators to remain in power. It enables them to buy the allegiance of cronies and the military equipment to oppress their own people.

When the troubles started in Zimbabwe's rural areas, opposition parties exposed the corruption inherent in many land reform policies. Zimbabwe escaped starvation only because donors chipped in with food. When the late Zanu founding member and luminary, Eddison Zvobgo, then told parliament: "We have turned what was a noble agrarian revolution into a racist enterprise," few of his colleagues quite grasped the import of his remarks. Zanu elites had ventured further to taint the agrarian reform by assuming the role of serial robber barons of farm equipment and implements rather than showcase their industry and acumen as competent farmers. The 'noble land revolution' had become an enterprise by cronies of the ruling elite to reap where they had not sawn veiled in dubious radicalism as "remedying the maladies of colonial land imbalances".

While it managed to forcefully secure the means of production, Zanu's power from this agricultural structure was actually weak because of low productivity. The only reason why it was important to Zanu was that it managed to deprive others of the opportunity to draw power from the agricultural structure because of its monopoly that was supported by a strong security structure. It can also be pointed out that it was within this power context that we can understand Zanu's desire to assume greater control of the mines and was hard on the local industry, setting the prices of essential goods and therefore levels of production and also its active participation as a shareholder in local industries, Gukurahundi, Murambasvina's destruction of the informal sector, citizen harassment etc.

By 1990 Zanu had already increased attempts to control the knowledge structure by enhancing control and interference with academic freedom at universities via the notoriously controversial University of Zimbabwe Amendment Act. The same efforts could be seen in the control of syllabi of key subjects that taught liberation history and also increasing attempts to take control of the private education sector. Similarly, re-education programmes and the national youth service constituted attempts to control knowledge.

More importantly, Zanu maintained control of power arising from the knowledge structure through a system of withdrawal of knowledge. This was the context in which we can understand the media monopoly of the Zimbabwe Broadcasting Holdings, the threats and actual acts of violence against the Daily News (it was bombed twice) culminating in the continued refusal to issue a licence and the dominance of Zanu's Zimpapers. The only power that Mugabe had no control over was the West and he exposed his weakness by rhetorical attack.

Judging from two case studies: Jamaica's assault on the American Bauxite Companies (1971-75) and Idi Amin's assault on the Asian merchants in Uganda (1971-1979), the Mugabe land experiment in Zimbabwe had no chance whatever of succeeding. Imperialists do exist and it is true that they do not wish Africa and Africans any good. Their methods are the same and similarly, the reaction of their victims has been foreseen and studied.

In Jamaica, Manley's attempt to partially nationalise the bauxite mines brought a swift reaction from the capitalists. The BWIs wiped out the $250 million surplus the Jamaican government had achieved by the act of nationalization within two years. The Jamaican monetary unit, which had been backed by the English pound, was no longer convertible. With shortages becoming a daily occurrence, it was the price of mortgages that finally impressed all young Jamaicans that they were better off as second-class citizens in New York than they were as militant nationalists in Jamaica. Today, there are more Jamaicans in New York than there are in Jamaica.

Then as now, black people sympathized with Manley. The great sugar company, Tate and Lyle, was driven away and their land given over to sugar sharecroppers. These sharecroppers could be seen standing by the wayside, selling one or two sticks of sugar cane. They regarded themselves as unemployed since the departure of their former employer, Tate and Lyle, despite the fact that they now owned the land.

AT its peak, Kondozi Farm, in the Eastern Highlands of Zimbabwe, raked in an estimated $15 million and employed 5,000 workers from the surrounding community. In 2004, Zanu forcibly took over the successful horticultural concern. Obsessed with revolutionary mantras and hatred for the West, government ignored the many voices of reason. And in keeping with tradition, a select few greedy senior Zanu politicians known for their ethical sense of a pack of hyenas pounced. Before anyone could say Kondozi, it was a free-for-all as influential politicians, most of whom had access to cheap loans for agriculture and subsidised inputs, systematically looted equipment from the farm. The farm never produced anything again and blame was apportioned to the West. Thabo Mbeki, and every normal man who has some African blood in his veins wished Mugabe's insanity success even if they knew that the facts were stacked against that possibility.

The issue of who owns the land in Africa is one of the biggest challenges for post-colonial governments, particularly in Zimbabwe and South Africa, where both whites and blacks consider themselves indigenous. It was without doubt unfair that most of the good land remained in the hands of white people 20 years after independence, but only a warped mind could call what Mugabe had done land reform.

After a hundred years of colonization, cultures had changed. The majority of young Africans want to make their career in the banking and air-conditioned world of the city rather than on the land. They showed their gratitude to Mugabe's redistribution of land by leaving the country in their millions for the UK, USA, South Africa and Australia. The elites were no exception as they surely considered their careers to be bound with politics, even if they wanted to visit a bushy place they call a farm over weekends for a 'braaie'. Because of technological advances, farming has become a specialized field for agronomists and chemists rather than an occupation of unschooled peasants and unscrupulous politicians.

Evidently, it was hoped that the eviction of the white commercial farmers from their properties would cause only a mild and temporary hiccup to productivity. This was a grave miscalculation and people like Minister of agriculture "Doctor" Joseph Made did not help matters by predicting bumper harvests on the basis of nebulous evidence collected by flying in a helicopter over two farms. The drought did contribute to the food shortages, but the bulk of the problem can be traced to government bungling. Zimbabwe had in the past seen more devastating draughts but had managed well.

The government was ill prepared for a major overhaul of a sector that had been the mainstay of the economy for so long. The hundreds of thousands of new unprofessional farmers had been unable to produce as much food as the 4,000-odd commercial farmers did before the tragedy of 2000. Zimbabwe's black owned banks largely withheld funding from black peasants resettled on former white farms by the government chiefly because, unlike their white predecessors, the blacks did not hold title to the land and therefore could not use it as security to cover loans. The new 'farmers' (Mugabe's cronies) record of efficiency and integrity, going by the sorry mess in the parastatal sector, was highly dubious.

Land redistribution should become a metaphor of what is possible with other sectors of the economy. Land redistribution should be pointing to what is possible for all of society. President Jacques Chirac had praised Bolivian land reforms in 2006 and Mugabe, ever the chancer he was, managed to slip in a line suggesting Bolivia's land reforms were similar to Zimbabwe's. But any similarity with Zimbabwe was in the eye of the beholder.

Firstly President Evo Morales of Bolivia had came to power in free and democratic elections. Bolivia's land reform programme was noticeably helping the poor. It was not used to reward VIP cronies such as police chiefs and judges. Mugabe racist remarked that no one questioned Bolivia's land reforms because the landowners facing expropriation were non-Caucasian was mischievous. In fact the land-owning class in Bolivia is of largely Hispanic descent not Caucasian. But the important point to note here was that the group of emergent leftist South American leaders had been careful not to associate themselves with Zimbabwe's chaotic and often violent land grabs. Even Chavez had never paid a state visit to Zimbabwe.

In Zimbabwe hapless peasants wallowed on the fringes, harassed, tortured, murdered; patiently waiting for their turn to move away from barren soils. It had become extremely difficult to differentiate between an emerging acquisitive ethic among the ruling elite and the colonial settler who expropriated land over a century ago and banished the indigenous people to wasteland.

There were many countries that nationalised what they call strategic industries, including Britain under Margaret Thatcher. So long as that is done according to the law and in the public interest, it is an issue of national consensus. It was difficult to prove the "correctness" of Zimbabwe's land reform in the wake of the poverty, murder and starvation it had spawned. Essentially, the Harare 1998 donors' conference stressed that one of the key aims of land reform was to alleviate poverty and empower the poor. None of that was evident on the ground.

Morales launched the land reform programme by distributing state-owned land to the poor. Thousands of the beneficiaries were immediately given title so that they could borrow money to use the land productively. None of the land distributed to the poor in Bolivia had been confiscated from large landholders. Six years down the line Zanu mandarins were still seizing land.

In the 12 months ending March 2005, 214 people had died from starvation, including 14 malnutrition-related deaths because of hunger-related illnesses as a severe food shortage inflicted a heavy toll on the city of Bulawayo; a city of one million people. After years spent trumpeting the "success" of the land grab, Mugabe finally admitted that most of the farms transferred to black owners had never been used. By June 2005 the Zimbabwe government was offering former white farms for free to Chinese state-owned firms in a desperate bid to revive the key agricultural sector. At the height of fuel shortages in 2002, the government signed a similar deal with 'born again' Qaddaffi who was to take large swathes of land in exchange for fuel. The deal collapsed as the Libyans preferred cash at that time.

"Our investigations have shown that a monkey caused damage to a transformer, thereby sabotaging our preparations for this coming season," Agriculture minister, 'Doctor' Joseph Made said 2006. A monkey! Desperate to say something in face of a pending disaster, Mugabe's cronies tried to cover the shortfalls by any means. Handing land to people who don't know how best to farm it decreases crop production in an already famine-prone region.

Black economic empowerment had created a narrow class of black capitalists rather than benefiting the majority that will result in resentment and resistance from the lower classes. Moreover, it creates opportunities for corruption and abuses of power. The problem with African leaders is they don't take the effort to initiate programs that spurred wealth creation.

On the international stage, Britain and America seemed to be more incensed by Mugabe's socialist policies since they feared that that might upstage the capitalist structures if the land reform was pursued to its successful conclusions. The international fight therefore seemed a battle against communist incursion and hence the pressure applied was necessary so that in the event that Mugabe was not scared into back-pedalling on the land reform or be defeated in a presidential election, the effects of the sanctions imposed on Zimbabwe's ruling elites would scare potential land or anti-imperialist reformists in other SADC states.

However the greatest threat was not Mugabe-style expropriation of white farms, but a less understood part of the Mugabe strategy: stealing land from poor blacks and handing it to political elites. The lack of a governing law or planning and transparency at the start of the fast-track land reform exercise in 2000 prompted many individuals to amass more than one farm. They took advantage of the chaos, whilst others simply acted out of greed. This was not confined to those in government and the ruling party, but also extended to ordinary well-connected Zimbabweans.

Politically motivated and illegal land reform leads to the emergence of the next generations of the deprived and the discriminated against. Resettlement has to be both fair and seen to be fair, based on unambiguous criteria and transparent and even-handed procedures. It has to be backed by sufficient agricultural inputs and machinery, financial and technical assistance, training, access to markets, and basic infrastructure. The proximity of services and institutions, from schools to impartial courts, is critical.

Above all, land reform has to look after people displaced in the process, both farmers and their workers, and thus enjoy near universal support or acquiescence. Legal title and tenure have to be established and recorded to allow the new settlers to obtain credits and invest in buildings, machinery, and infrastructure. Mugabe surely is to blame for the mess even though he was not the prime mover of this debacle. He merely encapsulated and leveraged insidious social forces in Zimbabwe and in Africa.

Nations that have made economic progress have, irrespective of ideology, undergone similar processes. Development has involved capital accumulation, industrialisation, the transformation of productive forces through machine technology and the introduction of factory systems of production. It entailed urbanisation; the rationalisation of thought and changes in social beliefs and institutions, including family life. Investment in physical and human capital has been indispensable. In all developed countries, the economy was given primacy in the political system. Perhaps most importantly, development has been underpinned by certain values, including efficiency, hard work, precision, honesty, punctuality, thrift, obligation to one's duty and wealth creation. All modernisation involved a move away from traditionalism.

There have been differences in the methods of organisation adopted by modernising nations. Nevertheless, both socialists and capitalists followed the same fundamental steps to economic development. "Development," said the economist J.K. Galbraith, "is the faithful imitation of the developed."

African nationalists find this basic idea difficult to accept. Despite the failure of African Socialism or Africanisation there remains a belief among some African thinkers and writers that there is an African way to development that is different from the universal path. No one has been able to describe this African way in any detail or even point it out. There is no way economic non-rationality can possibly result in development, which occurs in the material world and not the spiritual domain. Development is not an abstract art; what we have in Africa is a tragedy in which intellectual opposition to the West has prevented African thinkers from developing a coherent ideology for change. Ironically, in this penchant to criticise colonialism and defend the integrity of traditional African society ended up without a clear developmental ideology.

The search for an alternative African model continues, but it is unlikely that one will be found this side of the century. It is an uncomfortable truth that if the objective is to improve the material conditions of the people, then most of the institutions and values introduced into Africa during colonialism are more conducive and cheaper to modernisation than going back to traditional ones. Modern institutions and principles such as representative democracy, judiciary, banking and factories, provide more effective means for meeting the new desires of Africans than what existed in pre-colonial societies.

The Zimbabwe government did not have to give in to international demands for the reversal of the programme of land acquisition, redistribution and resettlement, for no such demands had been made. What it needed to do was to modify the programme, with retrospective effect, to be inclusive and impartial through involving all Zimbabweans, UN, AU, Commonwealth and SADC organs. It needed to enable displaced farmers and those wishing to return to the land to do so, and it needed to pay realistic, market-related compensation for improvements acquired.

Mugabe's attempts to formalise and legitimise his actions through constitutional amendments and new Acts of Parliament had not brought legitimacy or morality to his actions. Neither had they offset the massive injustices inflicted on the people whose personal endeavours, sacrifices and lifetime commitments had created the businesses that were mostly destroyed by the aggressive confiscation process. The land reform programme failed to empower the ordinary peasant and to liberate the country from neo-colonialism, but instead degenerated into a class struggle with the rich elite grabbing vast stretches of fertile land.

On crossing to Zambia, you cannot buy anything using a Zimbabwean dollar and vice versa; you need a U.S. dollar, pound, euro or yen to get by. The two African currencies cannot talk to each other; they have to be mediated by Western currencies, thereby becoming the perfect metaphor of Africa's relationship to the West. But the difference between Zambia and Zimbabwe, (and it is a big difference) is that in Zimbabwe the questions of inequality, who owns and doesn't own land and how historical imbalances and injustices can be redressed were being asked. As a consequence perhaps, tourism on the Zambian side was flourishing.

The great lesson of the 20th century was that tyrannical regimes such as the British Empire, Mao's China, Stalin's Russia, Mengistu's Ethiopia to name but a few, presided over enormous famines. Democracies didn't. Surprisingly by December 2005 Mugabe was tinkering with embarking on a new discredited Stalinist-style command agriculture programme to boost farm output and 'Jambaja' (confusion/invasion) on white owned factories.

But command agriculture was not the solution to Zimbabwe's food problems. The cash-strapped government did not have the financial resources or skills to successfully manage crop fields across the country and the corrupt politicians did not have the legitimacy to order people around and just as they had failed to keep teachers in schools and nurses in hospitals, they were going to find empty farms and factories.

Does land reform generally work? That depends on the region of the world. It has a poor record in places like sub-Saharan Africa, where it has led to lower output and even greater inequality. On the other hand, land reform was successful in Japan, South Korea, and in pockets of India. In China, land reform went through a series of stages, the most infamous of which is the harsh collectivisation under Mao in the 1950s which helped create an artificial famine that killed some 30 million people.

One reason land reforms faltered in Africa is that land was often seized from skilled farmers and handed to unskilled ones. Another problem is that the land most often redistributed to the poor is the lowest quality and least arable land available, which leads to lower agricultural output, leaving poor peasants open to criticism for poor farming practices. Further, many of the land holdings are not redistributed to the poor but to political cronies with little farming experience; so called "cell phone farmers." There are a number of other impediments to land reform, including climate, the rising costs of farm production, lack of funding and bank support, lack of title deeds and the volatility of global agricultural prices.

The Diaspora

"We would be better off with only six million people, with our own people who support the liberation struggle." Didymus Mutasa, Mugabe's corruption minister after Mugabe's ruling Zanu party claimed victory 2002, officials spoke openly of "taking the system back to zero" and halving the country's population in a chilling echo of what the Khmer Rouge did in Cambodia in the 1970s.

The word Diaspora is old Greek and it means "scattering" or "dispersion." The term refer to any people or ethnic population forced or induced to leave their traditional ethnic homelands, being dispersed throughout other parts of the world. It has almost always for hundreds of years been used to refer to the Jewish communities scattered all over the world from their homeland by Roman authorities after the Jewish revolt between 66 and 70 CE. Almost every country in the world today in the world has a Diaspora community.

How to consider Zimbabweans abroad: should they be called the Diaspora or the exiled community? Exile is a form of punishment and means to be away from one's home, being explicitly refused permission to return and being threatened by prison or death upon return. On the other hand, the Diaspora in most instances has a choice to return home after a serious conflict has been resolved.

Experiences of other countries like Jamaica, Uganda, Ghana, India and China clearly show that most of those that left these countries over the decades of conflict are still yet to return home. It is thus absurd for one to expect the four million plus Zimbabweans now based outside the country to return en masse someday.

How desperate does a person have to be to try and wade across one of Africa's major rivers, the Limpopo, in flood, that is teeming with crocodiles? 48% said they left Zimbabwe due to the economic situation, the lack of employment and around 26% said that their main reason for leaving was political. The majority, (82%) had arrived in the UK or South Africa with a qualification, of which 38% held a bachelor's degree or higher, 19 percent had a diploma or higher education certificate and 3% had a professional qualification.

However, many in the UK and South Africa had to take employment not commensurate with their skills or experience and this meant that in future years, some Zimbabweans returning from the Diaspora would return with a lower skills base than when they left. Given that many Zimbabweans in the Diaspora were key workers in the education and healthcare professions, their emigration, and the evidence of deskilling, created clear and obvious concerns for the longer-term future of Zimbabwe.

The Zimbabwean government's own analysis put the number of Zimbabweans who left the country in the first three years since 2000 at 3,4 million, 25 % of the entire population, a higher figure of over 4 million would be nearer the mark. What was clear was that Zimbabweans who went to South Africa or neighbouring Botswana were much more likely to disappear from the official statistics. Rather than seeking a work permit and getting on a flight to Europe or North America, most Zimbabweans simply slipped across the border, often doing so again and again after being caught and deported by the South African authorities.

Deportation was a waste of money and so was the building of electric fences by South Africa and Botswana.

Zimbabweans born abroad (and there were millions not accepted as nationals in the UK, USA and Australia) were not included in the official figures. This could mean that over 50% of Zimbabwe's population was outside the country's boarders. In addition, the vast majority of Zimbabweans in South Africa arrived before 1990 during and after gukurahundi, had no papers, making them illegal fugitives. Zimbabweans were the second largest group of foreign Africans in South Africa. By 2006 the authorities down south were deporting 76,000 Zimbabweans every year.

74% Diasporas sent remittances to Zimbabwe and of those that sent these remittances, 85% said the main reason was to support family members. Money was also more likely to be remitted by the informal routes of family, friends and personal visits to Zimbabwe than through formal financial institutions. Clothes (85%) and food (43%) also ranked high as non-monetary gifts sent home by expatriates. Eighteen percent of respondents said they remitted on average US$565 per month from the UK and South Africa. Another 18 percent said they sent between $377 and $563.

Mugabe's investment in destabilisation was paying off. The Diaspora was providing something of a buffer against the real anger of the people, because they were being kept from total poverty. The Diaspora also funded opposition groups and organized protests against Mugabe's misrule in Johannesburg, London and other expat centres. Britain was also the base for Zimbabwe Diaspora controlled SW Radio Africa, which beamed news into Zimbabwe and the weekly newspaper The Zimbabwean. Activists staged mock polls on Election Day in Johannesburg, London and Sydney to highlight the ban on expat voting. Still, most Zimbabweans abroad would rather be at home, but few seemed likely to make that journey anytime soon. For those who had legalised themselves in other countries, the longer they stayed, the more entrenched they became in their adoptive homes.

The first lot of these "Diaspora" arrived in the United Kingdom between 1990 and 1998   initially to study or on work permits. These were not political activists and their hatred of Zanu and Mugabe was slight to imagined, while their understanding of politics was low or non-existent irrespective of what they said. The second category was made up of people from the Ndebele extraction that arrived after 2000 and to this category nothing decent could ever come out of Zimbabwe as long as the balance of power was tilted in favour of the majority tribes.

Since 2000, a further economically important group of migrants had been white farmers; government policy changes led to the seizure of 4,000 white-owned farms, and many who lost land sought new opportunities elsewhere in Africa or overseas. White population dropped from 100,000 to a mere 20,000. By 2005 Murambatsvina had been a further reason for Zimbabweans to flee to South Africa.

Acknowledging that Zimbabwe's internal problems warranted granting asylum to its citizens would contradict President Mbeki's policy of 'quiet diplomacy' towards his northern neighbour. Hence by 2008 just 100 of the millions of Zimbabweans who had sought asylum in South Africa had been successful in their applications and zero elsewhere in the SADC region.

Zimbabweans in South Africa were vulnerable to crime and exploitation without redress; lived in appallingly overcrowded and unsafe conditions; didn't have access to basic facilities including health and had to adjust to being beggars. There were no ready jobs in the Rainbow Nation, so the vicious cycle of hopelessness continued and the youths easily turned to the only means that could keep them fed if for just a while; crime and women ended up in prostitution. That so many opted nonetheless to live a hard criminal life in exile, was an indicator of the severity of life in Zimbabwe.

Corrupt officials in South Africa, Botswana and the UK took bribes from Zimbabwean refugees in exchange for another day of not being deported. Zimbabweans who illegally entered Botswana were each given three lashes in public at a customary law court, while women were raped by soldiers before being deported.

As illegal immigration increased, four South African police officers were gunned down in central Johannesburg in a violent shoot-out with armed robbers. Eight armed robbers among them former Zimbabwean soldiers died during the bloody shootout. The South African police had often blamed the rise in violent crimes on former Zimbabwean soldiers fleeing economic collapse at home.

Like the rest of the world South Africa resorted to using brutal force in their quest to flush out "illegal immigrants". As police intensified their campaign against well-armed Zim-gangs of robbers in Johannesburg (which was preparing to host the 2010 World cup), their conduct in some of the raids was to come under mounting scrutiny. Police stormed blocks of flats and indiscriminately fired rubber bullets into flats occupied by Zimbabweans. Many civilians were injured. SADC governments were prepared to get tough with the victims of the crisis in Zimbabwe while continuing to appease the political leadership responsible for the situation.

It is understandable that the opposition was taking the initiative with the objective of facilitating the participation in the elections of Zimbabweans living abroad with the expectation that all or most of them support their party and cause. A sizeable number of the Zimbabweans in the Diaspora were asylum seekers, though a large number of Zimbabweans in the Diaspora did not leave the country because of the political situation, but primarily because of the prevailing economic situation. Some had gone into business and succeeded, mainly because of their superior education, training and resilience.

A Zimbabwean in the Diaspora holding a refugee status would lose that status automatically if the situation in Zimbabwe changed and will be required to return home by the host country immediately. That was dangerous when it came to elections as most were not interested in going back to Zimbabwe and could use the chance to maintain the status quo.

It began to sink into an increasing number of Zimbabweans that the struggle that faced them may be a long one, and that it certainly would not be easy. Those who had hoped that it will be waged and won by, "..Tsvangirai," while they watch from the relative safety and comfort of their homes and glass offices in Zimbabwe or from exile without getting hurt, only emerging to cheer, now realize that they may be forced to play a more active part than they would rather not. Zimbabweans preferred someone else to do the dirtiest aspects of cleaning up Zimbabwe. This "messiah complex" of hoping for easy, one-man solutions to complex challenges applied in many other aspects of Zimbabwean life as well, not just politics.

In a statement after a court verdict, Liam Byrne, the UK Immigration Minister, said, "…a robust and fair system. We recognise that there are Zimbabweans who are in genuine fear of persecution and that is why we have granted them asylum, but it is only right that we remove those who seek to abuse our hospitality. I am therefore pleased that the Asylum and Immigration Tribunal has today backed us and said that the involuntary return of failed asylum seekers to Zimbabwe does not put them at risk of mistreatment." As in South Africa, Zimbabweans in the UK often resorted to petty crime and fraud, as jobs were difficult to get.

Fixing Africa's problems is tough work, but at least some nations were taking the right steps. War-torn West Africa, in particular led the way in luring home expatriates with the skills to change the continent. Nigeria's finance minister, Ngozi Okonjo-Iweala, brought home from a top World Bank post, was now helping lead that country's futile battle against corruption. Ellen Johnson-Sirleaf, another international economist, was voted Liberia's new leader, which made her the continent's first democratically elected woman president. She quickly and correctly said Liberia's worst enemy was corruption.

The prospects of Zimbabwe's economy bouncing back from its crisis were dim if over three quarters of the parents of new graduates were urging their offspring to leave the country, mainly because their families depend on remittances from abroad and for fear that they will be forced into political party gangs. Hundreds of thousands of young Zimbabwean doctors, nurses, pharmacists, teachers and other professionals had already left the country. Most seriously affected was the health sector where 80 percent of state-registered nurses and medical doctors had left the country. The British, whatever their vision for Africa, whatever they did during colonialism, were not the reason why Mugabe had 52 unnecessary ministerial positions nor did they impose rigging elections and unfair electoral practice upon Zimbabwe. They may well be surprised why governments like Zimbabwe's still treat their citizens in so much the same brutal way they were treated by their rubbish psychopath white ancestors.

The degrees in violence and rigging elections

"It is the weak who are cruel. Gentleness can only be expected from the strong."
Leo Rosten, 1908-1997, US academic, teacher and writer.

'Our demand is just and legitimate. We demand a free and fair election where international observers will oversee." Josiah Magama Tongogara (1978).

"ZANU PF rules this country and anyone who disputes that is a dissident and should be dealt with." Enos Nkala (Zimbabwe Home Affairs Minister 1980)

Zimbabwe inherited a thriving and vibrant economy with adequate checks and balances to enable it to develop into a well-organised modern state. But surprisingly another Zimbabwean crisis was the use of law as an instrument of terror. The rule by law, as opposed to the rule of law. This very fact that law can be deployed as a medium to harass, as a medium to exclude, as a medium to oppress, as a medium to mark out from normal, as a medium to mark as abnormal and therefore subhuman or inhuman, therefore not entitled to rights.

Once you mark out a person as not human they cease to be human, they cease to be entitled to the civility that the law that you apply to yourself entitles them, because they are not normal. In Zimbabwe, once you call people 'stooges of imperialism'(chimbwa sungata), 'proxies of imperialist interest', 'Mutengesi', you mark them out from normalcy. You then say the youth militia can gang rape women who belong to this marked-out group. You then say the police can ill-treat, arrest, torture and kill without cause. Law ceases to be an instrument of empowerment; it becomes an instrument of terror.

The test of freedom is the ability of any citizen to walk to the town centre and say in public what they think of their governments and not suffer any consequences. Zimbabwe had 15 newspapers, 4 radio stations and one television channel. Of these, 7 newspapers and all electronic media were owned by the State, 6 of the other newspapers were owned by Zanu in various forms and only two weeklies were really independent. The State/Zanu media was tightly controlled and only carried news and information that was approved by Zanu officials. The news and other coverage were totally hostile to the opposition; any opposing views and its civic allies were used simply to promote the position of Zanu on every issue. Speaking to the average citizen who was not politically minded and who had no alternative sources of information, it astonished how effective this propaganda machine had become.

Never in the history of humankind had a government been so busy at chasing political trivia at the expense of pressing national issues. Zimbabwe was facing a crisis of impunity and immunity. The suggestion that in the name of the leader, the party and the revolution, you can create crime, commit crime and continually engage in crime and be immune from prosecution. This culture of criminality spread throughout the ruling class, down to the Beitbridge border guard who threatened or delay drivers if they were not given bribes, and the bribe-hungry police officers who stopped a truck 12 times between Harare and Bulawayo.

It's quite likely that had God even suspected to what devilish use humankind would put electricity and water He might have prevented the idea from germinating in the fertile mind of His most unique creation, one Robert Matibili-Mugabe. Water and electricity were used in the torture of two Zimbabwean journalists, Mark Chavhunduka and Ray Choto, of the independent weekly, The Standard. Soldiers of the Zimbabwe National Army subjected them to torture over a story they published concerning an attempted military coup against the government. The two men narrated how water and electricity was specifically being applied to their genitals to force them to disclose their sources. Chavhuduka and Choto stood firm. The price was high. For months, they had to undergo therapy. Chavhunduka died later from this trauma, and Choto left the country to work in the United States.

The assault on Chibebe, September 2006 conjured up memories of South African nationalist and Black Consciousness leader Steve Biko's death in police custody in 1977. The difference with Chibebe's case, and what made it more painful was that in Zimbabwe it was black-on-black violence in an independent country. Chibebe suffered head injuries, a broken arm and hand and extensive bruising in the street assault and subsequently in a police cell. Doctors had to remove one of the trade union chief's eyes. His colleagues also sustained broken limbs and other injuries.

It was patently absurd for Mugabe to boast about his 'degrees in violence' and then attribute it to someone else. The people who planned the attempted murder of Kuwadzana legislator Nelson Chamisa at the Harare International Airport on his way to a parliamentary business trip in Brussels, were known but the police were turning a blind eye to the case. The officers who fired live bullets into the car of an opposition leader were known but were free. Other cases included the sending of a live bullet to the offices of The Standard Newspaper and the murder of former Zimbabwe Broadcasting Corporation cameraman and technician, Edward Chikomba.

Chikomba was abducted from his home in Harare and his body was later found dumped by the roadside about 60km away. Chikomba was murdered for transmitting the images of a battered MDC leader, Morgan Tsvangirai, to the international media. Tsvangirai had been severely assaulted while in police custody and Mugabe had claimed responsibility for the torture to Sadc and Comesa leaders in Tanzania, but was applauded for calling the opposition terrorists.

Other outstanding cases include the bombing of the MDC headquarters in Harare in 2000, the bombing of the offices of Voice of the People Radio in 2002 and the bombing of The Daily News printing press in 2001. MDC activists Talent Mabika and Tichaona Chiminya were murdered in cold blood in 2000 but the suspects remained free despite mounting local and international pressure for them to be prosecuted. Central Intelligence Organisation operative Joseph Mwale, the alleged killer of the two, remains a free man at a known address.

Mugabe was an old cunning well-meaning politician at times, but his job was made even more difficult because he had foolishly surrounded himself with crooks, murderers and psychopaths. His former Minister of information, strangely but rightly believed that if he repeats a lie frequently enough it would settle as the truth in the minds of ordinary people. In addition to the untold human suffering resulting from the upheavals unleashed by draconian media laws under (AIPPA) the greatest damage was to Zanu and the country. It will take years for both to recover from the negative effects of Moyo's overzealous but amateurish propaganda campaigns.

Moyo's real motive in joining ZANU was to destroy the party from inside and many failed to understand how Mugabe could place so much faith in a spin-doctor who depended on out-moded totalitarian methods used by Gobbels, Vorster, Isreal, DRPK and Ian Smith. Moyo's virulent, costly, all-pervading, hate-filled, reality-defying and anti-everything-good propaganda did not bring a single political, social or economic benefit to the nation and failed on the art of winning international and local friends.

But what was frightening was the dangerous level of the government's paranoia. Anyone who was critical of its awful human rights record or its policies that had caused record unemployment and hunger was labelled an agent of Blair or Western interests or to be working with the enemy, an imperialist or a spy. Lack of transparency or corruption, greed for power and property, violence and racial bigotry, petty and major, is not only a hidden cost but also a continuous hassle to doing business in Africa.

For example, journalists in Zimbabwe could be jailed for two years for practising without obtaining a licence from the government. And a new law would see journalists jailed for 20 years for publishing false information, while under the security laws, Zimbabweans need police permission to gather in groups of five or more to discuss politics. Another law barred non-governmental organisations from carrying out voter education while civic groups wishing to carry out human rights or governance-related work were prohibited from receiving foreign funding.

The Ombudsman's Office was in total shambles as the office continued to be dogged by lack of adequate personnel, gross under funding and mismanagement. The office was under staffed at a time when human rights abuses were increasing. The Office was mandated to investigate cases of administrative malpractice and alleged contravention of the Declaration of Rights by members of the defence forces, police, government departments and the prison service on civil society. Rather, it was the UN and AU commissions that were reporting these human rights violation while the Ombudsman's office twiddled its fingers and spent more time refuting these allegations of torture and violations.

It was only a senile mind and one of shallow depth that would believe that because Zimbabweans wanted a fair and just country in which public officials and politicians are answerable for the way they handle public business, they were agents of another government and not their conscience; that they were un-African, pro-Western, agents of imperialism etc, etc.

2004 Zimbabwe's chief police spokesman Assistant Commissioner Wayne Bvudzijena killed a 10 year old boy in Chitungwiza after running him over with his car. Instead of rushing the victim to a hospital, Bvudzijena, who was drunk, dumped him at a secluded spot to die at an open space in Unit B Seke, Chitungwiza. This was the preposterous act of a senior police officer.

2006. The world saw shocking images of Mugabe's police brutalizing workers who dared to raise their voices. For simply exercising their democratic right to peacefully march in protest against unbearable levels of poverty, demanding an end to harassment of informal traders and calling for access to ARVs, ZCTU workers were brutalized by Mugabe's running dogs. Testimonies from the arrested workers told of unrelenting beatings and torture within cells. The ZCTU secretary general Wellington Chibhebhe was beaten until he lost consciousness. The Vice President Lucia Matibenga burst an eardrum from repeated clapping and her whole body bruised and blackened from beatings. Many others including the ZCTU President Lovemore Matombo got broken limbs. If the thuggish behaviour of the police was shocking, even more outrageous was to hear Mugabe audaciously and chillingly condoning these callous acts. This is the point history must record; the impunity and well-documented cruelty of the Zimbabwe Republic Police had blessings from the "liberator", Matibili-Mugabe himself.

March 2007: Grace Kwinjeh, an attractive single mom, was severely beaten and at one stage a policeman took an iron bar to her head. She lost part of her ear. An iron bar is a murder weapon. One cannot think of anything she might have said or done to justify such a beating. Then you have to look at the case of Morgan Tsvangirai; he and his PA went to the Machapisa Police Station to ask what was happening to others who had been arrested in the prayer march that morning. On March 12, 2007 with no crime committed, no charges laid, no violence at all, they were arrested and tortured. Just pure vindictive hatred.

What did the police do with the opportunity of meeting Morgan at their station? They just beat him until he fell unconscious on the floor three times so that when his wife went to see him, he could not see properly, could not feed himself and was almost unrecognisable. They knew that what they did would inflame the people even more outside the Police cell walls. The killing of that weekend and the bludgeoning meted out to about 100 other supporters was entirely standard. Violence of this kind had been enough to suppress Mugabe's critics outside and inside the ruling Zanu party. Yet Mugabe accused the opposition of violence and Sadc concurred with him. How did they sleep at night?

Most African leaders are in the range of 19 to 26 years in office. These leaders organized their own elections and win them. Nearly all of Africa has been headed into dissolution by unelected leaders and only four countries had religiously allowed free multi-party elections since independence that gave voters a choice but not more than 10, out of over 200 Big Man so far, had permitted voters to end their reign. Only Mauritius had done so on a regular basis.

It started with Rhodes (of Rhodesia) who said in a document that he wanted "every civilised man to have the right to vote. A civilised man who had some education and owned some property". This was applied, more or less up to 1964 when it was finally abandoned for a racially defined right to vote which excluded black people, from the voters' roll. The African Nationalist leaders had never been in favour of the qualified franchise. They knew that when this threatened the hold on power of the white minority, the standard would simply be raised and ambitions thwarted. What they demanded was "one man, one vote." It was the rallying cry of the liberation war; it defined the principal objectives of the struggle for power.

On 4th March 1980, 100 years after colonisation; 100 years after the first Whitemen set foot on Zimbabwean soil, for the first time ever, millions of Zimbabweans were afforded the opportunity to cast their votes and elect their leaders. This was of course a turning moment in the sense that until then, not many people had expected themselves to vote. No, not even in their lifetime. Over 85 per cent of the total population voted, many with tears of joy.

On the average, the result was as expected; almost every person in the country voted for the men and women who had brought about this unique opportunity. The old regime attracted less than 3 per cent of the vote. The transition was peaceful, the planned Rhodesian army coup did not materialize and the four armies that had fought each other gave up their weapons and went home. Not a shot was fired in anger; it was a short-lived astonishing achievement.

In contrast, fast forward 25 years later, in 2005, the pot bellied imperially wigged Chief Justice of Zimbabwe, a Mugabe lieutenant and appointee, sitting with a full bench of similarly appointed pot bellied wigged Supreme Court judges, said that the right to vote was not a fundamental right of Zimbabwean citizens! The universal suffrage that tens of thousands gave their lives for in 30 years of struggle was a sham. The behaviour of the Judiciary was itself a serious violation of human rights and fundamental freedoms enshrined in the Constitution of Zimbabwe, Sadc and international human rights instruments.

Some Big man like Samuel Doe and Robert Mugabe proclaimed themselves winners of elections they had rigged and lost and their commitment to democracy did not encompass the possibility that their citizens despise them. In both countries there was blatant fraud before, during and after the election; the electoral commissions kept in constant (every 15 minutes) contact with the leaders, ballot boxes were stuffed, unregistered voters allowed to vote; unauthorised polling stations set in military barracks; and raudy youths voted early and often. Ballot papers were found burnt by the roadside and independent courts were not allowed to adjudicate.

According to the 2002 national census Zimbabwe's population officially was at 11 631 657, broken down as 3,55 million and 2,39 million people of voting age in rural and urban areas respectively. Hence we had at most 3 million people in the country who were eligible to vote and might register and then physically turn out. The rest were outside the country (3,5 million adults) or were too young, or were ruled as being ineligible for one reason or another. The voters roll of 2005 had 5,6 million names on it, meaning about 2,6 million "ghost" voters. Some were dead; some were duplicates, others were now outside the country. In the 2002 elections more than 5 million people voted. All those who had left the country were denied the vote, they were a group that was potentially larger than the voters who remained in the country.

Zimbabwe was the only country in the region that denied their Diaspora citizens the right to vote. In fact when you work out who can vote and will be allowed to vote, it represented only about 42 per cent of potential voters who were alive. On top of this astonishing fact, the whole process of voter registration and maintaining the voters role was done secretly, partisan and controlled by officials paid by the State, but loyal to Zanu. The systematic exclusion of voters who might be sympathetic to the opposition was carried out on a regular basis. Voter registration was intensive in areas controlled by Zanu and where they believe they could control the vote in an election.

The government also adopted a narrow definition of the country's Citizenship Act to disenfranchise many Zimbabweans and children of immigrants from countries in the region such as Malawi, Mozambique and Zambia. Although such

"Zimbabweans" were born in the country and were residents all their lives and voted in all elections held before 2000, they could no longer do so.

The tragedy of Zimbabwe was that political violence, which flares up in the run-up to most elections, is one of the country's biggest curses. Since inception in the 60s Zanu (and all other parties black and white) employed violence as a systematic political strategy in general and in the run-up to elections; civil servants and rural villagers believed to support the opposition had been beaten up, kidnapped, tortured and some killed or labelled "Vatengesi" (sell-outs); homes and businesses of perceived opposition members burnt and looted; schools and clinics in rural areas touched or closed as teachers and nurses flee to the relative safety of towns; at every election time there was general fear of soldiers and war veterans, hired Zanu thugs and militia because of their capacity to instigate and inflict violence on the voters as they moved from one area to another; all-night forced Zanu political re-education meetings (pungwes) brutalised those forced to attend. Zanu had repeatedly refused to sign a multi-party code of political conduct outlawing violence.

In 1990 Mugabe declared: "If whites in Zimbabwe want to rear their ugly terrorist and racist head by collaborating with ZUM (Zimbabwe Unity Movement), we will chop that head off." He threatened to seize all white-owned farms, while his TV adverts depicted a car crash and announced: "That is one way to die; the other is to vote ZUM." Albeit to say ZUM was a legally registered black African nationalist party. Mugabe warned ZUM President Tekere, "You are playing with fire, my boy." Tekere turned to alcohol for solence and lost interest in politics soon after.

Tekere for his part, helped Mugabe escape Rhodesia and was a founder member of Zanu, was briefly a cabinet minister in Mugabe's government before an exhibitionist incident when he donned combat fatigues and announced he was "...going to fight a battle". He then went to a place outside Harare where supporters of Joshua Nkomo's ZAPU cadres were reported to be camping. Failing to find them, he went to a nearby farm and wantonly shot dead the white occupier, Gerald Adams. Two-boy Tekere was acquitted of murder.

Despite their quest for untainted, indisputable, free and fair elections, Zimbabweans had not, for the entire duration of their written or known history, been allowed to exercise their universal suffrage without enduring pain, grief, loss and sorrow. The poisoned political situation had been aggravated by an equally poisonous egotism of the parochial politicians who did not seem to realise that difference is a real factor not only in life but in politics too. Consensus of opinion is not a virtue in politics and people should always be free to agree to disagree.

The 1999 launch of MDC to contest successfully a constitutional referendum then parliamentary elections in 2000 and subsequent presidential elections in 2002, 2005 and 2008, had resulted in a Zimbabwean political reality that was focused on elections. On the side of the opposition, the very rapid rise to electoral prominence had meant that social movement, trade union and other energies had been considerably focused and squandered on an electoral project, on winning elections, on contesting in court the results of elections, and on preparing the ground for different elections and there had been a sense that everything will change at the "next elections". In a sense the strategy had been regime change through the ballot box. It failed because Mugabe was always a step ahead.

On the side of the ruling party the electoral rise of the opposition had led to an ever-narrowing siege mentality. Zanu only wanted elections whose outcome was pre-determined. Conspiracies were seen everywhere and the hastily launched land reform programme was less about land reform and more about seeking to consolidate the party apparatus and its electoral base. The unleashing of youth militias and other violence was also very much based on electoral calculations.

Soldiers whipped, raped and killed revellers in bars if they did not answer certain questions correctly. Gun bayonets were inserted into women's privates and revellers were paired and forced to have unprotected sex in full view of all. The idea was to show them that not voting for Zanu carried its own deadly risks. Some of the stories of retribution sounded as if they had been garnished for special effect. People were hounded out of their neighbourhoods, out of their jobs and, in bizarre cases, they were even hounded out of their marriages. Zanu was determined to remind the urban dweller that, in future elections they would know what fate awaited them if they did not vote for the 'right' party.

Aspiring Zanu candidates gave out free cash, computers and farming inputs in their respective constituencies towards elections (about the only time they visit their constituencies) and the manipulation of medical, social welfare benefits and scholarship packages against opposition supporters. People were told, "vote for MDC and you will starve", "vote for MDC and you will be kicked out of the community." Both were life or death issues in the countryside where there were no private property rights left and no food was available except through the aid agencies.

The MDC could not match the resources of Zanu, which had no qualms about plundering the state coffers, as well as using almost every branch of the civil service and security forces to ensure its continued rule. A law made it illegal to conduct voter education without government approval, requiring most election workers to register and clear electioneering materials with the state (e.g. all flyers distributed had to have the printer's name on them).

Earlier 2004, the government installed equipment, with Chinese assistance, on Zimbabwe's Internet service providers to monitor and censor e-mail messages. It bared the one cell phone company outside state control from routing calls outside the country, saying unsupervised foreign telephone calls were a national security threat. The company, Econet Wireless, was controlled by a government critic whose opposition newspaper, The Daily News, was by far the most popular publication in Zimbabwe. The government bombed the newspaper offices twice before closing it in February 2004. In October of the same year, it charged five of Econet's directors with illegal dealings in foreign currency tying down the company's resources and effective delivery.

Police and government vehicles were used to ferry Zanu candidates and their campaign teams to rallies and meetings with supporters and police stood by at such meetings while ruling party militants threatened villagers with severe retribution if they voted for the opposition party. At times people were killed or beaten by Zanu supporters in police stations.

Magunje and the surrounding Hurungwe, Maramba, Pfungwe, Bindura rural district were no-go areas for the main opposition with militant Zanu supporters hunting down and torturing suspected supporters of the opposition parties. A local Government minister (Ignatius Chombo) was shown on television saying that traditional chiefs should not sanction rallies by opposition political parties in the rural areas and that chiefs should take persons organising such rallies to task.

Mugabe set up an independent Zimbabwe Electoral Commission (ZEC) to run the ballot "...in compliance with the Sadc Protocols". The setting up of such an independent body had been one of the key demands of the opposition and constitutional reform activists. At first glance it seemed as though the government was capitulating to demands by the opposition, local human rights groups and the international community for measures assuring a free and fair poll. But closer scrutiny revealed that with the media under government control, and non-governmental political activity effectively outlawed, all forms of independent observation and analysis had been eliminated.

The new regulations did not preclude Mugabe from amending electoral laws as and when he saw fit by using his absolute power under the Presidential Powers (Temporary Measures Act). Election observers had to be accredited by a committee dominated by nominees of government ministers and the president's office, and only those invited by a minister or by the partisan Electoral Supervisory Commission were eligible. The justice minister, a Mugabe mouthpiece, could summarily fire commissioners, was himself a candidate in the election. The Electoral Supervision Commission (ESC), an older version commission in charge of elections since 1980 had the final say on whether elections had been run properly and had overall constitutional authority and took precedence over the bodies that run elections since the ESC was established by the constitution of Zimbabwe. It therefore tells you who was to supervise whom.

The various opposition parties tried to verify the roll in a few constituencies to confirm the accuracy of the printed roll on foot, going from house to house. The MDC's Stevenson said 64% of people in her densely populated constituency, Harare North, were not known at the addresses given on the voters' roll. She was the only opposition candidate who was able to finish the laborious audit ahead of the deadline for objections to the voters' roll. David Coltart, the MDC's legal secretary and MP for Bulawayo South, missed the deadline because his team, also going from house to house, was repeatedly arrested and tortured. Without a properly and transparently compiled voters roll, it would never be possible to hold free and fair elections despite what Mbeki would say to the contrary.

Several Zanu held seats were declared invalid by the High Court after opposition lawyers proved beyond any reasonable doubt that there had been widespread intimidation and violence, as well as outright rigging in the 2000 and 2005 elections. Through an abuse of the judicial system, the affected members appealed to the Supreme Court, which still had not heard the appeals, six years later. This allowed the fraudulently elected Zanu MPs to sit in parliament for its entire five-year lifetime, making laws, drawing salaries and enjoying benefits.

Mugabe, voting in Highfield, said "..the people are behind us". Indeed they were. He had jumped the queue and the ruling Zanu had 90,000 votes in the bag with the soldiers and the youth militia and over 2 million ghost voters on the electoral registers. Zanu could take those 2 million votes and use them in any district they wanted.

Even if the opposition were to win, under the Zimbabwean constitution, 120 parliamentary seats were contested and the president still appointed 30 members (25% unelected). That means the MDC could win a majority of the seats, but Mugabe could still control parliament. And even if the MDC could control parliament, it could not form a government by appointing ministers, as that is the prerogative of the president.

The opposition obtained a series of High Court Orders ordering Mudede to preserve the ballot papers and Election material and to bring them to his Head Office in Harare. However, the Registrar-General persistently refused to comply with these Orders and over three years after the presidential election was held. When he did, after jail threats, the room the papers were stored in was bugled twice rendering the whole exercise worthless.

This meant that Tsvangirai's party was unable to inspect the ballot papers and election material and the consequence of this was that it severely handicapped Tsvangarai in his election petition challenge to the outcome of the 2002 Presidential Election. The repeated failure by Mudede to comply with High Court Judgments indicated that he had something to hide. It also confirmed that Mugabe had lost the election.

Zanu was the referee, goalkeeper, match commissioner, player and spectator at the same time and expected the opponent to score, let alone win. Many remembered the shameless, but now obscure South African comrades who gave purported credibility to the 2000 parliamentary and 2002 presidential elections. As a matter of posthumous record, some of them have possibly attained their due desserts: Tony Yengeni, former ANC chief whip, was a convicted fraudster. He unreservedly endorsed the 2000 parliamentary election in Zimbabwe. Sam Motsuenyane perhaps understandably disappeared from public view. Few can forget the event in March 2002 when he had the international media collapsing in howls of derisive laughter when he pronounced that the election was "legitimate".

South Africa's Safety and Security minister Steve Tshwete, who was Mbeki's representative during Zimbabwe's presidential poll, died in April 2002. In hindsight, it is clear that high-ranking members of the ANC government, starting with Mbeki, had earlier laid down guidelines to the Motsuenyane mission.

Come March 2005 elections and the ANC expendable desperados were the nominated head of the Sadc observer mission, Home Affairs minister Mapisa-Nqakula. She was to purportedly ascertain whether the Zimbabwean electoral process was in keeping with the Sadc electoral guidelines. Labour minister Membathisi Mdladlana was to lead the parliamentary national observer mission. You could almost in advance guess that they were already busy fabricating an election report with imaginative wording. As it turned out Mdladlana was to proclaim the election free and fair the minute he stepped out of the SAA plane at Harare airport, two weeks before the actual elections, sparking a row with the MDC and other civic society. He ran away and hid in shame (leaving his comrades to apologise) only to reappear to re-emphasise his earlier point.

It is not by coincidence that Mugabe kept repeating his everlasting gratitude to the army and Sadc for keeping him in power. Mugabe had never thanked the electorate for voting him into office. He knew very well that Zimbabwean voters overwhelmingly voted against him and his party. During one of his Politburo meetings Mugabe said in Shona translated: "Where would we be now if it was not for the army?" Had the elections been free and fair Morgan Tsvangirai and the MDC would have been in power since 2000. Incredible as it may sound, Ian Smith and the Rhodesian Front of the settler colonial era had, when compared to Mugabe and Zanu (PF), emerged clearly and unambiguously the lesser of two evils that had befallen Zimbabweans for over a century. The so-called independence for Zimbabweans in 1980 was a giant leap from the frying pan of Ian Smith's dictatorship into the fire of Mugabe's repression and thuggery.

There could be no debate regarding Mbeki's attitude and blind sponsorship of the Zanu regime. Historical records speak for themselves. His conspicuous support of global retrogression could be seen from his "best-friends" list. The schedule of America's "outposts of tyrannical states" had been published. What had yet to be formally recognised were the inter-meshed supporter nations that facilitate retroversion and despotism via their umbilical connections to evil regimes; countries that provided succour, moral and material support to pariah states. Though Mbeki and his foreign minister Pahad had said Zimbabweans did not need the world to pre-judge an election that had not yet taken place; Mbeki had, in early March 2005, already said that the election would be free and fair despite all the documented problems on the ground amounted to pre-judging the poll.

The South African double standards were baffling and stupid at times. Pahad said he was confident that two weeks were ample for the mission to deal with allegations of pre-election irregularities. "If they do their work properly and energetically, two weeks should be sufficient for us to make our presence felt there." Yet the official SADC guidelines where the oxymoron Pahad himself should certainly have contributed enormously clearly state that the monitors had to be invited 90 days in advance.

In the 2005 election, Zanu secured 78 of 120 directly elected seats against the MDC's 41 but that did not reflect the will of the Zimbabwean people but the will of Zanu. So Mugabe and his party won what they describe as Zimbabwe's third Chimurenga. Like his predecessor, Ian Smith, Mugabe believed that this land was won by force and no one was going to take it from him, certainly not through some liberal Western construct such as a democratic elections.

Notwithstanding the claims and substance of foul play in elections, the reality was that the outcome was really representative of the now typical Zimbabwean and of generalised African autocratic culture. The declared results could not have been attained without massive complicity by assorted Zimbabweans, suitably compliant or press-ganged, pre-aided and abetted by none other than comrades such as found in Mbeki's regime in South Africa. Some residual Zimbabweans could be categorized as being imprisoned by circumstance. Otherwise, a growing proportion were seen to be morally sapless, racists, shameless, inept, looters, exploiters, liars, free-loaders, cowards, self-improvers, lazy, greedy, non-achievers, pathetic, mentally challenged, opportunists, blame passers, incompetent, delusional, beggars or state-enabled thieves.

Honest diligence remained unnecessary whilst there were still a few residual national assets to loot for interim sustenance purposes. The actuality is that well-proven cultural values, that had enabled the first world to mature and lead, were alien concepts to most African leaders and the ruling elites, since these evolved benchmarks, challenge, undermine and exposed the lack of capacity and integrity of despotic leaderships. Their parrot-cry is: "we are eternal victims of all others than ourselves" and "the West must forever give us compensation and access to loot for past evils". Some still fail to come to terms with the fact that African despots habitually keeps scratching their self-made festering scabs in the misdirected expectation that Western aid programs will heal them with easily convertible contributions that augment externalised asset holdings.

Certainly it appeared that the former Mugabe/Blair public battle had been transposed into a Mbeki/Bush row, and that Mbeki was responding defensively to growing Western criticism of his "quiet diplomacy", while desperately seeking the Mugabe's cooperation for a more formally open election process that would create new diplomatic spaces in the post-election period. Mbeki was either badly advised or was taking a dangerous political gamble. A favourable election result for Zanu was not likely to convince any but the already converted.

As things stood the script had almost been finalised for a continuation of the political crisis in Zimbabwe. There was unlikely to be sufficient consensus among the regional and international players on the outcome of the 2008 election and the stalemate, while slightly repositioned, was likely to continue. The ball for the most part was to remain in Mugabe's court and his relations with the South African government. It may confirm that the ruling party had its hands firmly on the levers of state, but could not deliver the broader legitimacy that would provide the impetus for a new political initiative in the country. On the other hand, a good election result for the opposition would be damaging for the regime and the region. Either way the region was between a rock and a hard place.

Africa and its leaders had to learn that the real complexities of the relations between outside pressures and internal dynamics could not be flattened by the simplistic encapsulation of blame in the figure of a British prime minister or on neo-colonialism diatribe. One gets the feeling that even within Zanu and the ANC, this message had become an amulet desperately invoked to hold back the accumulating fears in the ruling parties.

In the hands of Zanu, the idea of sovereignty had been translated into a legitimation for national repression and thuggery. A nationalism that once carried the broad hopes of an emerging nation had been transformed into an esoteric authoritarianism dressed in corrupt revolutionary fatigues. Every appeal to "the people" was a rhetorical device expounded to legitimise yet another attack on democratic space and individual liberties. The outcome was a greatly weakened sense of a common national identity.

One of the major lessons from Zimbabwe's history is that a dominant party cannot coerce a nation into unity or patriotism. Neither the physical brutality of political violence nor the symbolic onslaught of a monopolised media could create the consensual basis for the long-term creation of national belonging. In many ways we were witnessing traumatised subjects on hold, living daily with their anxieties, fears, loss and omniscient material deprivations.

"Ridiculous, rigged and rubbish", responded an angry opposition to a 100 percent election victory by incumbent President Ismael Omar Guelleh of Djibouti, in the horn of Africa, after the April 2005 elections. Francophone and Arab League observers commended the 'improved' operations at polling stations, as well as the peaceful environment during voting days, as compared to previous elections. The opposition was forced to shun the election on the grounds that the electoral playing field was uneven.

In Zanzibar, the main opposition candidate, Seif Shariff Hamad, did not qualify to contest the October 2005 elections because he had not stayed in his "constituency" for more than three years, as stipulated in a rushly passed law. The opposition was miffed.

Ethiopia had elections too. The story was not any different as there were reports of harassment, imprisonment and victimisation of the opposition. Over 100 people were killed by the police in riots that followed the announcement of the results.

Peace was on the horizon in the Ivory Coast after Thabo Mbeki successfully brokered a truce between government and rebel forces, that would see an end to two years of conflict and holding of a 'peaceful election' in October 2005. The main opposition candidate Alassane Ouattara had to prove both his parents were Ivorian, failure of which he could not stand.

In 2006 the Democratic Republic of Congo would hold their first "elections", in 40 years. Kabila's son, Joseph would stand, initially fail an African endorsed costomary 'landslide victory' but eventually "win". Togo's main opposition leader of the Union of Forces for Change (UFC) party was back in 2005 after over a decade in exile. Only that he could not represent his party because he was abroad for too long and in any case the elections were rigged.

Kenya in the end got rid of Arap Moi, but the new democratic government was not living up to its election promises, as there was no new constitution on the horizon by 2008 and corruption was more than Moi left it. And a member of parliament, Reuben Ndolo was detained for ridiculing President Mwai Kibaki.

After every aging murdering dictator was re-elected president, the international press was shocked. "Why," they all asked, "would Africans elect a crooked, murdering, philandering buffoon as president?" But the honest answer was, "Why not?" The sad truth is that African presidents, democrats or tyrants can do little in terms of what the West knows, but entertain, so they elected murdering entertainers. Elections in Africa are little more than a chance for poor people to sell their vote for a few bucks. Africans are very sceptical of politics and politicians. They know that all politicians lie. So they are pragmatic and vote for the ones who tell the best lies. Elections don't matter to the average African since they don't own anything or owe anyone. So things like interest rates, mortgages, money supply, unemployment rates and inflation mean nothing to them.

The political equation changes dramatically when the law protects a person's home and his life. Then, those who make and administer the law directly affect the lives of the poorest voters. Only at that point will they tend to select leaders rather than murderers, crooks and entertainers like Mkapa of Tanzania and Nujoma of Namibia. Economic opportunity fertilizes the growth of a civil society, which is the only real support for an electoral democracy. This is not to suggest that democracy be put on hold while the country becomes prosperous. Capitalism and democracy can run in parallel. But timing matters. One cannot rush democracy and slow-walk economic reform.

However, it was clear that the democratic process was once again exposing the fallacy of the belief that change was only possible via coups and other military means; that the electoral process had not countered the sense of disadvantage felt by opposition political parties who consider conditions were unfair and that governments had to work for national unity and economic recovery. As it was, it was dawning on the minds of many Zimbabweans that the solution to the crisis in their country lay way beyond the elections and alternatives were required; with options like armed struggle, peaceful resistance and marching on Mugabe. All workable but disasters.

Africa had no precedent on peacefully marching a dictator out of office. Tsvangirai criticised Zimbabwe's flawed elections, saying they had left the country at the mercy of "a determined tyrannical class ... a vampire and criminal clique". The true state of affairs was not far from that comment and the opposition leader was trying to shift the argument and focusing more on the actual practicalities of Africa. Focusing on imperialism had drawn attention away from internal forces that were crucial to the understanding of the African condition and which, unlike external demons, can change ordinary Africans.

A credible opposition in Africa must demonstrate that it is viable, credible and, above all, can focus on maintaining a national presence; a government-in-waiting fully capable of participating in the national life of the nation. Its philosophy and ideology must appeal to the largest and ethnically blind populace as possible to merit any relevance. The opposition must also work diligently to attract the best minds that can research, develop and apply political, social, fiscal and economic alternatives to national issues for the general good of the nation. Another ideal is the formation of a united opposition climate such as building national and regional alliances with oppositions that have won in other countries.

Doddering though he was, Mugabe had foiled the pressure of the United States and Britain and the quiet diplomacy of his neighbours in Southern Africa. So long as Mugabe reigned, his Zanu regime would survive. The international community tried to change things. It embarked on a strategy of concerted economic and diplomatic pressure to weaken the regime; trying to force it to either back down or submit to the democratic opposition.

That strategy failed as Mugabe went for broke. However the exit of Mugabe, whether through retirement or death, would leave the regime internally and externally vulnerable. Internally, the Zanu regime without Mugabe at the helm will be uniquely susceptible in an election. In sub-Saharan Africa, opposition candidates have won post-transitional elections only 5 percent of the time against incumbents but 33 percent of the time against regimes' designated successors. The most important reason for that is the incumbent's exit removes the regime's glue. The regime fractures into competing factions and is left with a substantially reduced capacity to repress the political opposition and rig an election.

The negotiated settlement

"ZAPU and its leader (Joshua Nkomo) are like a cobra in the house. The only way to deal with a snake is to strike and crush its head," Mugabe once said.

U.S. Secretary of State Henry Kissinger, "If you want to make peace, it's no good talking to your friends; you need to speak with your enemies."

What Zimbabweans were fighting for was rule by democratic consensus in which all major stakeholders and other interested parties felt that they were part of the process towards a new Zimbabwe. The reason there had been so much bloodshed and polarisation between the rulers and the ruled was that the latter had been excluded for a long time from decisions that affected their lives. The negotiations were seen as the beginning of a process that would lead to an all-inclusive watershed election towards democratic accountability and rule by consent.

What Zimbabweans had seen after independence in 1980 had been five years of reasonable government under a constitution drafted in London with the unholy help of the British. This creature of Westminster gave them all the trappings of a modern society; Parliament, the vote, a certain disbursement of power through the State and civil society. When drafted in London, none of the parties to the process had any stake in what was being created; the British just wanted to get out intact and clean, the Nationalist leaders did not believe a word but just saw it as a pathway to power. The Whites, defeated and tired after 15 years of sanctions and war, just wanted to get on with their lives and protect what they had.

They each got what they wanted, but the Nationalists lost little time in white-anting the legal and political arrangements so neatly laid out in the Lancaster Agreement and the British watched, enthusiastically fanning the flames of damage with rhetoric and withdrawal of much needed skilled manpower.

First the nationalists wiped out the opposition and by 1988 this was achieved. Then neutered the whites and reduced them to the place of serfs who pay tribute and have no say in anything to do with the way they were governed. This was achieved in very large measure by 1990. Then the elites moved from a modern, liberal State to a one party dominated political system and then to rule by dictate from State House. This was achieved by 1995. The state of affairs that prevailed since 1995 strongly resembles a feudal State; the government destroyed the modern economy, largely because independent business persons with assets and intellectuals with education were a threat to feudal power.

Many thought that Didymus Mutasa, a Mugabe worshipper, was simply playing devils advocate when he said to a reporter "...we would be quite happy to have a population of 6 million people who supported Zanu." The fact that at the time Zimbabwe should have had a population of close to 16 million was not an issue. So the feudal elite who ruled Zimbabwe since 1980 had systematically driven out of the country or killed any group who might threaten their hold on power; the educated, the business elite, independent workers, Ndebeles and private farmers, just as the Kulaks were a major threat to Stalin's power in the Soviet Union. Morgan Tsvangirai called this the silent Pol Pot revolution.

South Africa had numerous problems when it came to its 'northern province'. If South Africa were to admit that Zimbabwe was guilty of the human rights violations then it would have to change its policy on how it treated Zimbabwean immigrants, especially the asylum seekers. It would have to stop detaining them like criminals in detention centres and deporting them. It would have to adopt a position consistent with an acknowledgment that there was political persecution of a certain group of citizens in Zimbabwe. There were economic factors that meant South Africa had to play sugar daddy for its economic interactions in Harare to continue; the loans, pensions and company profits remittances.

In a sense South Africa's foreign policy indicated that it had to be motivated by considerations of human rights, consistent with the ANC Charter and its history of supporting democratic struggle and development. But there were some sentimental issues that were not necessarily economic which were related to history. And the sentimental issues took several strands. The one was the suspicion that to condemn Mugabe would be to affirm Tsvangirai as the legitimate successor to the aged Zimbabwean president.

The long sort after ANC solution was a reformed Zanu, with young progressive forces leading it. Different strategies were played by the South African government up to 2005. The whole fiasco with Mnangagwa and the young 'Turks' fell apart when they tried to go too fast for the "veterans" in Zanu was one such Mbeki move. Had Mugabe gone along with Mbeki in this exercise he would have made things very difficult for the opposition and might even have attracted some of the less principled members of the international community to his side. As it was Mugabe slapped him in the face, his heir apparent was tossed aside and Mbeki's spy ring inside Zanu incarcerated.

In 2002, Mbeki was in Zimbabwe on this perennial Mission Impossible, trying to bring together two political parties led by two people from different eras of time: The Cold War and The Global Village.

Every time as the talks between the Zimbabwean belligerents got underway, Mbeki's sorry image cast its shadow over the whole enterprise. Instead of the negotiations becoming a collective, inclusive drive towards a better Zimbabwe with Mbeki leading the discourse, it was reduced to a shadowy exercise exhibiting directly, his personal attitudes, moods, views and flaws. To kick-start an exercise of such a magnitude and importance with an individual's character holding sway was to fail at the outset.

What most people remember must be the bewildered sight of Mbeki as he looked at the shabby Joseph Chinotimba. Mbeki seemed to wonder: Was this weird-looking man part of the Mugabe delegation or an intruder? The impression many gleaned from Chinotimba's presence was that Mugabe wished for Mbeki to know that his 'people' were not the clean-cut, suave politicians who could fit easily at an international conference. His people were 'down-to-earth' and could not speak a single correct sentence of English. They were not stooges of the West, he wanted to say.

After absorbing the implications of this scenario, Mbeki decided Mugabe was not ready for dialogue with the MDC. Mugabe may never be ready for dialogue with the MDC. He oozed with such contempt for both: Mbeki for his indecisiveness and petty games and the MDC it seems he could hardly stand them.

Mbeki sometimes paid lip service to the principle of non-interference in the internal affairs of another sovereign state, but South Africa quickly sent its army into Lesotho in 1998 after a rigged election there. Would Mbeki have sent his soldiers into Zimbabwe if disaffected middle-rank officers threatened Mugabe's regime? He probably would though Nigeria, Ghana and Senegal might have objected. Part of Mbeki's reluctance to act on Zimbabwe had to do with Mugabe's residual status as a liberation hero. But mostly it stemmed from Mbeki's distaste for the Zimbabwean opposition the MDC, particularly its main leader, Morgan Tsvangirai.

In mid-2001, Mbeki told the British television show Hard Talk that he had tried persuading Mugabe to reform, but that the Zimbabwean ruler "..didn't listen to me." By November, Mbeki publicly attributed Zimbabwe's problems to "twenty years of wrong economic policies" but gave no details. Likewise, the ANC presidential spokesperson Smuts Ngonyama blamed the Zimbabwean economic mess on too many subsidies. Zuma gave a brief lecture on Zimbabwean political economics saying Mugabe's government embarked on a huge social spending spree without analysing social needs, which caused inflation to spiral.

When Mugabe controversially won the March 9 to 11, 2002 presidential poll, Mbeki and Nigerian President Olusegun Obasanjo visited Zimbabwe on March 18 and met Mugabe and Tsvangirai separately. Mbeki was at the time pushing Mugabe to form a government of national unity and diffuse the international criticism. Mugabe rebuffed the unity government calls. From Harare, Mbeki and Obasanjo proceeded to London for a Commonwealth troika meeting with John Howard on March 20 2002. Howard then announced Zimbabwe's suspension from the Commonwealth for a year because of a Commonwealth observer mission report that condemned the presidential elections as rigged. Mbeki and Obasanjo kept on pressuring Mugabe to talk to the opposition.

On April 3, 2002 Mbeki and Obasanjo brokered talks opened in Harare between the MDC represented by Welshman Ncube and Zanu represented by Justice Minister Patrick Chinamasa. Their envoys, ANC Secretary-General Kgalema Motlanthe and a respected Nigerian academic, Prof Adebayo Adedeji, represented Mbeki and Obasanjo. The talks collapsed soon afterwards after Mugabe withdrew his delegation, citing the MDC's decision to file a court application challenging his victory in the presidential elections.

Mbeki then spent 2002 trying to privately coax Mugabe into going back to the negotiating table, but to no avail. In February 2003, the Commonwealth troika on Zimbabwe collapsed after Mbeki and Obasanjo objected to any further meeting with Howard, saying the troika's mandate had expired.

An infuriated Mbeki later tried to get McKinnon voted out as secretary-general of the Commonwealth at the Abuja summit in favour of a former Sri Lankan foreign minister. Mbeki failed and McKinnon was retained.

Earlier, on May 5, 2003, Mbeki joined Obasanjo and then Sadc chairman Bakili Muluzi on a trip to Zimbabwe to help broker talks between Mugabe and the opposition. The opposition had successfully convened a weeklong strike that shut down the country. The three leaders separately met Mugabe and Tsvangirai. Their mission failed after Mugabe set tough conditions for resuming dialogue, including a demand that the opposition recognise his legitimacy and drop its electoral petition. The opposition refused and Mbeki failed to broker a deal ahead of the December Commonwealth summit. Mbeki visited Mugabe again after the Abuja summit, but to no avail.

A frustrated Obasanjo had already declined to give Mugabe an invitation to attend the Commonwealth summit despite reported pressure from Mbeki to extend an invitation. When the Abuja summit agreed to keep Zimbabwe out, Mugabe, without parliament approval, pulled his country out of the summit.

In July 2003, Mbeki stood smiling inanely beside George Bush and claimed that talks with the Zimbabweans were getting on nicely, thank you very much. He said: "We are absolutely of one mind about the urgent need to address the political and economic challenges of Zimbabwe." Mark the word 'urgent'.

So what had Mbeki been "..urgently," doing? He tolerated, clothed, fed and supported Mugabe with his tolerance for the man's penchant for arresting, beating and killing his subjects. Mbeki made it abundantly clear which side he was on.

In June 2003, weeks before Bush's visit, Mbeki had explicitly told the World Economic Forum in Durban that the Zimbabwe crisis would be resolved within a year. This did not happen. All Mbeki's interventions were punctuated by public support for Mugabe, such as a letter on his ANC online column condemning Britain for protecting "kith and kin" in Zimbabwe at the expense of blacks. Foreign Minister Nkosazana Dlamini-Zuma vowed that South Africa would never criticise Zimbabwe.

In March 2005, Mugabe proceeded to hold elections under the same conditions that Mbeki had been quietly urging him to change, and the opposition lost again. It emerged afterwards that the MDC's Welshman Ncube had been quietly talking to Minister of Justice Patrick Chinamasa and the two had produced a draft constitution that Mugabe and Tsvangirai had signed and were being urged by Mbeki to consider. Mugabe eventually went on the war path with the MDC.

For the greater part of 2005 and 2006 Mbeki was very quiet on Zimbabwe, having apparently given up. A Mbeki aide told the annual Tswalu dialogue that there was nothing more Mbeki could do and the "...situation in Zimbabwe would have to resolve itself".

In February 2007, Mbeki renewed his intervention in Zimbabwe by meeting Mugabe in Ghana for the first time in more than a year. In March 2007, Sadc leaders officially mandated Mbeki to intervene in Zimbabwe on the regional grouping's behalf after police brutally assaulted opposition leaders and supporters. Mugabe confirmed as much after he returned triumphant from the SADC meeting. Gloating, he said Tsvangirai 'deserved' to be savagely beaten up. "Yes, I told them [Sadc leaders] he was beaten but he asked for it... We got full backing, not even one criticised our actions," he said. "There is no country in SADC that can stand up and say Zimbabwe has faulted."

Mbeki failed in previous intervention attempts because of his hypocrisy in wanting an outcome that would preserve Mugabe's party in power and not one based on the popular will of Zimbabweans. So the first thing he emphasised was that the

154

only way Zimbabwe could solve its crisis was to have free and fair elections in 2008.

Mbeki had a warped idea about free and fair elections. His Sadc observe teams of 2000, 2002 and 2005 had shown and proved this. Zimbabweans were not calling for another election. They wanted Mugabe out and their isolation lifted. They wanted their dignity restored. They wanted jobs and a government that respected their human rights. Elections under the old bandaged Lancaster Constitution would not provide these demands and Zimbabweans knew this. Mbeki didn't seem to. For free and fair elections to be held, the government had to change a lot of things that gave Zanu a far superior advantage over others.

What was even more amiss was that Zimbabwe could not expect any help from the European Union either. The old liberal spirit had been wiped out of Europe and the United States by a concerted effort of propagandists like Rupert Murdoch. But even if Europe wanted to help, they could not help unless Zanu was in a predicament from which it had no escape.

Mbeki assumed that his offer of a US$1billion credit could influence Harare elites, aiming at installing a neo-liberal regime that would sideline Mugabe by 2008 at the latest; permit a reformed Zanu to share power with a technocratic president and then open the economic borders to Johannesburg capital. But Mugabe didn't play along. Showing a desire to hold on to power at all cost, Mugabe visited China and then snubbed Mbeki in a brutal diplomatic manner at an African Union (AU) meeting in Addis Ababa. Mugabe then pulled a card from his sleeve no one thought he had; he came up with US$135 million and paid the IMF a substantial down payment, enough to earn a six-month reprieve on the expulsion threat and vowed to repay the full amount. By all accounts, this was an irrational and costly egoistic gesture by Mugabe for it served no economic or political purpose.

It was not for love of peace that Ian Smith negotiated with the black nationalists. White South Africa had pulled its troops out of Rhodesia under pressure from the USA. Nor was it for the love of peace that Prime Minister Margaret Thatcher negotiated with the liberation forces. It was Nigeria that had threatened to nationalize BP's 5 billion dollar investments in Nigeria that drove Thatcher to negotiate. From a white population of 250 000, Smith was left with a remnant of 100,000 mainly hard core racist. Mugabe had been told by Samora Machel not to return without an agreement. The white population was facing annihilation from an insurgent guerrilla war. To step out of this quagmire needed courage.

The 2002 negotiations entailed the setting up of a truly independent electoral commission, the removal of the 30 presidential appointed seats, the establishment of a bicameral Parliament and reserved seats for women on proportional representation. The negotiations also had to involve setting up a land commission to look at the land reform to rationalise the process and the interim government had to sort out a new truly representative, inclusive and democratic constitution.

Mbeki and Mugabe had agreed on this route to try and end the crisis in Zimbabwe and, as usual, Mugabe reneged on this by end of 2002 and was pursuing the repressive legislative route with amendments to AIPPA, POSA and the NGO Bill. Negotiations did not meet Mugabe's needs and he avoided implementing them as long as he could.

Meanwhile Mbeki's line of engagement with the Zimbabwean crisis remained the only faintly credible international one, but continued to have a major weakness in that it was never backed up by real measures but largely by fraternal political persuasion and revolutionary solidarity slogans. In international politics, diplomacy and foreign policy normally work when they are supported by credible capabilities, usually military and economic. Nigeria is able to influence the West African region because it is usually willing to use its military and economic leverage to back its diplomacy.

Perhaps of more relevance, is how the South African government of P.W. Botha put the squeeze on the new government of Mugabe in the early 1980s. Shortly after coming to power Mugabe had assured South Africa that he would not provide military assistance to the ANC. Ever rhetorical, Mugabe continued to deliver speeches attacking the "racist Pretoria regime", criticised Zimbabwean migrant workers working across the Limpopo and banned any of his Ministers from having any dealings with the South African government. The hawks in the South African government responded by threatening to send the 40,000 Zimbabwean migrant workers home at the end of their contracts.

Eighty wagons borrowed from South Africa and desperately needed to shift Zimbabwe's record 1981 harvest were abruptly recalled. In the early morning of the 9th December 1981 a South African recce commando blew up the oil depot at Beira, destroying two and a half months of fuel supply for Zimbabwe, leaving the country with just two weeks domestic supply and facing economic ruin. An alternative rail route for oil from Maputo was also sabotaged by the MNR. This left South Africa with a grip on all of Zimbabwe's oil supplies, whether purchased direct or from Maputo. The resulting chaos hit Zimbabwe over Christmas. Mugabe admitted his total vulnerability. After diplomatic intervention by the United States fuel supplies were restored and the pipeline repaired, but South Africa had made its point.

Mugabe would have been moved by Mbeki's diplomacy if he knew that South Africa was willing to deploy its capabilities against him. Although South Africa is the superpower of Africa with huge military and economic capabilities that could be deployed to sort out the Zimbabwean issue, Mbeki failed to harness his resources to his advantage. A country may fail to influence another, even though it is a regional superpower, if its capabilities are not credible and relevant.

One way of using those capabilities would have been refusing to bale out Zimbabwe economically, with electricity, finance and fuel, unless Mugabe addressed certain fundamental issues. Mugabe seemed to think Mbeki had given him a blank cheque and that was sabotaging South Africa's diplomacy. It made it impossible for Mbeki to strengthen his hand by threatening to bring into play his capabilities. If he did, as he did in 2003, Mugabe resorted to blackmail, claiming Mbeki was now being influenced by imperialists; was an imperialist stooge etc.

Mbeki could not even contemplate switching off electricity and fuel permanently as he'd have refugees at the boarder the next day. Mugabe was buying massive armaments from China and training thousands of militias preparing to fight it out with any "Dog of imperialism". "The programme is going ahead . . . we are actually aiming to produce more graduates than we have managed before," Chimutengwende, responsible for the militia, said in April 2005. Zanu was using its only trump card on South Africa; the threat of massive waves of HIV/AIDS infected and criminal militia refugees. South Africa was already busting to the seams with these types of Zimbabwean refugees.

For Mbeki to pick a fight over the embattled Zimbabwe white farmers would be unwise when you put his political situation in South Africa into account. Where the percentage of white-owned farm acreage in Zimbabwe was put at about 70 per cent of the arable land before the appropriations, in South Africa it was actually much higher at above 80 per cent. Mbeki was not so daft as to imagine his own constituents were not watching how he handled the Zimbabwe situation.

The illusion of Zanu and South Africa was that they both thought Zanu could solve the country's problems when they lacked legitimacy, knowledge and the will. However the 2005 election Zanu win outcome raised a number of issues for the region:

i)   That the legacy of liberation solidarity, in the face of criticism and confrontations with former colonial powers takes precedence over issues around the internal despotism for post-colonial states. In such situations the concerns of local dissent around human rights questions were considered of little importance. That the discourse of Pan-Africanism and anti-imperialism serves as a controlling structure whose parameters had largely been set by the authoritarian nationalisms of Mugabe.

ii)   That the Sadc electoral norms and standards would be interpreted according to the broad political requirements of the region at any one time, sadly and unfortunately with issues around national accountability of secondary and little importance.

iii)   That Sadc needed a lesson on the obligations of states to their citizens; that Governments are responsible for the safety, security and well being of their people, wherever they maybe. Otherwise they have no need to exist.

iv)   The muzzling of the media was a demonstration that while the Sadc idea of conflict resolution was modern, the tools and spirit employed to achieve this all belonged to the liberation era.

By 2007, with declining international popularity, the British and American governments did not need to add Mugabe and Zimbabwe to their gallery of crises. Hence South Africa persuaded the British and US governments to support the creation of a framework for a government of national unity in Zimbabwe, promising each faction within the MDC (apparently the MDC had by then split into two tribal factions) a part of the political fortunes on condition that human rights abuses be swept under the carpet, Mugabe keeps his loot and be granted immunity.

As an insurance policy, Mugabe agreed to retire with the condition that the international community accepted his appointed successor and that key hardliners within the party and public service continue their tenure. The training programme and supply of vital helicopter parts agreed upon between the South African and Zimbabwean air forces was meant not only to secure Mugabe's retirement but to provide protection and military assistance to the ailing Mugabe government in the event of a now very eminent military-sponsored uprising.

Repression, restrictive legislation and the deployment of security forces to quell street demonstrations was no longer a viable approach. On the economic front, South Africa could not afford for the Zimbabwean economy to totally collapse. With problems of its own the South African government was unable to shore up the Zimbabwean economy over the long term. The further collapse of the Zimbabwean economy, coupled with the threat of internal strife, would invariably tie up South Africa's and the International Community's resources.

Therefore the emergence of a coalition government was the main objective. Mugabe in exchange 'accepted' to adopt economic reform, the lifting of price controls and acceptance of IMF economic reform measures and UN demands for access to build permanent housing for those displaced and rendered homeless by Mugabes social reconstruction policy. To make sense of Harare's willingness to pay the IMF and to compromise on all these issues, peer pressure from Mbeki was certainly a factor, but the initial refusal of Pretoria's $1 billion loan suggests that Mugabe's ego was so large that he paid simply to massage his pride.

Two major obstacle to this grand scheme were the intransigence of the opposition leader Morgan Tsvangirai and the non-involvement of the main faction MDC in the senate and the rank and file of Zimbabwe's war machine was becoming increasingly dissatisfied with their conditions of service and desertion from the army ranks was at an all time high. Senior army officers were being harassed by their juniors as entire fields of corn were slashed down on the confisticated farms. Between 2004 and 2008, 3 coup attempts by middle ranking soldiers were foiled.

South Africa's Zimbabwe policy called "quiet diplomacy" (actually supportive diplomacy) believed the MDC would destabilise Zimbabwe even further as the army threatened to revolt if the opposition won and therefore wanted rather to co-operate with "progressive elements" within Zanu to speed up reform. The six provincial chairman, Information Minister and others fired by Mugabe late 2004 for holding a meeting he wasn't invited to, were generally seen as part of the "rebel" element, sponsored and encouraged by South African agents.

That strategy having failed, the ANC and Sadc grasped at minimal electoral reforms as a basis for recognising Zimbabwean elections, notwithstanding the immense damage that was done to the election process since 2000. South Africa had to be pragmatic in making the best of a bad deal in the hope that somehow, after a flawed election, a victorious Zanu would be more magnanimous and a reduced MDC would be more realistic.

It may not be inconceivable that Mugabe received the buy-in from the Sadc Heads about his understanding of the broader context of the Zimbabwean crisis to the extent that they may all have agreed about the need to defend his legacy. It was unlikely that Zanu would be persuaded, even through the Mbeki mediation, to commit political suicide and agree on any changes that would weaken the party by removing its most potent weapon, Mugabe, from the scene.

The MDC was advised by leaders in Africa and Europe to fight the poll, even with a thoroughly one-sided playing field. African leaders wanted to validate the polls so that election observers could declare it to have been free and fair and bring the whole sorry saga to an end. The West lived in the misguided hope that after all they had been through, the voters would turn against Mugabe, which would end the crisis from their viewpoint. Both sides were misjudging the situation.

The West would instinctively not recognise another or more flawed Zanu victories, while Zimbabwe's voters lacked the organisation, material and the stomach to insisting Mugabe step down. Under those conditions it was highly likely that Zanu will win such flawed elections in the future, thus legitimising the broad process of authoritarian consolidation that had characterised the politics of Zimbabwe and Sadc.

The raft of Western measures against Mugabe's regime were bound to fail as long as Zimbabwe's rulers' iniquities were shielded by Mbeki's inaudible diplomacy. Thus, while the EU/USA smart sanctions presented the stick, they lacked the carrot; the crucial ingredient of reaching out to the obdurate octogenarian ruler. Mbeki's approach offered the carrot but there was no stick. Neither targeted sanctions alone nor Mbeki's behind-the-scenes scheming or internal pressure had managed to nudge Mugabe.

In the same vain, the Blair government played directly into Mugabe's hands by failing to counter-respond to Mugabe's consistent "Blair-baiting." UK's Tony Blair had been reduced to what the Americans call a cheese-eating-surrender-monkey. Totally against his conscience Blair had allowed himself to be bullied and abused by Mugabe and his friends via rhetoric like colonialist, imperialists, gay gangster, and other unmentionables. Blair miserably failed the leadership test set by John Stuart Mill who said "...the only purpose for which power can be rightfully exercised over any member of a civilised community, against his will, is to prevent harm to others". British efforts, like those of the rest of Europe, simply and urgently needed to be focused on Harare's neighbours and push for peer pressure to be applied more forcefully.

The British government clearly lacked backbone and resolve and had failed to stand up to the African bullies. Blair's expressed revulsion at Mugabe's brutality looked more hollow with every asylum seeker deported from the UK, intimidated, tortured, maimed, killed or disappeared within Zimbabwe's boarders and jails. Blair had to be more hawkish and be able to use his financial and political muscle as the leader of the most powerful EU country to counter this threat.

By 2005 Mugabe's image-makers appeared to be winning the propaganda war and Blair had allowed the devil to run away with the gospel. Great leaders are not those who pander to the whims of powerful media dynasties, but those like Bush who acted decisively even at the risk of losing the good public ratings for the good of humanity.

By 2006 Mbeki suggested he had pinned his hopes on a draft constitution and the attendant political process. Did he seriously believe Mugabe was ready to be legislated out of power? Mugabe only agreed to Mbeki's and Sadc's initiative to buy time and not to secure a resolution of Zimbabwe's crisis. Mugabe's principal negotiators said their mandate was to ensure the talks failed and hence tabled the rejected 2000 constitution for negotiation with the opposition. The Zimbabwean question was widely seen as a litmus test for Mbeki and it was also a test case for

Nepad and Mbeki's African Renaissance project. The collapse of Mbeki's "quiet diplomacy" on Zimbabwe left Nepad and the African Renaissance dream in tatters.

Mugabe had never been an honest statesman when it comes to talks and he was leading the MDC up the garden path to legitimising another fraudulent election in 2008. Overtures from the Mutambara camp about backing Tsvangirai's single candidacy was part of a ploy to set him up for the 'great fall' if he were to lose the election again. Mutambara was an unintentional Mugabe decoy. The MDC had to withdraw from the Mbeki led talks and demand Mugabe slackens on violence. As it was, Mugabe's principal negotiators had to be coerced by Mbeki on several occasions to attend the talks in Pretoria.

Mugabe's palpable contempt for British Prime Minister Tony Blair, George Bush, Obasanjo and Thabo Mbeki was understandable. He had yet to lose a round against any of them and there was no reason to imagine that this was going to change any time soon. Mbeki's spell as US president George Bush's point man on Zimbabwe had meant four wasted years, as Mugabe took advantage of the South African president's reluctance to move beyond quiet diplomacy. Under the cloak of "quiet diplomacy" Mbeki displayed incredible levels of muddled thinking.

Mbeki was no poker player. One reason why Mugabe had run rings around him was because Mugabe had always known what cards Mbeki and Sadc held. Perversely, Mbeki had obligingly shown his hand: no smart sanctions; no disruption of electricity supplies however tardy Zimbabwe was in paying its bill; no disruption of Zimbabwean exports; and no condemnation of Mugabe's human rights abuses.

The 2007 Sadc initiative was a new round but the deal was virtually unchanged. This was not because the Sadc countries had any ideological commitment to restoring democracy to Zimbabwe. It was because they feared the fallout from the impending final collapse of the Zimbabwean state would have a serious impact on the fortunes of the region. Sadc could not pretend not to know that the Mugabe regime had institutionalised violence as a survival strategy. Mugabe gloated about the battering of opposition leaders in Dar es Salaam, making it clear that his regime was not being falsely accused of perpetrating these atrocities.

Zimbabweans, Sadc and Mbeki's people would come away from any negotiation convinced there would be no real dialogue with Mugabe in his lifetime. Which probably makes you wonder if they had to create the proper circumstances for Mugabe to listen to them or for Mbeki to treat the crisis in Zimbabwe as seriously as he treated the others. History had shown that Mugabe resented documents of discussion. Think of the Chihambakwe report, CCJP report, Zimrights report, African Union Human Rights Commission report, Constitutional Commission draft Constitution etc. To want to negotiate was to miss the fact that what was obtaining in Zimbabwe was not a battle of minds. It was something less about views but more about murder, brazen repression and madness.

The duped and the African dancers

"We are people in suits by day but in uniform at night. We fought a liberation war," Museveni President of Uganda said. *"Don't play around with freedom fighters."*

African rulers have tried to justify their suppression of their people's political rights arguing that what is more pertinent in Africa is the promotion of rights such as the right to health, housing, education and other social services. And yet what African people have been insisting on since colonial times has been the right to express themselves precisely over issues of access to health, housing, education etc! It appears, therefore, that the suppression of political rights is not because they are naturally antithetical to the delivery of rights. Rather, it is functional only in the context of a sitting regime's political survival prospects for it effectively undermines the organization of any meaningful political opposition to it.

Saleshando, who headed the Botswana Congress Party, said while colonisation had contributed to Africa's problems, Africans must take their fair share of the blame. "I do not think the looting of African economies by its leaders is a function of occupation by imperialist forces. It is a product of irresponsibility and greed among other things. It is also an outcome of the failure of African institutions like the African Union to act on the delinquency of some of its member states." The Botswana politician said one of the reasons that compounded the problem of mal-governance on the continent was the exclusion of the people from the decision-making process.

Meanwhile Mozambique's past president, Joachim Chissano, welcomed the idea of an African Union Government, saying such an institution would help Africans to "proudly identify themselves so that the problems facing the continent would be things of the past." How this would be, he did not say.

Urged on by that well-known African, the Guide of the First of September Great Revolution of the Socialist People's Libyan Arab Jamahiriya, the AU devoted the entire three days of their Accra summit to a "Grand Debate" on creating a United States of Africa, complete with a federal government with a 15-member cabinet and a two million-strong continental army under the command of none other than Muammar Qaddafi himself. He said: "In Accra, the voice of the people must be heard. At least this summit will be different from others because the leaders are forced to listen to the masses." Qadaffi called for a single army, a single currency and a single president for Africa. The trouble is that he fancied himself as that president too. The Accra summit was a waste of time as more important and pressing issues such as HIV/Aids, human resources depletion and trade failed to be considered.

So what qualities would the head of an African Union Government need to have to be acceptable as a rallying point to enable the 'people' to deal with abstract and diffuse issues? What "masses" wanted an United States of Africa, the brotherly leader did not say. Did it include the Diaspora; the hundreds of millions of blacks scattered all over the world; the black Americans, those in Cuba, Brazil? Who is to say which blacks are to be included in the debate and how are the elections for this 'President' to be conducted? Did it include Porta Farm residents? Or had he ever heard of them? Obviously a referendum was required to ascertain whether 'Africans' wanted a USA of their own.

Qaddafi would not give up bribing and bullying African governments and "masses" to support his Big Idea. What he did not tell any of the masses that greeted him like a hero in Accra was that the Big Idea was his "insurance" against the day when his barren land runs out, not only of oil, but also of water. Libya, he tells his people, would cease to exist in a US of Africa, but Libyans would have the run of the "paradise" of Africa's natural wealth.

The so-called AU had failed to take any specific decisive action in resolving the Zimbabwe and Sudanese question. The "AU" is an amorphous body of nations divided and operating without a single specific voice at all times. It would appear that to the opposition parties and the average African, the "international community" consisted predominantly of the West and this was the only rallying point for the despots.

On the other hand, feeling ostracized by the West, the despots had deliberately constructed their world-view through the lens of the East. The sad fact is that real Africans did not seem to realize that they were mere pawns in a game of the Big boys. If there is one thing that unites the divided community of nations, it is that each nation's attitude, position and action in relation to any issue was motivated by self-interest, corruption and the search for scarce resources.

There was little evidence of foreign sabotage (British or American) on Zimbabwe's political, social or economic systems. But there was substantial evidence that because of failure to take charge of its destiny, a single senile old man had taken the whole nation for granted. For some powerful Western countries, the Zimbabwe question had become a matter of prestige and they would not accept any reforms that would leave Mugabe posturing as the final winner in the standoff. This partly explains why it was for South Africa and the AU to lead a 'no action' motion at the United Nations and maintain quiet diplomacy over the crisis in Zimbabwe. It also partly explains why Sadc did not condemned Mugabe in spite of the overwhelming evidence of his reign of terror, torture and rigged elections.

Throughout history, the greatest threat facing ordinary citizens comes from their own government. One need only think of the millions who were murdered by Hitler, Lenin, Stalin and more recently the thousands of minority Tutsis who were murdered by the Hutu majority government or the thousands of the Ndebele who were murdered by Mugabe to understand this.

The modern notion of countering this threat is that of an independent judiciary backed by a constitution. It is not at all clear why any rational person should believe that these, in the end, provide any protection at all. These were wholly ineffective in Nazi Germany, Stalin's Russia and Zimbabwe.

If a judiciary is to prevail, it can only do so very early in the attack. It is the first line of defence. The attack against individuals usually starts with an attack on their liberty and property as in Nazi Germany. Tyrants first start by corrupting cronies to remain in power and when they run out of tit-bits to buy their way, they will use the only available tool left; conscription camps.

However, the writing was on the wall. The remaining tyrannies would eventually perish and the world would move slowly toward greater freedom. The United States was right to push this trend forward. However lessons had to be leant. Mugabe, who had ruled Zimbabwe since 1980, was yet to be persuaded to accommodate constitutional amendments that would really keep dictators in check. The AU had failed dismally and the presidents had no moral or legal right to call for a USA. How could a band of discredited despots claim any right to such a noble idea?

The African Union Commission report (rubbished by Zanu as imperialist funded and controlled) adopted by the AU stated that laws such as the Public Order and Security Act (POSA) and the Access to Information and Protection of Privacy Act (AIPPA) would have "....a 'chilling effect' on freedom of expression and introduced a cloud of fear in media circles". The African Commission's report stated: "Legislation that prohibits the public participation of NGOs in public education and human rights counselling must be reviewed. The Private Voluntary Organizations Act should be repealed."

Since the African Commission visited Zimbabwe in 2002 no reform whatsoever of the police service took place. Youth training centres remained operational. The government intensified its repression of NGOs and human rights, yet the AU and Sadc kept its silence despite its own commission's reported findings.

Some African leaders were not enthusiastic about Mugabe's open defiance. President Kufuor of Ghana regarded the crisis in Zimbabwe as "...embarrassing". "I know personally that presidents like Mbeki tried desperately to exercise some influence for the better. Please do not think Africa is unconcerned. But what can Mbeki do? Are you proposing that Africa compose an expedition team and march on Zimbabwe and oppose? It does not happen like that. We in our various ways are trying very hard". Ghana was however considered by many to be Africa's 'weakest link' in its fight against the machinations of Bush's neo-conservatives in Africa. And how was Kufuor, "....trying very hard"? Had he visited the suffering masses in Zimbabwe?

Mbeki had spoken of this dooms-day scenario of militarily marching on Mugabe and his inability to do that. No one had ever requested him to do so, yet most African big men kept on the mantra that someone wanted them to militarily intervene. All Zimbabweans wanted, it seemed, was economic, moral and verbal pressure to be applied on Mugabe to stop torturing and murdering them and cheating in elections.

The AU and Sadc were a pariah regional block not recognised as democratic organisations. Mauritius lost all its Sadc Chairmanship powers in the goings-on in the election observation team to Zimbabwe, which was stuffed with ANC lieutenants. Opposition organisations could harness this growing discontent and derail South Africa's chances to land a permanent seat in the UN Security Council.

Although the idea of a borderless, continent wide entity had been accepted by most African countries, it remained no more than a slogan due to disputes on how to proceed; the despots wanted international power, the masses wanted more human rights, food, shelter and jobs. In the conference rooms, no one was talking on behalf of the ordinary African. What was apparent was that the AU was mainly donor funded by the very Western world they were castigating in the conference chambers. And if any continental government was to be launched, then begging bowls were heading in only one direction.

163

SADC and the AU

The African Union (a misnomer) with 53 member states was a classical example of size having no bearing on the end result. What did the AU have to say about anything? Nothing, because the body was broke, disunited and awash with members who played truant with impunity knowing too well that African brothers and other dictators around the world could always find kind words to justify the unbecoming behaviour.

So the 2006 AU summit meeting in Sudan suddenly was very significant to a lot of Africans in general and misguided Zimbabweans in particular. What to do with despotic leaders breaking the AU's sparkling new constitution? There was a sudden unseemly brawl over the chairmanship; Chad accused Sudan of hosting rebels trying to unseat the N'Djamena government; while other African leaders charged Sudan with being responsible for a crisis in its Darfur region. While the leaders were squabbling, the United Nations announced that Africa would need food aid that year, which would cost US$2 billion to supply. Meanwhile, Ugandan rebels in the Democratic Republic of Congo were killing eight UN peacekeepers; and insurgents in Nigeria's oil-rich delta were launching a new wave of attacks on public and commercial buildings.

The following year the conference was held in Accra and yet again Africans were to see the despots, led by the eccentric Qadaffi, arguing over a useless United States of Africa. Their rivalries and twisted priorities eclipsed discussion of such vital issues as war and peace, famine and starvation, oppression and freedom, unity, HIV-Aids, continental trade and economic development. Just like its predecessor, the African Union had failed the people of Africa and was becoming a sick joke to many inside and outside the continent.

One of the first individual test cases of the new AU's formal commitments was Zimbabwean human-rights lawyer Gabriel Shumba, who was arrested and severely tortured by the government for defending in court a member of the opposition. The Zimbabwean judicial system failed him. He was threatened with death and fled to South Africa. In 2003 he approached the African Commission on Human and Peoples' Rights (ACHPR) directly. "Nothing about the AU has changed but the name", said a bitter Shumba. "We can only conclude that the African system, as a legal system to enforce rights, is hopeless."

The long-delayed presentation to the African Union assembly in July 2004 of the ACHPR's 2002 fact-finding mission to investigate human-rights abuses in Zimbabwe was met with protests from the Zimbabwean delegation, supported by the South Africans and resulted in the report's adoption being postponed. This indicated a clear lack of political maturity at the AU and it was a shame that South Africa, so soon out of oppression from apartheid with the help of Zimbabweans, would not lift a finger to help other oppressed people of the world.

However the AU with leaders such as Teodoro Nguema, the despotic head of Equatorial Guinea, the likes of DRC's Joseph Kabila, and Museveni of Uganda who shot their way into power, little was to come out of that absurd body. These were some of the people who decided on human rights for Africa yet they didn't know the meaning of the words 'Human rights'. Several of these African rulers would not even sit in the same room as their putative continental partners with whom they were engaged in bitter border struggles or outright wars and generally the AU summits were attended by as little as a third of these rulers. Those who religiously attend them, like Mugabe, were seen dozing on TV with boredom as nothing concrete usually came out of people who were used to do nothing.

The United Nations condemned Zimbabwe's actions and the country's braver religious leaders said they were shocked by the havoc and persistent attacks on ordinary citizens' rights. It was no wonder that the demolitions, tortures, murders evinced no word of protest or condemnation from South Africa or from any of Zimbabwe's neighbours. In response and buoyed by this comradeship Mugabe growled in a ten-point resolution summarised bucking: No more wide-eyed envoys from Annan (UN), warning that Zimbabwe would no longer welcome any nosy envoys from Khoffi Anan's UN office, whether they were black and female or white and male.

Africans were angered by the continued unwillingness of African rulers to deal with human rights issues. With much fanfare and rejoicing in South Africa the new body proceeded to establish an impressive array of organs and instruments purporting to deliver human rights to the continent's oppressed millions. The Constitutive Act of the AU explicitly espoused the promotion of 'democratic principles and institutions, popular participation and good governance' and the promotion and protection of "....human and people's rights in accordance with the African Charter on Human and Peoples' Rights and other relevant human rights instruments".

Most significant was the agreement by member-states to limit their sovereignty with specific regard to respect for democratic principles, human rights and the rule of law. "Good governance" and "peer review" were the new buzz phrases. In a further erosion of state sovereignty, the AU even gave itself some teeth, allowing it to condemn and reject any unconstitutional change of government and to impose sanctions against any member state for failure to comply with its decisions and policies.

But the fact that they held the 2006 summit in Sudan in the first place showed their disdain for human rights. The fact that they were passing the African Union chairmanship to a coup leader in Congo made them laughable. It was seen as a vital leap forward into the 21st century for the 'dark continent' with its tragic millions of poverty-stricken, starving, fly infested diseased people, and its coterie of elite, portly-bellied, bemedalled, ageing dictators.

However the African Union's failures as an organization were plain to see. From Rwanda, to the Democratic Republic of Congo, to Sierra Leone, to Nigeria, to Ethiopia and Eritrea, to Liberia, Somalia and to Zimbabwe, death and economic destruction continued to be the rule rather the exception. The reluctance of the union to condemn the iron-fisted governance of dictators throughout Africa had become the clarion call of growing numbers of people in Africa. Yet the Big Man discussed AU succession issues avoiding vital issues such as HIV-Aids, Dafur, NEPAD and human rights.

At every AU "Summit meeting" African leaders called for further trade liberalization. But, although they urge an end to protectionist policies in rich countries, African leaders refused to open their own markets to foreign competition. For example, the AU meeting in Libya June 2005 called for the abolition of "....the rich countries' subsidies that stand as an obstacle to trade." The meeting produced no concrete results on intra-African trade liberalization, however. That is unfortunate, because Africa remained one of the most protectionist regions in the world. Strikingly, other African countries impose the highest tariffs on African exports.

It took opposition master minded widespread bloody riots on the streets of Kenya in 1997 to compel President Daniel Arap Moi, who had ruled Kenya with an iron fist since 1978, to accept a constitutional amendment limiting the president's tenure. And when shortie Frederick Chiluba of Zambia, who had promised to vacate the presidency at the expiry of his second and final term by the end of 2001, started taking dodgy steps to abridge the constitution to extend his term of office ad infinitum, it took similar intensified opposition to stop him. In all this the AU stood by. By 2005 in the United States, the demand for a reassessment of foreign aid was becoming more intense as it dawned on the American public that their tax was going into a bottomless pit.

The AU and the South African government tried to justify quiet diplomacy by arguing they wanted to avoid antagonising Mugabe so that he will be more amenable to persuasion to mend his ways. This collegial approach was based on the flawed premise that Mugabe was a reasonable man who didn't realise that what he was doing was wrong. But Mugabe was aware he was transgressing all Zimbabwe's and the AU's human rights principles. He was doing so because he had to and knew that there would be no punishment.

Most African Heads of Government agreed that the British Government was the root cause of the problem, and called on Blair to honour the obligations to compensate Zimbabwe for the historical injustice. In sum, instead of demonising Mugabe, African heads condemned the British and the Americans and yet insisted that the Zimbabwean problem was an African problem which could best be resolved by the sovereign African people, using African strategies of conciliation within their regional and continental organisations.

Doffing their race-laced caps to an old revolutionary, African nations had become complicit in the killing of a neighbouring people. Taking action against Mugabe would essentially mean siding with white Western leaders, apparently a sin worse than genocide. To African leaders, Mugabe was a godsend. He was the master crusader against neo-colonialism and other stinking isms. He was the bulwark against the bullish West. He said all the harsh words against Tony Blair or George Bush that African leaders would not dare utter publicly. In the larger context of global politics, Mugabe was the weapon of choice for the cowardly.

Southern Africa has had a unique relationship with the whites, which makes it less receptive to suggestions from the northern hemisphere. Namibia, Zimbabwe, and South Africa suffered the horrendous last experiences of white domination in the last century and their memory of white exploitation needs no refreshing. Tanzania, though fairly farther off in Eastern Africa, was a 'Frontline State' against apartheid and other anti-imperialist struggles. It is not difficult to see where Tanzania's sympathies would lie.

Mugabe had tortured Tswangirai and boasted about it at AU and Sadc summits, intimidated and killed political opponents, judges and journalists. He had rigged elections to cement his preference for a one-party state. He had razed shantytowns where his opponents lived. Zimbabwe was not just an economic basket case. It was a nation of brutalised, defeated people. Dissent was met with violence and death.

Mbeki said Zimbabweans should be responsible for solving their problems. That was a very welcome statement but made in bad faith and full of deceit. He seemed to forget that the South African independence came not because political parties sat down and came to an understanding, but because there was external pressure for a political settlement.

From an economic standpoint, it was to the advantage of the South Africans for Zimbabwe to remain on its knees because this would result in companies and Non-Governmental Organisations relocating to that country. Industries, which lost confidence in the investment climate in Zimbabwe, would naturally relocate to South Africa. South Africa also needed about 69,000 senior managers, 1,000s of builders, electricians, plumbers, and surveyors etc to function properly. Zimbabwe had these in abundance and South African advertisements in Zimbabweans newspapers for skilled personnel were in abundance.

In addition, Zimbabwe had become a supermarket for South African goods. Zimbabwe, which was the only credible competitor for South Africa in the area of regional investment, had fallen behind its neighbour, which had ventured into regional markets unchallenged. This meant that South Africa could go and invest in emerging markets like the Democratic Republic of Congo, Mozambique and Angola, made safe by Zimbabwean soldiers' blood, knowing that it had no challenge. South Africa would favour a situation whereby Zimbabwe continued to deteriorate because the Zimbabwean economy was until 1990, one of the strongest in the region, posing a direct threat to South African ideological supremacy.

As members of Sadc, South Africa and Zimbabwe were signatories to that organization's Mutual Defence Pacts. Article 7 of the agreement stipulates that "No action shall be taken to assist any State Party in terms of this Pact, save at the State Party's own request or with its consent." Thus, Mugabe could continue to run a police state and his neighbours couldn't do anything about it without his permission. Conversely, if Mugabe felt that the opposition posed a threat, he could theoretically ask Sadc members to help him stamp it out. That is the only way to understand why Sadc leaders applauded Mugabe for beating Tswangirai. Of course, just because treaty language allows an intervention doesn't mean it'll happen. But, given how close the countries were, it was hardly impossible.

In 2005, South Africa and Zimbabwe established a Joint Permanent Commission on Defence and Security, which aimed to coordinate military strategy. At the commission's inaugural meeting, the South African intelligence minister, Ronnie Kasrils, stated that "The history of the liberation struggles of Southern Africa and the resultant shedding of blood for a common cause ... cemented our cooperation on the way forward in the development of our respective countries." Sadc maintained a "Regional Peace-keeping training centre" in Harare that had trained well over 1,000 troops from member countries

The socialist/nationalist mindsets (the extreme left) in Africa was becoming more dominant and Africa, especially with the AU functioning and being led by South Africa would move further and further away from the Western sphere of influence. One way it affected the Western world was in the demand for more money via NEPAD and the British African Commission to uplift Africa and continued calls trying to lay the blame on the West for Africa's failures. Socialist influence and failure was causing them to blame everything on "the legacy of colonialism" or the "legacy of Apartheid" and "slavery".

The blame game is a lovely political game to play; first lay the blame at the door of the West, then come with begging bowls and ask for money, money and more money. And the West would never be able to give Africa enough money to satisfy its greed and corruption. Of course, a large portion of that money would never reach the poor people at whom it was aimed but back in European banks. The West needs to give up on this guilt conscience. It was not helping anyone, less the poor and vulnerable and the despotic leaders were milking it for all its worth.

Africa was sliding backwards, economically, politically and socially. If the West was to completely ignore Africa, then it wouldn't affect the West too much although there was one effect of Africa's implosion that the West couldn't ignore: The continual fleeing of millions of people to Europe especially and America from Africa. This would continue and will get much worse over time. This implosion of Africa will be of concern because it is the West who ultimately had to help foot the bill. Civil wars were becoming more common and the West was playing a bigger role in sending in peace keeping forces (or financing them) into parts of Africa.

The African Union which is a model of European Union, costs about US$100 million per annum; a cost which most of Africa can't afford. The AU existed in anything more than just a name. Whites, through colonialism and domination, became a common enemy and it united Africans. But with white power broken and gone, Africans would return to fighting each other. The War in the Congo involved almost a dozen African nations and millions died and billions of dollars wasted. When it came to peace keeping in the DRC, Zimbabwe was not contributing even a cent or soldier. There seemed to be many wars in Africa that would continue for a long time, with the West only called upon to finance reconstruction and refugees after the Big man had made their pointless points and fortune.

In 2004 Tsvangirai was received by the Presidents of 6 African countries, with full honours that such visits normally attract to significant visitors and this again revealed a changing climate in Africa. Senegal and Botswana were fairly strong critics of Mugabe, while relations between Nigeria and Zimbabwean were lukewarm following Obasanjo's support for the continuance of Zimbabwe's suspension from the Commonwealth and Nigeria's warm embrace of disgruntled former Zimbabwean white commercial farmers. This came as a bitter pill to swallow for Mugabe, as Obasanjo had been an arbitrator alongside South Africa's Mbeki, in the bitter Mugabe-London standoff.

Even the UN had to get its act together when it came to issues of democracy and human rights. John Danforth, the U.S. representative to the UN, had this to say when South Africa, for the second time, blocked UN debate on Zimbabwe, "The message from the General Assembly is very simple. You may be suffering, but we can't be bothered. One wonders: If there can't be a clear and direct statement on matters of basic principle, why have this building? What are we all about?"

If a World War were to be fought today, then South Africa would side with the enemies of the USA; this was apparent during the Iraq war. If the USA wanted South Africa on its side per se, it had its work cut out for it. The West can't tell their friends from their enemies as most politicians in the USA and West believe the ANC were their friends. One day they will see how completely wrong they are as they will be stunned later when they see what, Mugabe, Mbeki, Obasanjo and other Africans really stood for. Mugabe was just the tip of the ice bag. The decay of Zimbabwe and of South Africa needed more attention.

NEPAD principles were quoted frequently by Africa sympathizers who advocate more foreign assistance, and they even boosted Mbeki's profile marvellously. Mbeki had become a fixture at the rich countries' annual Group of Eight summits. He had been treated by George Bush and Tony Blair as a player; America's point man in Africa. He felt emboldened to advance South Africa as a candidate for a permanent seat on the U.N. Security Council. The preparations for an ideological world war were being set and the connection was again the little African banana republic called Zimbabwe.

Mbeki was a centrist, intolerant and cold manager. His mistrust for the media, his refusal to open up to new ideas and his persistence on his so-called 'quiet diplomacy', all conspired to lend credence to this image. As the talks between the Zimbabwean belligerents got underway Mbeki's sorry image cast its shadow over the whole enterprise sending the signal that this could be yet another waste of time, diminishing into a shadowy exercise exhibiting directly, his personal attitudes, moods, views and flaws.

To Mbeki, the likes of Welshman Ncube and Morgan Tsvangirai of the MDC would do well to join Zanu. To him these were rebels who should be readmitted and not politicians with a different worldview seeking an electoral mandate. Mbeki thought the 1987 Unity Accord between PF Zapu and Zanu was enough and its only mistake was that it left out the young revolutionaries. Hence to him the MDC was occasioned by the frustration of the young revolutionaries whose upward mobility was thwarted by the unyielding seniors. So Mbeki's approach would be to convince Mugabe to create space for the new blood and prepare for the party's continuation after he left.

From the outset, Mbeki's agenda was at variance with the aspirations of Zimbabweans as he sought to preserve the revolutionary aspirations and to renew his own party back home while the Zimbabweans hope for a new dispensation free from the Big man mentality of the post-liberation aristocracy. That is why he worked in the shadows with no journalist reporting on his attempts to reform Zanu.

The Pan-Africanists 'ideological' positions of the Sadc leaders would never side with the imperialist West over their own brother. They saw no reason to support the West in its drive for regime change because they were insecure and didn't know what the future holds. The whole idea of regime change in Zimbabwe in the eyes of the Sadc leaders was a Western-driven idea, and the MDC was viewed as championing a Western cause rather than that of the Zimbabwean masses. Sadc leaders were not convinced that the MDC was the way to rescue Zimbabwe from the road to ruin on which Mugabe had taken the once prosperous country.

South African Xhosa nostras

"I said (in 2004) that the Zimbabweans were talking to each other and would find a solution ... they were actually involved in negotiating a new constitution for Zimbabwe, and they did and they completed it." Mbeki said 2006, "They had done this constitution, they gave me a copy initialled by everybody, done."

In the end we will remember not the words of our enemies, but the silence of our friends. LUTHER KING JR.

South Africa was spared the post-independence trauma that most African countries were plunged into because Nelson Mandela prevailed upon the younger leaders of the new country not to take the path of revenge like was happening up north. To be sure, not all revenge could be prevented. Attacks on lonely white farms continued, with landless blacks claiming they had a legitimate right to reclaim their birthright. Yet, although South Africa was counted among the most violent places in the world, most of that violence was not steeped in the politics of intolerance personified by the Dutch-born racist, Hendriek Verwoerd.

Most of the violence stemmed from poverty. Mandela, for all his huge-heartedness, could not make a dent on the poverty inherited from nearly 500 years of occupation. When he stepped down as president in 2009, Thabo Mbeki hardly had made much difference to the poverty of the majority of the people of South Africa. Mbeki's successor would need to be someone willing to take advice on how to end South Africa's major problems, among them poverty, the HIV/Aids pandemic and unemployment.

65% of taxes in South Africa were paid by less than 500,000 people out of the entire population of 44 million. That is socialism and it's backward. Crime, corruption and AIDS were spiralling out of control and government policies were making all of the above worse. If South Africa had a more committed progressive outlook, then it would have done better. But they weren't and socialism/Marxism was slowly sucking the country. Though it looked like it was making progress, South Africa was actually stepping into Zimbabwe's spore; the difference was that South Africa was moving just a bit faster towards disaster as murders spread from the cities into the farms unchecked. Though the economy looked in great shape, so was Zimbabwe's in the late 1980s and early 1990s. It would only take a threat from the opposition in South Africa to trigger the inevitable collapse as the ANC showed its true colours.

But in Zimbabwe, the infinitely much smaller number of white farmer deaths had created uproar whereas the South African murders were not common knowledge; international media did not report them and Western politicians had turned their gaze elsewhere. While acknowledging that there was no evidence that suggests the A.N.C government had sanctioned white farmer murders, it was still worthwhile to look at the reason why there was such a discrepancy in how the two situations were received and perceived in the West.

The reason why the West had latched on 15 white murders in Zimbabwe and skated over South African 1,500 murders was complex. There was an intersection of racial mythology, natural rights and entitlement, colonial history and legacies, politics of reparation and redistribution and ideology of private property. In South Africa, the contradiction of a country with a black leadership that protected a large body of white racist interests and a growing black elite, whose role was to give individual success the illusion of collective success, had yet to come home to roost. True there were murmurs to be found in the COSATU led strikes and the growing radicalisation of those calling for land reform in South Africa, but they had as yet to rise to an extent where they forced the A.N.C. into taking radical measures that would end neo-apartheid.

Therefore in South Africa, the myth of white skin, of a naturalized racial hierarchy, where class and power find expression through race had not yet been violated. And even though the murders were atrociously high, because the A.N.C. government had not made it a matter of conscious policy to violate this socio-economic order, the murders could be ignored. It is a paradox of sorts. To put it crudely, in South Africa, white lives were being taken, but white property was not.

Zimbabwe on the other hand had violated the myth that naturalizes racial hierarchy. It seems, therefore, that Zimbabwe's original sin was indicating to a world full of oppressed blacks and racist whites that there is nothing inviolable in the myth. More than threaten the whites in their very own homes, in Zimbabwe white natural right to vast land and property was being threatened as a matter of governmental policy.

It is important to briefly note that Zimbabwe, while threatening white property and life had not violated the basic principles of capitalism, family values and Christianity. Capitalism in general was well and alive ideologically. What had been threatened was white monopoly but monopoly over the production of wealth remained alive. There were still whole sections of Harare and suburbs that were predominantly white. Certainly, Western media and politicians had drummed up the racial-nationalism that had been unleashed on Zimbabwe. President Bush, Prime Minister Blair, Merdoch, the BBC and the New York Times were, rightly or wrongly, at the forefront of the save white Zimbabwe agenda.

In Zimbabwe, eleven million black Zimbabweans suffered under the rule of an undemocratic, exploitative elite and of repressive state machinery serving the class interests of a few tens of thousands of well-connected bureaucrats, military, and paramilitary leaders. And this was in the context of unprecedented economic crisis. In South Africa, it was not difficult to posit a similar trajectory of material decline, ruling-party political illegitimacy and ascendant opposition, as the rand crashed by more than 50 percent over a two-year period and trade union critiques of neo-liberal policies hardened.

In South Africa political power may have been handed over to the blacks, but in terms of ordinary life the whites still had it made and very blatantly and offensively so. The whites, who still wielded economic power, won't allow economic power into black hands, and if they reach the conclusion that the necessary degree of radical redistribution and/or expropriation was unavoidable, they will get out, taking their money with them. Such then will be the passions released that no democratic government will be able to contain them. Nothing short of a sledgehammer will work and South Africa's Mugabe would rise and shine in the Rainbow Nation.

A grievance so profound and so deeply rooted cannot be put to rights democratically, by due process, within the law. The blunt truth was that henceforth the white minority were fated to be obvious scapegoats for anything that went seriously wrong in South Africa. As soon as Mugabe got into trouble, he turned on his white minority; so it will be in South Africa.

Justice Minister Charles Nqakula who described whites who criticized Mbeki's lack of policies as unpatriotic moaners said, "They can continue to whinge until they're blue in the face or they can simply leave the country." Over a million whites left South Africa by 2006, more than 1,600 farmers killed and millions of blacks lived in the shadow of lawless gangs. Christian leaders were pleading with their arrogant and aloof president to do something. In Zimbabwe, it was government policy that created the conditions in which farmers were killed. In South Africa lack of government policy led to the conditions in which 1,600 farmers had been killed and millions of Aids sufferers to die. It was part of the same movement.

Mbeki wanted to make Africa as a whole stable, democratic and less poor, and this was a good moment to try. By 2005 he had the ear of world leaders. George Bush called him America's "point man" in Africa, and seemed inclined to channel more aid and help. Late 2004, Britain's finance minister toured the continent to promote the ill-thought out Britain's Commission for Africa. And indeed it was Britain's as Africa was not to deposit anything into this Fund. Mbeki's side of the ANC wanted annual aid from rich countries doubled to $100 billion and poor-country debt worth $80 billion to be written off, much of it to Africa's benefit.

Only Mbeki, who though himself was still unknown to many Africans, stood much chance of influencing other leaders on the continent. And yet he had extremely worryingly autocratic and reactionary instincts, which were clearly on display in the way he ran his own country. If they were a clue to his future leadership, then the hugely ambitious plans of the developed world could probably be consigned to the dustbin brimful with previous ideas marked "Save Africa".

Abroad, Mbeki was willing to use his weight to knock heads together in the name of peace. It was often a losing game, but at least he tried. By 2005 he had been to Kenya, Sudan, Congo, Gabon and Côte d'Ivoire for peace parleys and truce-signings. 2003-4 he made 22 trips inside Africa. If the continent was becoming less bloody, it was sometimes nothing to do with him. But in other places, especially Congo, his efforts had made a difference. In 2004 his spies foiled a coup plot against Equatorial Guinea. The year before, he helped organise the exit of Charles Taylor, a brutal tyrant, from Liberia and helped reverse a coup in São Tome and Principe. He hosted talks between warring parties in Burundi, Côte d'Ivoire and elsewhere. He used his influence to nudge leaders in Zambia, Malawi, Namibia and Mozambique to quit office when their constitutions or voters said so.

Yet he had notably failed on Zimbabwe, which he likened to the intractable problems of Northern Ireland. Sadc and the South African government in particular had been attempting to walk the tightrope of keeping South Africa's continental ambitions alive by not coming out in opposition to Africa's popular Mugabe's regime without totally sacrificing Western support. It was reflected in Foreign Minister Dlamini-Zuma statement that Zanu was a "progressive" regime, which she considered beyond criticism. The main concern of Mbeki was to preserve quiet diplomacy, which meant trying ineffectually to find a graceful exit for Mugabe, without letting Tsvangirai take over.

The South African government had no drive to do anything serious about the situation across the Limpopo as its dominant political elites were not affected by it. Those elites were only concerned with wealth redistribution, and the millions of Zimbabwean refugees pouring into South Africa only affected the country's poor, who had to compete with them for jobs. In that situation there was no need for South Africa to take any action about what was happening in Zimbabwe because it didn't affect their interests.

The South African president's stance over AIDS might have been forgiven as unfortunate ignorance but tolerating Mugabe was seen as either plain stupidity or deliberately condoning the dictator. Africa's failure to deal with the Zimbabwe crisis proved its leaders were either unable or unwilling to tackle problems in their own backyard which had a huge bearing on Nepad and other programmes for political and socio-economic renewal. The collapse of "quiet diplomacy" was also part of Mbeki's legacy in regional politics.

On a balance sheet therefore, Mbeki's policy was a failure insofar as it did not change the situation in Zimbabwe. The point was it did not resolve the situation but left it far worse than it was in 2000 when he started dabbling in the Zimbabwean issue. But in the end Mbeki's failure stemmed largely from his inability to realise that in international politics, diplomacy without the backing of credible and deliverable capabilities does not work.

Back in 1994, when South Africa gained independence, whites of South Africa, and particularly the Afrikaners, thought they had a deal: if they gave up political power, their position would be guaranteed. Nelson Mandela went out of his way to court the Afrikaners. He spoke excellent Afrikaans and had several close Afrikaner friends and advisers.

Thabo Mbeki came from a different generation, and a different background. Most of his life was spent in exile, much of it in Britain and Zambia and was never a frontline combatant. In the ANC, he was often seen as a remote outsider and more of an intellectual. He knew it did him no harm to criticize the unreconstructed attitudes of many whites. Little things as well as more important ones continued to grate on the white community. White South Africans hoped the capital would keep its old name, Pretoria. But under the ANC it had been renamed Tshwane. Black empowerment, which was essential if the country was to prosper, meant that whites were losing their jobs throughout the economy. Crime seemed as bad as ever, yet the government sometimes gave the impression it was just a white myth.

Just as what happened in every other African country more and more whites were leaving South Africa; some temporarily, some for good. Although it is essential to bring black people into the economy in large numbers, South Africa was in danger of losing the talents of its whites, who often felt it was no longer their country. Perhaps it was inevitable. Until less than 1994, black people were still legally inferior in South Africa. The apartheid system was just as cruel and stupid as its critics maintained, and simply handing over political power was not enough to wash away the after-effects. Plenty of whites understood this.

Most young white South Africans, and particularly Afrikaans-speaking ones, seemed fully committed to living in a society where the colour of people's skin was of no importance whatever. They were proud of their country, and wanted to make it better. Most of those who were living in Britain or other countries were determined to go 'home' as soon as they could. But this would not happen if the ANC reversed all its principles and regarded South Africa as essentially a black people's country, where everyone else lives on sufferance.

He was no "Big Man" like the others north of him, but Mbeki was undoubtedly Africa's most powerful politician. Earnest, academic and remote, he lacked the charisma of his predecessor, Nelson Mandela. Yet, under him, the African National Congress (ANC) scooped a record 70% in April 2004 election, and his poll ratings were ever high. By 2005 he still had 3 years in office, presiding over Africa's richest and best-organised country. The ANC had managed to subordinated Parliament to the party and squashed and frustrated both it's own and opposition MPs' aspirations to make law and oversee the executive just as Mugabe and Zanu had done in Zimbabwe.

The South African public broadcaster was training its reporters as performing lap dogs, and the official opposition's representatives were unjustifiably and routinely ridiculed and bullied within and outside South African boarders. The ANC declared it's intention to extend it's influence to "all levels of power" to counter potential sabotage by "forces opposed to transformation" and was poised to strike at the White enemy and imperialists.

Unlike Zanu before it, the ANC project began from an alternative understanding of freedom and democracy, rather than from an antagonism towards those values. All conceptions of what it is to be free share the underlying idea that freedom is diminished when black people are unable to realise their intentions. The liberal tradition, understands liberty as the absence of external and personal constraints on our ability to act as we please. On this view, Africans are un-free when states fail to respect and protect a realm of individual liberty defined by our civil and political rights and by our right to enjoy our property due to poverty.

ANC veterans were likewise alert to the importance of political freedom. However, their experience of apartheid and their extended immersion in socialist and developmental traditions had convinced them of the limitations of the liberal ideal. To them constraints on freedom need not be external and personal. To protect rights and liberties is never enough. A consequent lack of self-belief, until redressed, is a powerful constraint on a person's ability to realise his or her purposes. Thus even if blacks are no longer denied political rights, their lack of assets and skills may still leave them effectively in chains.

Rather than celebrating democratic elections, constitutionalism and political rights as triumphs in themselves, the ANC viewed these as instruments in a larger struggle: the "national democratic revolution" towards "the creation of a non-racial, non-sexist, democratic and united Africa". Second, the democratic revolutionary project had helped neutralise the potential for dramatic ideological polarisation within the ANC. The ANC had used the language of national democratic revolution to protect the wealthy from revolt by the poor. Many communities languish in poverty, appalled at inequality and poor public services. Yet the revolutionary timetable dictates that fiscal prudence and minimal redistribution is needed "in the current phase", when international capitalism must still be accommodated. Communist intellectuals introduced the doctrine to the ANC to avert the destruction of socialist ambitions and organised labour by rapacious nationalist elites

Sadly, notwithstanding its achievements, the doctrine has two overriding weaknesses. First, the political accommodation that it accomplishes between diverse interests and values lacks intellectual and moral coherence. It may lead to the worst of all worlds: a messy compromise between over-regulated labour, rocketing social welfare expenditure, and rampant elite enrichment. Second, the moral authority of the revolutionary conception of democracy inevitably comes at the expense of respect for liberal institutions and political rights. In the face of grinding poverty and entrenched historical disadvantage, political liberty and its guarantors in representative democracy and the rule of law, can come to seem minimal and impoverished achievements.

The ANC is really an amalgam of three political institutions; the ANC itself, COSATU and the South African Communist Party (SACP). While the ANC drew its intellectual and other strengths from within, its real political muscle was drawn from the SACP and COSATU. In fact in this political game COSATU was the senior figure with its 2 million members and national infrastructure.

The real testing of liberal institutions would come when the ANC finally faced a genuine electoral challenge. Suddenly the incentives to obstruct free political activity, stifle editorial independence and curtail political freedoms would escalate. In such circumstances the lack of genuine enthusiasm for liberal democratic ideas and institutions, instilled across generations of revolutionary equivocation, could prove liberal democracy's undoing.

Now that the struggle against apartheid was over, the unifying forces that this brought to the ANC alliance had gone and in their place were the normal political forces of policy and programmes. The ANC was in power and with this had come new wealth and privilege; wealth and privilege that they only imagined in the days of the struggle. Not so for the poor working class in South Africa from which the membership of the SACP and COSATU were drawn. They were, if anything, more marginalized and felt left out of the new South Africa. The tripartite alliance was under strain.

COSATU had gone so far as to visit Brazil to see for itself what a "Workers Party" can do in a developing country. They were impressed and even came home with a draft constitution. This was blowing a chill wind under the South African President's chair. Mbeki hence feared that an MDC victory in Zimbabwe, followed by the formation of a government, which restores Zimbabwe's economy and their rights as a people and then goes on to be a real success in social and political terms, would have serious implications for the ANC itself. Zimbabwe's needs as a country were hence being subordinated to these perceived ANC interests.

For example, Mbeki's perverse stance on HIV/Aids, his insistence that immune deficiency was caused primarily by malnutrition and poverty, rather than a sexually transmitted virus, was ideologically driven. It offered a defence of the dignity of the black majority; absolved the ANC of moral responsibility and placed the blame for the epidemic back onto the apartheid era.

In the 1960s, very few people in the world knew who Nelson Mandela was. His detention was not a threat to world peace. The African National Congress (ANC) used every possible strategy, including the Security Council, to make the world aware of his plight. When the United Nations Security Council was asked to condemn the human rights violations in Myanmar, including the detention of Aung San Suu Kyi, the opposition leader, South Africa was one of the few countries that voted against it.

Mbeki had sought to portray himself as the champion of democracy and good governance, but his refusal to criticise Mugabe was rooted in his humiliating failure in 1995 to persuade Sani Abacha, the Nigerian dictator, to spare the life of the Nigerian activist and playwright Ken Saro Wiwa. That was post-apartheid South Africa's first real foray into African politics and it was a disaster. It was his own intolerant character, sharpened by bitter experiences as an ANC exile that had rendered him unable to criticise leading figures of the struggle to end white minority rule in Africa - such as Mugabe. He was terrified of laying himself open to taunts of being close to and hence a stooge of Western imperialism.

So as Zimbabwe began to implode during the late 1990s, and as Mugabe appeared to have squandered both political popularity and the legitimacy to govern, the ANC leadership must have looked north and observed the following:

i)   A liberation movement which won resounding electoral victories against a terribly weak opposition, but under circumstances of worsening abstentionism by, and de-politicisation of the masses;

ii)   Concomitantly, that movement's undeniable failure to deliver a better life for most of the country's low-income people, while material inequality soared;

iii)   Rising popular alienation from, and cynicism about, nationalist politicians, as the gulf between rulers and the ruled widened inexorably and as numerous cases of corruption and mal-governance were brought to public attention; growing economic misery as neo-liberal policies were tried and failed; and

iv)   The sudden rise of an opposition movement based in the trade unions, quickly backed by most of civil society, the liberal petit-bourgeoisie and the independent media - potentially leading to the election of a new, post-nationalist government.

If all such events had happened in Kenya, Zambia and Malawi a decade earlier, if they had ultimately misfired in Zimbabwe, and if the were preparing to happen in South Africa, then it was logical for ANC leaders to panic. At that point, around February 2000, three options emerged:

i)   Hunker down and mindlessly defend the Zanu government against its critics;

ii)   Or move into a "constructive engagement" mode that might serve as the basis for an "honest broker" role on some future deal-making occasion or

iii)   Actively support Zimbabwe's social-justice movements, so as to ensure Mugabe authorised genuinely free and fair elections -

176

presumably did not warrant attention; no doubt for fear that the last bullet would inspire South African trade unionists to do the same, and in the near future.

The ANC leadership moved from the first (all out support for Mugabe) to the second ("honest broker") strategy. Attempts during 2000 by ANC parliamentary leader Tony Yengeni, ANC secretary general Kgalema Motlanthe, and other nationalist ideologues to stitch together the old boys of Southern African liberation movements into a regional grouping, and Yengeni's own June 2000 parliamentary electoral observation mission, characterized by blatant pro-Zanu utterances, came to naught. Reality finally crept up on Pretoria: apparently the key incident that facilitated the move was the overreach by war veterans in April 2001, when for the first time they started occupations not simply of white Zimbabweans' rural farms, but also of white South Africans' Harare factories, farms and plantations.

However there is a very strong hangover of cold war era ideology watered by contemporary Western inconsistency and brazen hypocrisy that makes many Africans instinctively suspect any African leader liked by the West while adulating the one that is hated by them. Mugabe, because of the land issue, initially had a legion of support base within the ANC masses and rural areas of Zimbabwe and further across Africa where he was referred to as "the Liberator".

Further, there were disturbing similarities between the ANC and Zanu. The ANC had been far more restrained and reconciliatory, but their continued deep-seated resentment of whites was often apparent. They were also deeply intolerant of criticism and opposition and also quick to demonise their opponents as reactionaries and enemies of the people.

By mid 2004, a war of words had erupted between Mbeki and the Nobel Peace Prize laureate Archbishop Desmond Tutu over Mbeki's handling of the crisis in Zimbabwe. The ANC and its ruling alliance partner, the Congress of South African Trade Unions, were also clashing over Zimbabwe, leaving South Africa's ruling alliance on the verge of disintegration. So why did he have such an incredible, unfathomable, bizarre blind spot about Zimbabwe?

Mbeki and Ngonyama's response to the perfectly reasonable and polite criticism by Cosatu's Vavi and by Archbishop Desmond Tutu; the insulting nature of the remarks signalled an extraordinary arrogance and intolerance that made Africans fearful of what could happen when the ANC's majority in parliament was actually threatened one day. Mugabe said very similar things about his country's trade union leader to what Ngonyama said about Vavi. Mbeki famously despised the leader of the South African opposition, Tony Leon, refusing to respond to him or even to acknowledge him.

The parallels might explain the why. The main beneficiaries of the farm seizures in Zimbabwe were high-ranking associates of Mugabe's ruling party. In South Africa Mbeki announced one of the biggest black empowerment deals in history and the main beneficiaries were a handful of politically connected and politically active associates of the ANC, including chief party spokesman and head of presidency. Proposed deals by the South African black economic empowerment Nkululeko consortium to buy billions of rands worth of shares in Zimbabwe's Zimplats with the backing of South African banks had the blessing of Mbeki. Surely this is not the reason parliaments come up with laws to drive black economic empowerment, nor the reason voters expected when they marked their crosses.

The dominant tone and message of Zanu campaign revealed an inability to accept the presence of a legitimate national opposition. Casting its campaign as "anti-Blair" and demonising critical voices as "traitors", the Zanu president and his party continued to narrow the space for productive national debate. Like Mugabe, Mbeki also used party and state structures to bolster his own power and he attacked a mysterious cabal of rich whites who, he suspected "set the agenda" of debate against him.

Mbeki had a fierce desire for party discipline and centralised, presidential control and there were claims that the space for debate was rapidly narrowing, both within and beyond the ANC. The state broadcasting company was docile and uncritical of the government. Journalists, judges and others were told to work together to build the nation, rather than carping at the government or uncovering corruption. Many opposition politicians were co-opted into the ANC. Most alarmingly, Mbeki used organs of the state against party rivals. In 2001 he told the police to investigate three men, Ramaphosa, Tokyo Sexwale and Matthews Phosa for plotting to "overthrow" him, a typical Mugabe tactic. It was a ludicrous accusation, but it pushed the three men out of politics. Mbeki was creating a narrow "capitalist, black-consciousness party" obsessed with promoting the interests of one racial group.

In the run-up to Zimbabwe's election, when the regime's thugs were denying food to suspected opposition sympathizers, Mbeki actually undercut the international pressure for a fair contest. He expressed a serene confidence that the election would be free and fair. Fair enough. But he then allowed his labour minister, who was serving as the head of the South African observer mission in Zimbabwe, to dismiss the regime's critics as "a problem and a nuisance." He quarrelled with the Bush administration's description of Zimbabwe as an outpost of tyranny. He did everything, in other words, to signal that mass fraud would be acceptable and Zanu obliged him.

On New Year's Day 2005 Mbeki visited Sudan and addressed that country's government. If ever there was an opportunity for some peer-to-peer truth telling, surely this was it: Sudan's Arab leaders were engaged in the systematic killing of ethnic Africans in the western province of Darfur. Mbeki spoke understandingly of "the challenges facing the government," and reserved his toughest comments for the easy scapegoat of imperialism. "When these eminent representatives of British colonialism were not in Sudan, they were in South Africa, and vice versa, doing terrible things wherever they went," he lectured.

The last thing Mbeki wanted was to look like the bully boy of Africa, and although it was easy to criticise South Africa, it was not so easy to come up with solutions. Zimbabwe's opposition had failed to impress. When the opposition party split, Mbeki tried to bridge the gap by bringing the leaders together in Pretoria. Tsvangirai refused to attend the meeting, and then claimed he had never been invited, prompting an exasperated phone call from Mbeki. The opposition's ineptitude had left Mbeki turning to Mugabe's Zanu in the hope of finding a so-called "Zanu-lite" figure to replace him. But the Zimbabwean ruling party itself was bitterly divided between three rival successors.

Although some Western governments were cautious about the growing mood of anti-Western thinking taking hold in the southern Africa region's ruling elites, there was little doubt that Mbeki, Nunjoma, Mkapa, Qadaffi and Mugabe were in no doubt about the popularity in Africa of their anti-Western policies. The West was facing a dilemma when it came to Mbeki though. They took the view that he saved South Africa from a descent into communism and steered it towards global free-market economics and they saw Mbeki as the only game in town.

The West had been forced to learn that the only way it could influence Rhodesia and Zimbabwe's future was through other African allies, particularly South Africa. South Africa holds the key to SADC. But Blair and Mbeki incremoniously fell out over Zimbabwe at the Commonwealth Summit in 2003. Bush and Mbeki over Iraq. Since then Mbeki had shown little sign of changing his mind. In the meantime panicking and obviously red faced British diplomats carrying the poorly thought out and knee jack reaction Africa Relief Commission on Africa to the top of the agenda at the G8 summit found their route littered with prickly obstacles marked "Zimbabwe".

In reality Mandela had done nothing just like all the other African big man. His major contribution was South Africa was not turned into a blood bath. Mandela spent his years out of office defending Saddam, Castro and Qaddafi. He had never had a nice word about democracy, but plenty for Leftist dictatorships.

What makes you think that Mbeki's AIDS approach is apart from common world view? Look at the deal that Mandela's ANC did with Inkatha - a corrupt deal with people who had murdered thousands of ANC activists that lead to a division of the spoils of office. Look at the deal the ANC did with the Nationals - again the party that created Apartheid was allowed to join the ruling Party. There was no low that the ANC, under Mandela and after, would not stoop as long as it meant gaining and holding power.

"Hell no!" said Mbeki to all those non-Africans who dare to "instruct us how we should think, speak and behave, regardless of the dictates of our principles, our consciences, our best interests, our knowledge, and our dignity as human beings," Mbeki in March 2005 urging Africa and its institutions to take responsibility for their own welfare and troubles in sharp contrast to what the British were trying to achieve via their African Commission. In particular Mbeki urged the Pan African Parliament, to consider ways to "complete the anti-colonial revolution" in Zimbabwe; to adopt "appropriate socio-economic programmes" and to "manage the political evolution in our countries....to guarantee democratic practice."

Taken seriously, the policy attitude of Mbeki and his colleagues in the region was a dereliction of responsibility. His comments in early 2006 that South Africa would adopt a hands-off approach to the Zimbabwean question reflected a leader who had failed to demonstrate leadership at a time when his expertise was perhaps most needed. The size and importance, in political and economic terms, of South Africa in the region demanded meaningful responses from Mbeki. It was a serious mistake to blame victims of a crisis for the cause of that crisis. South Africa needed a peaceful region for the 2010 World Cup, not turmoil along its northern border. It was pointless to try to solve the problem by 'fixing' the migrants. The solution was clearly political. It required regional leaders to begin to approach the issues differently, with the real interests of Zimbabweans at heart.

The tigers vs the nights.

To those who beg, it's never enough.

"We envision an Africa where peace is known by all, where freedom is shared by all, where opportunity is expanding for all, and most importantly, where responsibility is embraced by all. Because we stand together with Africa, America today is helping more people across the continent to build lives of hope and dignity than ever before in history". USA Secretary of State Condoleezza Rice

The whole world was abuzz with the explosive economic rise of Asia, particularly China and India. In the process, all that the world had taken for granted about international power relations in the last few centuries was being turned upside down. This was the first time in the modern age that the Western world had had to look over its shoulder in trepidation at the first sign of real competition for power and dominance. It was no longer as unthinkable as it might have been just a hundred years ago to imagine a future world in which the centre of power and dominance is in Asia rather than in Europe and the Americas. Virtually every Western news outlet had some story every few hours showing the West's reaction to this new explosion and examining its implications for the present and the future.

The West, used to calling the shots, was undergoing a fundamental, steep learning curve in regards to dealing with countries that would soon be on a par with it but that in many ways were very different from it, and without any sense of obligation that they must adopt the Western perspective on anything. It was not at all difficult to understand why the West would be both excited and nervous about this emerging force in the world. We cannot compare monkeys and peacocks, but Africa's dysfunctionality and failure to thrive became more stark and inexcusable in the shadow of Asia's boom.

Meanwhile in Africa, Tanzanian President Benjamin Mkapa (Blair's point man in Africa) grudgingly stepped down November 2005, complying with his constitutional term limits. At the same time that Mkapa handed over power as required by the law, he urged his colleagues to discard the political system that was driving him out and warning other African leaders to be wary of the competitive global political and economic order because globalisation threatened to "..exploit, denigrate, and humiliate Africa."

This message particularly smacked of a return to the pre-independence rhetoric that made the creation of political kingdoms a greater priority than development and fed the overwhelming urge of many leaders to remain in power. No wonder President Yoweri Museveni of Uganda had cunningly severed all ties with his country's constitution since he managed to give himself a de facto third term. At a time when the continent strives to liberate itself from the expansive powers of postcolonial governments and the politicisation of society brought about by them, the real need of the day was economic freedom and human rights. Alas, the economic situation was so bad in so many African countries that young men were fleeing their own governments, trekking through the vast and dangerous Sahara desert and struggling over heavily guarded barbed wires to look for better opportunities in Europe, the imperialists.

What Asia was now reaping were the fruits of decisions and investments made decades ago. One of the depressing lessons for Africa was the certainty that just as much as Asia was benefiting from the enlightened leadership of decades ago, Africa would be paying for the colossal disasters of the Big Man era for a long time. Much of Africa is not only saddled with repressive governments, but they are also generally totally incompetent. Asia no longer needs to feebly cry about "sovereignty" as some weak African leaders do. That is because the fact of their increasing sovereignty, on the strong foundation of economic strength, is obvious to all and does not need to be defensively stated.

Some African leaders tried to compensate for their countries' growing relative weakness with a kind of rhetorical machismo abroad and a repressive bullying at home. Asia can increasingly assert its growing power and confidence more calmly because the world recognises and respects it anyway. This is the quietly assertive confidence that comes from achievement, not the shrill lashing out borne of insecurity, weakness, failure and doubt.

Globalisation can hardly be blamed for the fact that only 10 percent of Africa's trade takes place among African countries themselves. With 750 million people living on the continent, the potential for the expansion of trade must be enormous. Very little trade has been allowed in this poorest of continents where tariffs are almost as high as 50 percent and where highway robbers dressed as policemen, customs officials and corrupt politicians masquerading as warlords block the little free exchange that exists.

Did President Benjamin Mkapa of Tanzania know that African farmers use less than one-twentieth as much fertilizer as those in the West in part because import duties and red tape make fertilizer eight times as expensive as in Europe? For the same reasons, ordinary Africans pay ten times more for air travel than those on other continents. Every ordinary African faces innumerable government-created bottlenecks in any enterprise they attempt. As the government has become the majority employer in these countries, the range of employment opportunities has been reduced and the government's limitless public borrowing to finance cronyism has crowded out the private sector's access to capital. One would have thought that African leaders would be better advised to use resources to build the infrastructure that will increase the volume of trade within the continent and thereby improve economic activity. But Africa's rulers are too busy harvesting where they had not sown.

Asian on the other hand and India in particular were running a charade when it came to Africa. India values democracy and the rule of law at home but said nothing about its violation abroad in countries with which it expresses solidarity. India did not believe its own freedom complete until freedom had been fully gained in Africa and with South Africa's democratic revolution that process was now complete as far as India was concerned.

But what did India say about Africa's slide into dictatorship and poverty? What contribution had India made to the struggle by real Africans for the same liberties that Indians had enjoyed since 1947? The answer was absolutely nothing. India had practised the politics of solidarity with tyrants abroad while turning a blind eye to mis-governance, corruption and human rights violations. The rest of Asia including Taiwan, Korea, Malaysia and Indonesia pursued a similar policy of complicity through complacency in genocide.

Europeans and especially liberals like Britain's Chancellor Gordon Brown and Tony Blair believed the reason Africa had problems was because Africa was not getting enough money and help from the West. Time and again, you'll see Africa's problems do not stem from poverty alone. Many parts of Africa are extremely rich and in actual fact two of the wealthiest countries in the world would be Angola and the DRC in terms of wealth per square kilometre. How then did Japan, with no natural resources to speak of except good leadership and brains get the second biggest economy in the world? Even the World Bank, one of the few remaining organizations still doling out free money to governments, confirms that of the twenty countries in the world where it is most difficult to do business, seventeen are African.

Compare post-colonial Africa: In Rhodesia and South Africa for example, sanctions and a ban on material goods did not cause much damage to each country; they were actually an incentive to substitution industrialisation. But handed over to unskilled corrupt rulers and even with lots of monetary assistance and free trade the results are disappointing. The real issue is lack of skills, incompetence, dishonesty, bad leadership and corruption. These are the real enemies in Africa that need to be tackled through sustained peer review systems, constitutional changes and open, people oriented governments and leaders. The real problem in Africa was human resources depletion, corruption, Big man mentality and not material or financial.

Maybe the M15 and CIA were not doing their job effectively to inform their leaders before they had put their African aid budgets together. But in the early 2000, the whole of SADC region was on an unnecessary arms race. Zimbabwe, on the United Nations' blacklist of countries to which no weapons may be sold commissioned 12 Hongdu K-8 state-of-the-art jet trainer aircraft bought from China. The K-8s joined 4 MiG-23s (bought from Kabila of the DRC) and 8 MIG 25s on loan from Libya in exchange for nuclear technology stolen from the DRC, together with the 12 Chengdu F-7M. Mugabe also placed an order for a dozen Chengdu/PAC FC-1 lightweight multi-role combat aircraft worth US$240 million. With a higher payload, longer range and a more advanced avionics and weapons suite the FC-1s certainly set the standard for air superiority within SADC. The country also took delivery of fourteen MiG-29s and an undisclosed number of state-of-the-art helicopter gunships from Russia.

Neighbouring air forces had also been rearming quietly. Zambia received eight K-8 fighters from China. Two MiG-23s, two Mi-8s, two Mi-24s and 12 K-8 trainers were delivered to Namibia. Botswana bought 12 second hand CF-5 fighters.

Perhaps the most significant order for new military aircraft was signed by the regional alpha male, South Africa, which ordered 28 Saab JAS-39 'Gripen' fighter, 24 BAe Hawk fighter trainers and 30 Augusta helicopters. An order of this magnitude was a very clear indicator that South Africa intended to transform itself into a military powerhouse in Africa, south of the Sahara and the South African Air Force would become the undisputed lord of the skies with absolute air superiority amidst poverty and squalor.

Britain and the US may not be driven by malice nor was Tony Blair likely to be pursuing a sinister neo-colonialist strategy. The British prime minister might have believed that the colonial past belongs to the history books. The visit to Africa by UK finance minister Gordon Brown in late 2004 may have signalled a fresh look at the battered continent. He was coming to learn, his advisers said, after all, it was his first ever visit to Africa. He must have been a very quick learner, for no sooner had he landed than he was coming up with policy suggestions, ranging from a Marshall plan for the continent to more debt relief. All good news to the ruling elites and more misery for the poor citizens of Africa. And if Brown had taken back to London a better understanding of the continent, its problems and its sensitivities, it was partly because he was wearing his historian's hat. For Africa, its history has, for the most part, been written by its conquerors, and truth, accuracy and perspective are casualties.

There were no doubts about the UK's sincere desire to help cut poverty in Africa through The Commission for Africa project. But if African countries were to make the great leap forward, the manner in which bureaucrats and officials across the continent lined their pockets on a daily basis needed to be addressed. The Sadc re-armament was wasting five times more than the aid the West wanted to put into the region and if the money had been used appropriately, Sadc nations could easily have wiped out the debt they owed and fed and housed their populations for over 20 years.

Clearly, one problem is that food aid was very big business, worth US$3-4 billion a year, and therefore highly political. Countries with surplus food, like the U.S. and Canada, tied their gifts of rice or wheat to their strategic objectives. It had been used in the past to dump heavily subsidized grain surpluses to improve trade figures and to reward favoured groups of farmers and transporters. The European Community had made the link most clearly, phasing out food aid as far as possible in favour of cash grants. But there was a sense within humanitarian agencies that cash was psychologically threatening, even dangerous. Giving people money means letting go control and power, and it fundamentally changes the relationship between the donor and the beneficiary. Giving food may have hints of superiority, even echoes of colonialism.

When trying to rein in the misbehaviour of roguish regimes, be it nuclear proliferation, support for terrorism, or internal repression, the United States increasingly turns to a policy of economic sanctions. A quick survey: economic embargo against North Korea in 1950, against Cuba since 1962, Iran during the hostage crisis in 1979, apartheid South Africa, to Burma beginning in 1990, froze the assets of Sudan beginning in 1997, Travel sanctions against Zimbabwe in 2003, against Syria beginning in 2004 and against Milosevic's Yugoslavia, Saddam's Iraq, and Taliban Afghanistan.

America's sanctions policy is largely consistent, and in a certain sense, admirable. By applying economic restraints, they label the most oppressive and dangerous governments in the world pariahs. The USA then wash their hands of evil, declining to help despots finance their depredations, and wincingly accept the collateral damage that falls on civilian populations. But as the above list of countries suggests, sanctions have one serious drawback. They don't work well.

Though there are some debatable exceptions, sanctions rarely play a significant role in dislodging or constraining the behaviour of despicable regimes.

Sanctions tend to fail as a diplomatic tool for the same reason aerial bombing usually fails. As Israel was again discovering in Lebanon 2006, the infliction of indiscriminate suffering tends to turn a populace against the proximate cause of its devastation, not the underlying causes. Fed on a diet of propaganda, they don't know what's happening inside their borders or outside of them. By increasing their seclusion, sanctions make it easier for dictators to blame external enemies for a country's suffering. And because sanctions make a country's material deprivation significantly worse, they paradoxically make it less likely that the oppressed will throw off their chains.

The cornerstone of the US policy on Zimbabwe had been the Zimbabwe Democracy and Economic Recovery Act. Section 4 of the Act directs the Secretary of the Treasury "to instruct US executive directors to multilateral development banks and international financial institutions to propose review of, the cancellation or reduction of indebtedness owed by, or the extension of loans, credit, or guarantees to, the Government of Zimbabwe (until) the President's certification to the appropriate congressional committees that: (1) the rule of law has been restored in Zimbabwe; (2) certain election or pre-election conditions have been met; (3) the Government of Zimbabwe has demonstrated a commitment to an equitable, legal, and transparent land reform programme that is consistent with agreements reached at the International Donors' Conference on Land Reform and Resettlement in Zimbabwe held in Harare, Zimbabwe, in September 1998".

In the face of sheer intransigence on the part of the Mugabe regime to adopt democratic reform, the US government formulated and implemented a set of benign measures; the travel ban and asset freeze, in an attempt to induce Zimbabwe's ruling elite to re-think their strategy. To compliment the US commitment to democracy the US turned the dial up on rhetoric calling for regime change in Zimbabwe with Former Secretary of State Colin Powell putting Mugabe on notice, pledging US support for Zimbabwe's transition to democracy and Condolisa Rice calling Zimbabwe an outpost of tyranny. Following the Bush's visit to Africa in June of 2004, and subsequent consultations with Zimbabwe's southern neighbour, the USA adopted a back seat approach in calling for change, allowing Thabo Mbeki's policy of quite diplomacy and African Renaissance to take centre stage in Africa. Mbeki failed as he was supposed to and as usual the black ruling elites in Harare had out-witted the world's super power in a game of smoke and mirrors.

Britain and America clearly saw it as a 'fight to the finish' since a lot more than land was involved. Mugabe had not buckled and in actual fact rolled up his sleeves for more. He also warned Britain and the opposition in Zimbabwe that "..we will never ever allow ourselves to be colonised again, and we will deal firmly with those bent on promoting anarchy". Mugabe in fact accused the opposition of being an instrument of imperial penetration in the pursuit of 'regime change', and thus had no apologies to make for having used violence on the opposition.

The typical response to dictators who go about summarily monstering their own people is feigned concern following an isolated news report. Then the world gets busy doing nothing about it, apart from the occasional sports ban. Mass murders of civilians by their governments normally rate a mention at the United Nations and it will often denounce such actions, sometimes even in very serious tones, but in the end it will almost always do nothing. It's a hard job saving thousands of innocent people from cruel deaths. It would require setting foot beyond six-star accommodation with top notch debating facilities. Downright miserable that would be.

The vicious police beatings of opposition leader Morgan Tsvangirai and 100 others who attended a prayer meeting triggered a familiar response. Western leaders loudly condemned Mugabe's iron-fisted tyranny. Mugabe told the West to "go hang" and portrayed Western criticism as mere evil colonial interference. Black African leaders such as Ghanaian President John Kufuor whispered that the situation is "...very embarrassing". South African leaders spoke meekly about Zimbabwe needing to respect the rule of law. Zambian President Levy Mwanawasa said Zimbabwe "...was a sinking titanic", but it was for Zimbabwe to fix. Much to Mugabe's pleasure.

When Zimbabwe was suspended from the Commonwealth, Mugabe waved the race card, denouncing the group as an "Anglo-Saxon unholy alliance". So-called smart sanctions imposed by Europe, including travel bans on him and his cronies, had not so smart loopholes. Soon after they were imposed, the despot headed to Rome to attend a UN world summit on, of all things, how to feed the hungry. He zipped through London to get there and went through Paris on his way home.

He hanged out at UN love fests in New York, delivering speeches that drew a standing ovation when he talked about "...an unprecedented era of peace and tranquillity" dawning in many parts of Africa. Tranquil for some. His wife apparently still shopped for swank clothes in Spain. Mugabe was back in Rome at John Paul II's funeral and managed to snick a handshake with "I talk to flowers" Prince Charles. The more the West condemned him, the more he played mischief and the race card.

So what's next? The West stiffened sanctions to include children and companies linked to the Harare elites. Cricketing nations black-listed Zimbabwe. But none of that bothered Mugabe. Condemnation from the UN counted for something to old man. The old megalomaniac appeared to crave the junkets, the stage and the applause the UN offered him. As with its predecessor, the UN Human Rights Committee, the neat regional grouping of African nations acted as a block against action, effectively mandating UN failure on Zimbabwe.

Let's suppose the UNHRC woke from its pathetic slumber. A resolution was, in practice, meaningless; full of multiple appearances of "whereas" and earnest expressions of disappointment with Mugabe's evil regime, it would be about as effective as Hans Blix's very, very angry letters to North Korea's Kim Jong-il. 2007, Mugabe won a phyrric victory at the United Nations General Assembly to chair a fairly impotent, innocuous commission on the environment against Western protests. African countries rallied to Zimbabwe's support, perhaps precisely for the same reason that the election meant absolutely nothing in terms of influencing the thrust of the UN in any decisive manner.

Hence the USA had rightly placed the onus to revive the continent on Africans ourselves. Bitter experience suggests that even if huge sums of money were multiplied tenfold, they would do more harm than good. On the other hand, Africa was not saying how much they were putting on the table through savings and investment to foster development further. Neither was the continent to do anything financial for itself. As usual the rulers were supposed to do nothing at all, their usual past time.

What was now required was a continent-wide referendum on whether Africans wanted these Western debt cancellation actions to continue. Because if actions by Zimbabwe, Malawi, Uganda, Cameroon, Ethiopia and many other African countries are anything to go by, then all that money saved by these governments was to be used to kill Africans, would be back in foreign bank accounts the following day, or used to rig elections, buy partisan support or wasted on some useless schemes like presidential statues, palaces or self named stadiums and useless bling-bling war planes.

2004 Bush said in his speech to the world's democrats, "When you stand for your liberty, we will stand with you." But when democratic Taiwan stood up to communist China 2003, Bush publicly admonished it, siding with Beijing, a communist dictatorship. When brave dissidents in Saudi Arabia were jailed for proposing the possibility of a constitutional monarchy in that country, the administration barely mentioned it. Crown Prince Abdullah, who rules one of the eight most repressive countries in the world, was one of a handful of leaders to have been invited to the president's ranch in Crawford, Texas. The elected leaders of, say, India, France, Turkey and Indonesia have never been accorded this courtesy. The USA president had met with and given aid to Islam Karimov, the brutal dictator of Uzbekistan, who presided over one of the nastiest regimes in the world, far more repressive than the Taliban.

This does not mean to suggest that in all these cases the US president should invade or break ranks with or even condemn these leaders. There are understandable reasons why the United States must look after its security, as well as its political and economic concerns. But Bush suggested in his speech that there was no conflict between America's ideals and its interests. From an African perspective the record of his administration, as all previous ones, highlights the opposite. According to statistics published by the American Census board, American imports from Zimbabwe accounted for 4.1%, of Zimbabwe's export earnings in 2002, placing America as one of Zimbabwe's major export destinations.

America was not without peers in trading with the outpost of tyranny. According to trade statistics tabulated by the Indigenous Business Development Centre of Zimbabwe, European Union member states accounted for 14.6% of Zimbabwe's export earnings in 2002. The reality of trade agreements between America, the European Union and Zimbabwe, severely undermined the effectiveness of their collective calls for Mugabe to adopt democratic reform. Zimbabwe had also managed to sign an asset protection agreement with France. This explains the French government's invitation of Mugabe to Afro-French summit in 2003. For the impoverished people of Zimbabwe, who often went without fuel, electricity, health care, food and freedom, this apparent duplicity was tantamount to betrayal and was viewed as aiding and abetting Mugabe in his murderous agenda.

Americans believe that every country is great or small according to how much its economy can provide for its people. The US State Department, therefore, had done lots of research on the vulnerability of the Zimbabwe economy. Since the year 2000, US businessmen Reynolds and Brown and other associates had attacked Zimbabwe tobacco sales by saying that the quality of tobacco was below that of Malawi and Mozambique and that the amount of tobacco had declined to below one third of what it was. With this attack, they managed to reduce Zimbabwe's foreign income from tobacco from U$600 million to below U$200 million by 2005. Similarly, the US State Department issued three tourism warnings in two years, scaring American visitors from touring Zimbabwe, thus reducing foreign currency revenue inflows from U$750 million to U$150 million (1999-2004).

Unfortunately, the Americans were ignorant of the African psyche and the resilience of African despots. Nevertheless, they were by late 2005 following a scorched earth policy. As long as Mugabe held sway in Zimbabwe, there was to be no revival of the monetary value of the Zim dollar. This effectively killed the wealth and pensions of any Zimbabwean and greatly disrupted mortgage holders. The governor of the World Bank, C Wolfowitz, a Bush neo-conservative strongman, swore to teach Zimbabwe a lesson so that no other African country would dare follow its example. The Zimbabwe dollar slipped from US$1 to ZW$25 to US$1 to ZW$400 million within 5 years.

Zimbabwe, like many other African countries, was not servicing its debt at all; the US$7 billion in debt that it owed was virtually free money. African countries have had access to European markets on an extremely preferential basis for 25 years and yet only a tiny minority had taken up the opportunities available. Zimbabwe, for example had beef, coffee, tea, sugar and many other preferential quotas with the EU plus contracts to supply Tesco, Sansbury and many other supermarkets in the EU for its fresh vegetables and flowers. Zimbabwe exported manufactured equipment like batteries, DVD players, radios, TVs, VCRs, small planes, Wind generators etc to the USA and rails wagons, steel and iron etc to the rest of Africa. Zimbabwe had the most diverse economy on the continent but managed to destroy it for cheap ideological reasons.

In all cases, Africa was seen as a charity case, completely dependent on aid. Africa is thus an object rather than subject of any policy of engagement with the EU or the USA. USA interests in Africa went far beyond simplistic aid and humanitarian considerations. Africa was increasingly becoming a major supplier of energy, both oil and gas. The danger was this massive revenue was going to be squandered on useless Swiss accounts, wars, genocide, white elephant projects and useless propaganda.

An example was the Chad-Cameroon oil pipeline which was meant to be different. It was the largest foreign private sector investment in Africa. Central to the effort was a law assigning most of the oil revenues to reducing poverty in Chad. December 2005 Chad changed the law to include spending on defence. The World Bank promptly shut down its operations in Chad and blocked the overseas account holding the oil money. This was a sound decision, even though some thought it an overreaction, as if bankers were expected to invite defaulters on mortgages for a friendly drink.

Four months later, the bank backed off when Chad's president, Idriss Déby, threatened to close the pipeline altogether. The geopolitics was understandable but the political impact and moral consequences were poisonous. Direct military assistance would have been better than allowing the government a free hand with the oil revenues.

Western countries had taken great steps to protect themselves (in Afghanistan and Iraq), and had stirred up a hornet's nest when Israel jumped on the bandwagon by attacking Lebanon. Africans may rightly ask how the West can respond so forcefully to the deaths of 3,000 Americans in New York, Virginia and Pennsylvania on 11 September 2001, and yet hesitate to send troops into Sudan after the killing of 180,000 people and the displacement of two million others. How Israel could be allowed to murder 100s of Lebanese because 3 of its soldiers had been kidnapped yet Israel had kidnapped 5 Palestinian elected members of parliament and 9,000 Palestinian civilians.

Constructive engagement, which often sounds like lame cover for business interests, tends to lead to better outcomes than sanctions and invasions. It was nearly three decades from the passage of the first U.N. resolution urging sanctions in 1962 to Nelson Mandela's release from prison in 1990. Apartheid South Africa was unusually amenable to this kind of pressure because it retained a functioning multiparty democracy and because, unlike many other pariah states, it didn't actually like being a pariah.

Trade prompts economic growth and human interaction, which raises a society's expectations, which in turn prompts political dissatisfaction and opposition. Trade, tourism, cultural exchange, and participation in international institutions all serve to erode the legitimacy of repressive regimes. These forces contributed greatly to undermining dictatorships and fostering democracy in the Philippines, South Korea, Argentina, Chile, and Eastern Europe in the 1980s. The same process was arguably under way in China.

The United Nations was suffering from irrelevance and it had two great crises: one was of efficacy and the other a moral crisis. The Human Rights Commission, which had 53 members, nearly half of those members were dictatorships of one kind or other, torturing and killing their citizens and vetoing debate about it. It's a shame. Its predecessor didn't work so well either for the same reasons. U.N. as a peacekeeping force doesn't work well either. All you have to do is think hard about the fact that there were 7,000 to 9,000 Bosnians who were simply slaughtered in Srebrenica and they were killed with U.N. peacekeepers in the area. In Rwanda, there were 800,000 Rwandans slaughtered simply in cold blood by waHutus who were not provided help by the U.N. peacekeepers on the ground. In Iraq the Secretary General himself was supposed to resign over corruption charges in the Oil for Food program. Because of these, plus more UN blunders, the organisation won't be there in its present form 25 years from 2000.

African Gono-mics

"The causes of financial crises and poverty are one and the same; if countries do not have good governance; if they do not have a complete legal system which protects human rights, their development is fundamentally flawed and will not last."
James D Wolfensohn, then president of the World Bank 1999.

"You cannot rig the economy - it operates strictly on the basis of the truth."

A question is not often asked; why are there people who appear to support the ruling elites despite their obvious failings? People or entities that toe the line do so because by doing so they secure access to facilities within elite controlled financial infrastructures. Looked at another way, if they chose to reject it they would be creating their own parallel source of power. In this context, the parallel (black) market was no more than a refusal to succumb to the power of the Big man controlled financial system. If all the funds circulating in the parallel market were in the formal system, it would greatly enhance the power of those in control of the finance structure. It had to be destroyed.

By the late 1980s, Zimbabwe was overwhelmed by the rise of a new bureaucratic-financial elite within and around the Finance Ministry and Reserve Bank, unprecedented property and stock market speculation, an increasingly desperate search for external markets due to local stagnation, creeping but often definitive policy influence by IMF, World Bank, and USAID missions and very high levels of foreign debt, followed by diminishing capacity to control the contours of the economy.

The early 1990s witnessed domestic financial markets imploding, as international financial interests gained dominance in the local economy and successfully removed trade and financial restrictions. This sunk Zimbabwe into a profound economic depression. Droughts in 1992 and 95, unconstitutional, unbudgeted for wars and rampant corruption exacerbated the situation.

Since independence, all of Zimbabwe's national budgets had featured economic stabilisation measures, yet nothing tangible had happened. Initially, the government had 5-year development plans. In reality this translated to an average of an economic reform programme every four years. First there was ESAP in 1991, then Zimprest (Zimbabwe Programme for Economic and Social Transformation) in 1996, MERP (the Millennium Economic Recovery Programme) in 2000, and NERP (the National Economic Revival Programme) in 2003 and The 2004-2010 Industrial Development Policy (IDP). Then there was the "Towards Sustained Economic Growth" which formed part of the Macro-Economic Policy Framework for 2005-6. None of them worked as expected or will work because government allowed populist posturing to take precedence over fiscal prudence.

As elsewhere in the developing world the Zimbabwe government implemented a so-called "Home Grown" Economic Reform Program (aka ESAP) that was supposed to guide Zimbabwe away from socialist, central control, towards a market-oriented and less regulated economy. Zimbabwe then had an excess but obsolete Rhodesia era manufacturing capital, some lying idle.

In 1989, with the full blessing of Mugabe and Bernard Chidzero, Zimbabwe established "task forces" and there was extensive and very wide-ranging interaction between the task forces and the key players in each of the economic sectors. After in-depth inquiry and evaluation, Chidzero required his advisors to assess the extent to which the proposals were similar to those applied in other countries under similar circumstances and to seek advice of those within the international community with experience and expertise in achieving successful economic structuring. Based thereon, the government formulated ESAP and then solicited international support, inclusive of the BWIs.

African despots, notorious for doing nothing, had found a way of seemingly doing something. Implementation of ESAP was a disaster. To minimise the hardships, ESAP was to include the establishment and operation of a Social Dimensions Fund. That barely happened, with only minimal consideration of creating such a fund, and even more minimal operation of the fund. Zimbabweans suffered the foreshadowed hardships, but were not aided with the intended compensatory medication. Because of the purposeful, lethargic and apathetic approval to ESAP by the government, the years of the programme yielded little of the targeted benefits albeit made a lot of the elites rich.

The point was that in a country where 4 percent of the population owned 90 percent of the wealth, market approaches would concentrate more wealth in a few hands, thereby making the rich richer and the poor poorer. In 1994 the government doled out $50,000 gratuities and $2,500 monthly pensions to each of the veterans of Zimbabwe's 1970s liberation war without planning where the funds would come from. It also got entangled in Mozambique and the DRC wars and occupied white farms. What followed was an economic implosion whose economic effects had never been seen on earth before.

ESAP was stopped in favour of ZIMPREST launched in 1997 aimed at correcting the deficiencies of ESAP. While the fundamental thrust of controls remained the pillar of the strategy, ZIMPREST placed great emphasis on social development. Unfortunately, just as these reforms were being launched, Zimbabwe found itself in the throes of broad and unprecedented economic difficulties illustrated by the depreciation of the exchange rate of the Zimbabwe dollars against the United States dollar and an inflation rate of over 1000%. The trigger was a series of internal and external shocks that intensified the pressure on the balance of payment and buttered business confidence. The effects spread throughout the economy, with once more the poorer populations bearing the brunt of the burden.

In February 2000 the Zimbabwe Millennium Economic Recovery Programme document was released and expected to steer the country towards restoring economic stability. The Programme aimed to remove the fundamental causes of inflation, restore macro-economic stability, create an environment conducive to low interest rates, bring about stable incomes and reduce poverty among the masses. Again the poor and vulnerable came worse of and the ruling elites started to openly fly out of the country with bags full of money to Swiss Banks.

In 2004 a desperate and clueless government had come up with the 2004-2010 Industrial Development Policy (IDP), founded on the baseless and unprincipled principle of tripartite participation in decision-making and goal setting. Zimbabwe hoped the IDP would ignite meaningful commercial activity, arrest massive de-industrialisation. But the program needed labour's input and agreement, which was not forthcoming as the government and the ZCTU were already at logger-heads since 1989 and the ruling elites of Africa don't listen to anyone anywhere and the entrepreneurs were coward Mugabe praise-singers. Simply put, these programs were never going to make the average Zimbabwean better off as long as the discredited and distractive rulers were in place due to their lack of care, laziness, greed and corruption.

After the 2005 elections, and his wife having bought a property in Malaysia, Mugabe increased his rhetoric about the "Look East policy" to circumvent the international isolation. The so-called "look east policy" was not a policy. It was an empty political slogan necessitated by Mugabe's conflict with the West. There was no established framework for Zimbabwe's economic engagement and integration with Asian countries except ad hoc measures largely dictated by Mugabe's whims instead of economic realities.

Gideon Gono was put in charge of this so-called policy, but then crooked tea-boys turned Mugabe banker, turned Reserve Bank Governor, never made any sense, let alone economic sense. "Inflation and corruption have become the two major chronic diseases in our national economy but you cannot prevent or fight any disease without tackling its causes," the Reserve Bank governor said. He further said he had to eliminate the causes and treated the symptoms of inflation and corruption just like a medical doctor! He slashed (like the doctor he was) three zeros from the local currency and went on to print tons of useless money.

Lets have a small economics detour at this point. Lets look at Yugoslavia for the simple reason that Mugabe's troops used to be trained there. Under Tito, Yugoslavia, like Zimbabwe, ran a budget deficit that was financed by printing money. This obviously led to a very high rate of inflation. After Tito, the Communist Party pursued progressively more irrational economic policies. These policies and the break-up of Yugoslavia led to heavier reliance upon printing money to finance the operation of the socialist economy. This created hyperinflation. By the early 1990s the government had used up all of its own hard currency reserves and proceeded to loot the hard currency savings of private citizens.

The Yugoslav government operated a network of stores at which goods were supposed to be available at artificially low prices. These stores seldom had anything to sell and goods were only available at free markets where the prices were far above the official prices. All of the government gasoline stations eventually were closed and gasoline was available only from roadside dealers whose operation consisted of a car parked with a plastic can of gasoline sitting on the hood.

Most car owners began to rely upon public transportation but the Belgrade transit authority did not have the funds necessary for keeping its fleet of buses operating. Delivery trucks, ambulances, fire trucks and garbage trucks were also short of fuel. The government announced that gasoline would be sold to farmers for harvests and planting. Famine followed. Potholes developed in the streets, elevators and traffic lights stopped functioning, and construction projects were closed down. The unemployment rate exceeded 70%. The government power company had to order blackouts to conserve electricity. The hospitals had no heat, there was no food or medicine and the patients were wandering around naked. The government tried to counter the inflation by imposing price controls. But when inflation continued, the government price controls made the price producers were getting so ridiculous low that they simply stopped producing.

In October of 1993 Yugoslavia created a new currency unit. In effect, the government simply removed six zeroes from the paper money. This instead made things worse. Many Yugoslavian businesses refused to take the Yugoslavian currency and the German Deutsche Mark effectively became the currency of Yugoslavia. On January 24, 1994 the government introduced the 'super' Dinar equal to 10 million of the new Dinars. The Yugoslav government's official position was that the hyperinflation occurred "...because of the unjustly implemented sanctions against the Serbian people and state."

Mugabe, who leant a lot from Yugoslavian during the war years, had dismally failed to draw the line between his revolutionary, public posturing and reality. While it is a good idea to widen economic opportunities for the country, economic practicalities in the local and international context should be the guiding principle. It is no use trying to persist with a dreadful charade in the hope that the reality will vanish and be replaced by wishful thinking.

Such was Zimbabwe, whose ruler since 1980 was awarded a University of London MA degree in economics, albeit by correspondence. With an annual inflation rate of 4,000% a year, the nationalist leader who had cheated his way into power in at least seven general elections vowed to keep on printing money and not follow the "...bookish economics" of the Ministry of Finance.

Price controls that had been imposed by the government regularly since 1980, had not worked as intended. This was so because price controls are a reactive and short-term measure, which in the long term has little impact in keeping the prices of goods and services at affordable levels. Price controls lead to shortages of basic commodities on the market as industries affected by them simply stop producing those goods. The consequence of price controls was unemployment, more shortages of goods and a thriving parallel market. Mugabe threatened to nationalise all "...under performing companies", yet on the other hand refusing them permission to charge realistic prices, starved them of foreign currency, forced them to employ uneducated corrupt party cadres and always threatened them with compulsory acquisition.

Mugabe's response was straight to character, to blame everything on "sabotage" by retailers and manufacturers "unhappy" that Zanu won; imperialist and neo-colonialist led by British Premier Tony Blair. Mugabe accused retailers and manufacturers financed by the imperialists of wanting to incite the public into revolting against him and claimed, just like Yugoslavs, he was having problems running the country "....because of the unjustly implemented sanctions against the Zimbabwean people and state."

The developmental and stabilisation paths which Argentina, Bolivia and Brazil transversed during the mid to late 1980s are also noteworthy examples of how what may, per se, seem as intractable macroeconomic imbalances can be brought in check over very short spaces of time. In Brazil, monthly inflation rose to 82% between 1989 and 1990. Through the vigorous pursuit of well-thought-out macroeconomic programmes, the annual inflation rates in Bolivia, Argentina and Brazil dropped to single digits. Mugabe never visited those countries to learn how they did it. There have been many other countries which, during the past 30 years, have successfully achieved substantive economic turnarounds, including Malaysia, Italy, Israel, South Korea and, closer to home, Zambia. Clearly, therefore, positive economic transformation is possible, no matter to what low levels an economy may have degenerated.

The reality was that Zimbabwe inherited a set of international economic and political relations that still, and in all probability will continue to, heavily influence its future. Political relations are defined by inter-governmental links and are easy to refashion to suit the political agenda. However, economic relations are forged by a combination of a complex history and network of external factors such as financial-commercial links, international markets, commodity regimes and trade treaties.

The reality of the Zimbabwean economy is that it is dominated by British, South African and US companies that hold sway across a vast swathe in nearly all key sectors. It is not helpful to try to deny this on the basis of political calculations that would not bring any meaningful economic benefits to the country. Further the World Bank and the IMF are American institutions and hosting them was like hosting the USA government. They were not going to do anything against USA policy and USA policy required that formerly white-owned land be returned to its titled owners or there be adequate compensation. The IMF did not care about Zimbabweans or the Zimbabwean economy; all they wanted was to be paid irrespective of what Gono said or did.

While China had some investments in Zimbabwe and there was significant trade between Zimbabwe and Asian countries, these paled in comparison to links with the West. This discrepancy and dilemma can easily deteriorate into a crisis if a country is run by an unpopular regime preoccupied with inflammatory demagoguery that defies logic. Populist regimes always try to appeal, arouse and exploit the sensitivities of the people in the name of justice and economic equality. This is where Mugabe had tried and failed. His actions were motivated not by his desire to help the country, but by self-preservation.

Zimbabwe's sizeable government budget deficit was the main cause of the country's hyperinflation. The state was borrowing and printing money to make up for the gap between revenue and expenditure. Because the government had wiped out savings by borrowing at below the inflation rate, its only option was printing money. The second major cause of Zimbabwe's inflation was the loss of export earnings that had created a foreign currency shortage that was driving the parallel market. The third cause was pressures emanating from the high money supply growth, which were largely inconsistent with economic activity, supply bottlenecks and periodic adjustments to prices of fuel and electricity. These pressures had seen the demand for currency for transaction purposes rising.

Historically there simply is no other country that appears to have suffered such a sharp decline without having been militarily attacked by a foreign enemy or by domestic insurgents. A war had been waged in Zimbabwe, but it was not the result of an attack by an external enemy and neither was it because of an attack from within. What happened in Zimbabwe was best described as the effects of a ruling party decision to violently withdraw the protection of the law from a specific economic bloc. Then the same political party enthusiastically joined in the resulting looting and pillaging of the unprotected business assets.

Mugabe's criticism of the former governor, Leonard Tsumba did not relate to any incompetence or dereliction of duty, but to embracing fiscal policies anchored in tried and tested principles. Gono's style was almost eccentric when compared with Tsumba's. Tsumba's was a staid, sober, cautious and ultimately well-reasoned approach to finance. Gono's was almost as if it had been choreographed by the grubby Chinotimba, which it probably was.

Gono was behaving no differently from any military coup leader, mafia and pocket book politician in one. He was exasperated by government's failure to back his monetary policies with anything other than rhetoric. Farm and industrial occupations led by Dydmus Mutasa and some lunatic called Chinotimba continued unabated. Gono was isolated. He was still looking West, to the IMF, World Bank and Diaspora while Mugabe was facing East. Mugabe had never hidden his hostility for the IMF and diasporas.

Gideon Gono's call for 'Operation Tell the Truth' in his preamble to the Fourth Quarter 2005 Monetary Review Statement was a pack of lies meant to mislead the gullible middle class voters. He accused the media of being "..a penal tool" responsible for the economic meltdown. He said bad publicity had dealt Zimbabwe's tourism a "...painful blow" and tried to ascribe the country's ills to sanctions imposed by the West. If the introduction of another useless ZW$50,000 bearer cheque* was indicative of Gono's grasp of Zimbabwean economic realities, then Zimbabwe was in even more trouble than initially thought.

He conveniently forgot Black Friday, November 14, 1997 when the Zimbabwe dollar crashed after the payment by Mugabe of an unbudgeted $4 billion to war veterans, and then the dispatch of troops to fight a costly unconstitutional war in the Democratic Republic of Congo the following year. Both actions personally sanctioned by Mugabe without parliament approval or government budgets. The balance-of-payments position was already evident well before the imposition of targeted sanctions or farm occupations and was the IMF's call for years in the 1980s and 90s.

*Zimbabwe had had no monetary unit to speak of. Instead it was using 'monopoly money' that had an expiry date printed on them. Though this was initially a temporary measure, it became permanent as the country struggled and failed to raise foreign currency to print money. The bearer cheques were a world first as no other country in the world had ever been so ingenious.

Gono knew who the real saboteurs were and it was foolish of him to try to make anyone believe otherwise. The threat to property rights was not a creation of the media, nor was the chaos at Air Zimbabwe, the Mugabes' private airline. Tourists do not conclude only from what they read. They conclude from what they experience, they don't want to be thrown off the plane just because Mugabe and his cronies had decided to go somewhere they fancy.

Since his assumption of office, Gono had always used words meant to placate the suffering masses, whereas he was the enemy who had recommended some of the most heinous crimes such as 'Operation Murambatsvina' that left thousands homeless, jobless and much poorer than they were before. The same military tactics reminiscent of the way 'Operation Murambatsvina' was implemented were evident when hordes of youth militia and State security agents manned roadblocks and subjected Zimbabweans to all forms of torture under the guise of searching for bearer cheques.

As Zimbabwe's six-year-old hard currency crunch bites, Gono and Mugabe took the podium to shift the blame game from banks, individuals and the tourism industry, hoteliers whom had been their earlier scapegoats, to foreigners living in Zimbabwe whom they accused of abusing the government's hospitality by engaging in illegal foreign exchange transactions that threatened his economic turnaround programme. "Some of the purveyors of this trade are non Zimbabweans who have come all the way from their mother countries in the region, some from West Africa, South East Asia, and beyond, under the banner of the 'friendly' relations existing and being forged between Zimbabwe and their countries," said Gono. "We cannot, and will not, allow any shadow forces to interfere with, or derail our turnaround programme, which we are putting back on the rails with immediate effect," Gono declared. Which 'rails' he spoke of; your guess is as good as anyone's.

Foreigners from China, Asian and West African had cornered Harare's CBD putting most Zimbabwean traders out of business. Apart from the illegal dealings that the Nigerians and Chinese nationals were allegedly committing, Zimbabweans also condemned their cheap quality products, which had flooded the local market and had driven local traders out of business. But the blame game and the seizures would not translate into foreign currency.

The preaching Gono had reneged on an undertaking to reduce inflation and introduce 'real money'. He offered no apologies and appealed, for the umpteenth time, to Zimbabweans to tighten their belts. The price of belts had, like all other prices, shot through the roof and those who could afford them soon found out they had no more waist or trousers to use them on and the 'fat cats' found them too small for their portly bellies.

It was clear Gono was resisting the need to link politics and economics and was dancing to his master's tune, the master puppeteer himself Robert Matibili-Mugabe. But claiming that the media, foreigners, journalists, ordinary citizens, NGOs, Parastatals, cross-boarder traders, students, farmers, miners, manufacturers and Western sanctions were responsible for the economic crisis, while letting the bungling political elite off the hook, was downright devious. Equally, flattering corrupt army generals and their political principals by quoting their irrelevant high sounding nothings in a serious monetary policy statement was downright unprofessional.

The problem with the Zimbabwean average person is the lack of analytical concepts to determine what was actually happening to them both financially, politically, mentally and socially. A case in point would be by 2007 arguments were still raging in bars and other meeting places, including in the Diaspora, that Zimbabwe could go it alone and did not even need Western assistance. The amazing thing was some even went on to fully believe that ever since independency the country was self financing and that shortages of food, fuel, electricity and so on had everything to do with sanctions and draught and nothing to do with the land reform program or Mugabe's rule or incompetence. The average person did not appreciate the level of assistance he received from the Western world in their everyday lives in the cities.

Service delivery and the general standards of living of people in urban areas started to degenerate in 2000 when major donors withdrew financial support to most councils and local authorities. The withdrawal of international donors exposed most local authorities. City Councils in the past used to receive stabilisation funds from the USAID (United States Agency for International Development), Oxfam, CIDA, DANIDA, SIDA, Save the children, Unicerf and the World Bank for developmental projects and social welfare assistance. All Zimbabwean, as all African town and city councils cannot generate enough revenue to keep themselves afloat as all funds are diverted towards war, preserving political power and Swiss accounts.

So, the residents of Harare, Bulawayo and other cities castigated un-elected local commissioners running their affairs, but little did they know that the problem lay somewhere else far, far away; in offices, chambers and parliaments down-town Berlin, London, Paris, Oslo as they withdrew or diverted equipment donations and financial packages to more appreciating citizenry elsewhere in Africa and other parts of the world; to Tsunami and earth quake victims and New Orleans.

And the preacher Gideon Gono took to the podium: "If, as a nation, we do not resolutely stamp out growing corruption, especially among us people in positions of authority and influence ...we will soon discover, too late, that policy formulations, implementation, monitoring and decisions have been based on self-interest, racial overtones, regional and tribal considerations, at the expense of national good..... Economic opportunism is now at the heart of everything we seem to be doing day in, day out, and this cancer needs to be stopped as we open a new chapter in a new year full of new prospects," he said especially because an IMF team was due in the country the following week. He did not explain how he had come by the millions of US$ in his own overseas bank account and how he was financing his AU$40,000 per year children's tuition fees and expensive life styles in Perth, Australia.

In reality it was pointless to rail against corruption without addressing the environment in which corrupt practices flourished. Gono was desperate and shooting in the dark without a consistent and cogent policy in regard to securing foreign currency. His statement was not economic policy but merely addressed issues that had to do with morality. And still on that point of morality, it seemed the Governor and Zimbabweans had suddenly developed amnesia and lock-jaw as Gono was a self proclaimed Mugabe's personal banker.

As for the question why conventional economic theory was not working in Zimbabwe, the answer lay in a combination of unrelated factors. First and foremost was the explicit and tacit support of Zimbabwe's neighbour, South Africa.

Secondly, Mugabe had the benefit of an unplanned windfall in the guise of his 5 million disaffected citizens working abroad. Third was the blind eye that the Government turned on the way Zimbabweans kept their shelves stocked through an informal and unsophisticated train of 'runners', individuals who were given mostly black market foreign currency to travel to neighbouring Zambia, Botswana, South Africa and Mozambique to buy both necessities and luxuries. Fourthly, Zimbabwe was not finding it too difficult to sell its deposits of chrome, gold, silver, platinum, copper, asbestos and believe it or not diamonds.

Parastatals

Zimbabwe had more than 30 parastatals, a crony infested monstrous bureaucracy which gobbled up a huge chunk of the national budget, and a bunch of bloated and incompetently-run industries which had been so steeped in corruption since independence nobody could calculate accurately how much they had cost the tax payer, yet offered essential services to the economy. Some of the strategic, but most under performing parastatals included the National Railways of Zimbabwe, ZUPCO (National bus company), Air Zimbabwe, the Zimbabwe Electricity Supply Authority (ZESA aka Zimbabwe Electricity Sometimes Authority), the Zimbabwe Iron and Steel Company (ZISCO), the Agricultural Rural Development Authority (ARDA), the National Oil Company of Zimbabwe (NOCZIM), the Grain Marketing Board (GMB), Zimbabwe Broadcasting Holdings (ZBH). Cotton, Milk and social services, health and education boards.

All parastatals in the country were ill managed by corrupt teams that were appointed by corrupt ministers, to whom they owed loyalty and for whom they would bent over backwards to please and safeguard their interests. Some had even lined their pockets in addition to running down the parastatals. These institutions were set-up to pro-up Zanu and to get jobs for 'right thinking' well connected people.

Air Zimbabwe (aka Tendawasvika; Thank God we are there) inherited 20 functioning and profitable aeroplanes from Air Rhodesia at independence. By 2006 it had three old, oil licking machines and some Chinese donations that didn't fly so well.

The national airline had witnessed a high turnover of chief executive officers and skilled workers. Most, if not all, chief executives were appointed not on merit, but on party patronage, regionalism, favouritism and tribalism. The result was chaos of the highest order where business ethics were ignored totally. At times the airline was run like the personal property of the Mugabes. The Minister of Transport and Communications (who was awarded a master's degree yet he had failed his examinations) should have just resigned. It was chaos.

If there was a Parastatal disaster you need only look at the brother-in-law of Mugabe's run ZESA. By May 2005 Zimbabwe was plunged into darkness as power stations broke down and with no foreign currency for spares, the situation became long term. South Africa's Eskom terminated electricity exports to the region in 2007 because it was bungling big time as well. The need for new infrastructure could be lessened if ZESA could optimise the use of existing facilities but ZESA found it difficult to source funding for new projects when it was failing to repair and maintain existing plants. It needed US$4 billion.

There had been plans to expand Kariba power station so that it produced an extra 300 MW. On Mugabe's orders, ZESA entered an ill-fated deal with Malaysia's YTL in the hope of expanding generation at Hwange by an extra 333 MW but nothing came of it; but Mugabe and Sahuto, who had become major share holders, benefited. The attempt was part of an earlier "Look East" policy. It was a disaster and it scared away other potential investors in the country's power sector.

The Batoka project, with a potential of 800 MW, and on the drawing boards for over 40 years was expected to go on stream in 2010 but that would not happen. Plans to develop the 1,400 MW Gokwe North plant, in which ZESA was in partnership with Rio Tinto and government, had also been deferred. The power station should have been built in 1990. If Rio were to externalise the profits it made, it would be less than what the country was externalising every month paying external sources. It would be less than the elites were externalising without doing anything.

The failure of the three huge capital projects to get off the ground typified the state of industry in Zimbabwe. There was no new investment of note coming into the country.

ZESA's finances were a victim of the country's bad politics and corruption. Considering the strategic position electricity occupies in industry and commerce, the energy deficit that had been exacerbated by the shortage of petrol and diesel was now a major threat to economic regeneration. Piecemeal measures that had been proffered by the parastatals and government had not made an impact. With limited resources to hand, the parastatal had been left to wait for handouts from the fiscus resulting in inadequate upgrades and network maintenance. The results were manifest in the broken-down of plant and equipment.

But Zimbabwe's energy sector was not suffering simply because the country was broke. The parastatal had been riddled with controversy since its unbundling. It had gone on a huge rural electrification drive without developing new power sources and it had sought deals with the Chinese, the Malaysians, Libyans and Iranians with very little to show for it. ZESA had become a political playing field where prudent business decisions had been superseded by political posturing. No energy minister had been able to solve the country's energy crisis. It was bound to get worse and ZESA was to bring the economy down with it.

Interestingly it seems African Big men had failed to link electricity (energy), de-colonisation and development. Africa continued to export huge amounts of oil to the Western world yet failed to realise that if people had electricity and fuel the development would be easier to achieve.

The point is, if people at the top, people who should lead by example are not themselves up to scratch, what do you expect of their subordinates? Like many of the parastatals in deep financial crisis, the GMB had been used more or less as an illicit milk cow for the Zanu high echelon. African governments must know that farming is not a philanthropic endeavour. Every potential farmer is in it for profit. To expect them to be motivated simply by the "national duty" of feeding the nation is unrealistic.

So what needs to be done to kick start the economy again?

The parastatal sector should evolve into contract systems for engagement of top management, where each contract is renewable upon satisfactory performance with remuneration being performance related. For meaningful investment to flow into the country, particularly in the strategic parastatal community it is imperative that government rids itself of the gross mentality of entitlement where management resist implementation of prudent turnaround strategies clinging to the past with no sound financial management norms.

For the economy to grow, governments must show that they are committed to stopping violence, restore the rule of law and respect private property. Those in positions of authority and power should be held accountable to those they are supposed to serve and a free media is fundamental to ensuring such accountability. Both The Public Order and Security Act (POSA) that allows police to restrict freedom of assembly and the Access to Information and Protection of Privacy Act (AIPPA) widely seen as a bid to muzzle independent journalists, were contrary to international treaties Zimbabwe was a signatory of and scare off investors. Investors like a third view. Both were bad laws and should have been scrapped.

What was extremely important was to reduce significantly the political temperature and equally reduce the intensity and volume of populist rhetoric that accompanied many government actions. Nobody wants to visit a rogue state where they could be targeted by government supporters because of their presumed country of origin or colour of their skin.

Appoint a Special Investment Advisor from an Investment Bureau to run behind all the regulatory approvals and paperwork for foreign investors, from visas to work permits business certifications etc. Reduce the amount of procedures required to do business and centralize as many of the approvals as possible in a "one-stop" shop. Government and local governments should hire teams of technocrats to curb corruption by making the public accounts more transparent and physically auditable.

Focus Government's limited resources on fixing the basic infrastructure of roads, lights, water, sanitation, telecommunications, postal services and airports. Quality of life in doing business abroad is as important to most foreign investors as potential return on investment. US$300,000 spent on fixing the street and traffic lights in central Bulawayo will do much more to attract foreign investors than US$300,000 spent on Ben Muneshe, a crook, lobbying in Washington.

Conduct a massive domestic PR campaign to educate the public and government employees in particular at all levels about the importance and sensitivity of foreign investors to national development. Let people know that the US$5 bribe someone is demanding from a visitor could be the last straw that drives away a multi-million dollar investment that could have employed, fed, clothed and trained hundreds of their compatriots.

There is no doubt Zimbabwe has some of the most breathtaking tourist resorts in the world. There is also no doubt that, in normal times, it is a paradise on earth. What this country needed was to create the kind of environment that compels foreigners to tell their fellow nationals about the natural wonders waiting to be explored here. This is about ensuring that people live in a society where there is no siege mentality, where locals and visitors alike feel secure and can always count on police for protection, if the need arises.

Tap into the large pool of African Diaspora with a deep-seated and vested interest in seeing their own country recover who were scattered in businesses all over the world. This should be the Government's first line of offence in attracting foreign investors, both for the contacts they have as well as for their capital, know-how and access to foreign markets. And treat every potential Zimbabwean investor as well as foreign investors.

Government should encourage the attraction of labour-intensive outsourcing industries such as basic manufacturing, light industries, tourism, data processing and information technology. Appealing for equipment and assistance in high-tech training from some of the wealthy high-tech companies around the world who may see a benefit as well as humanitarian long-term rewards in having Zimbabweans trained on their products and services. Some East African neighbours were already benefiting from this strategy.

Agriculture should be given high priority for it's ability to be a source of large-scale employment, it's export cash generation and for the benefits of imports-substitution and down stream industry it can provide for many basic staples. Issues surrounding land reform should be dealt with through the UNDP coordinated Technical Support Unit and discussions between all potential stakeholders in conditions free of violence and intimidation. Land redistribution is essential for sustainable development and national reconciliation but the process must be guided by principles of equity (in terms of race, gender, access to rural infrastructure etc), transparency, participation, fairness (beneficiaries of resettlement are to be selected by clear process, and not determined through racist, ethnic, regional party affiliation, or anti-'foreigner' sentiments) and at the same time, a need-based strategy.

The Zimbabwe Government could ask the US and other Developed Countries to grant special holidays on profits earned in Zimbabwe to their corporations for the next 10 years to go along with the tax holidays the country was granting these companies on profit earned. Zimbabwe cannot wish away Britain and the European Union or North America because they are some of its established trading partners.

Mugabe and his advisors seemed impervious to this reality. We have to engage economically as directed by our national interests, not individual ideology or party interests and we should know there is nothing to be gained from irrational hostility or publicity-seeking showmanship.

There is no way a full economic recovery can be achieved when Zimbabwe is still isolated from the world's powerful economies and when multilateral lending institutions were reluctant to resume business with the country. The point in the end was trying to patch up differences with major trading partners and avoid self-destructive politics that undermined the very national interests that we purport to be promoting. One thing we can learn is that it is possible to forge successful links across the ideological divide.

Zimbabwe: The other scenario

"Now some of them are crying, saying they were beaten up. Yes, you will be severely assaulted. When the police say move, move. If you don't move, you invite the police to use force." President Mugabe commenting on the vicious assault and subsequent torture of ZCTU leaders and MDC officials by the police September 13, 2006.

In May 2000, speaking at a UNICEF function Mr. Mandela said, "Ordinary people, should depose leaders who enrich themselves at the expense of their countrymen by picking up rifles and fighting for liberation." He also said ordinary Zimbabweans were not bound by the diplomacy of South Africa and other nations. "That is the lesson of history. The tyrants of today can be destroyed by you, and I am confident that you have the capacity to do so."

Jesus told the Jews to destroy the temple and he would rebuild it in three days. There is an age-old theory that one must destroy in order to build. That is why in order to build new lives, old ones have to be pulled down. It is important sometimes to destroy the old person in order to live a new life.

Zimbabweans had been gallant in their struggle to try to topple Robert Mugabe and rescue their country from despair and destruction. It can be argued that the power in Zimbabwe lied in a zone that was beyond electoral formations. The majority of Zimbabweans and Africans were fed up with the Zanu regime and other guises all over the continent, but for many reasons, they passively put up with the political rot.

Mugabe's state machine was simply too powerful and corrupt to be defeated by weakened, self-pitying and demoralized citizens. The escalating humanitarian crisis required an immediate and forceful international response. Even by Lt-Gen Romeo Dallaire's standards, (Canadian commander, UN 1994 Rwanda,) warned there was urgent need for regional and international intervention to prevent Zimbabwe's political crisis from further deteriorating. He said lack of such action was a perfect example of a lack of political will to prevent a civil crisis. The right to vote, in secrecy and safety, must be the most important single political right a citizen can hold. It is by these means that they can change their leaders and the policies they represent. Apart from the gun or street violence there is no other way in which Africans can seek to improve their lives and protect their human rights and interests.

All Zimbabweans talk very politely, diplomatically and will not show frustration at first. It is not in Zimbabweans nature to throw tantrums and this is a result of 140 years of strong and hush rule by foreigners; Ndebeles, Ian Smith and Mugabe in modern times. Everyone was afraid of Mugabe's spies and Zimbabweans do not trust people easily. They will talked about what was going on and but would never get worked up and call for Mugabe's overthrow. They all acted in a very "civilized" manner, and were all genetically very diplomatic about things.

There was very little or no chance for an uprising inside Zimbabwe itself because the people were not armed, and Mugabe had a water-tight control on the army, secret-service and civil service who were loyal to him by giving them huge pay increases, land and threats. He had an extensive Central Intelligence Organization (CIO) network similar to the "KGB" and they were everywhere. The only resistance that could ever occur inside the country was passive resistance as that offered by the MDC. When it was formed the MDC said it was aiming for peaceful change and it did not want to engage in war. That had been the MDC's stance ever since. This was the official position of all opposition parties in Zimbabwe so far.

The use of violence to achieve political objectives had, more than anything else, been responsible for the chaos Zimbabweans found themselves in. Mzilikazi used violence to get a foothold in what was shona land; the colonials used violence to overthrow Lobengula and used violence to maintain their power for decades. Zanu and Zapu used violence to wrestle power from the white minority. Zanu used violence to achieve its goal of a de facto one party state and to suppress the opposition since 1980.

The MDC did not have sympathetic neighbouring states that would provide bases. China, the USA and Russia were not falling over each other to provide arms of war to the opposition. Most angry young men were reasonably well employed in South Africa and the UK and weren't exactly jumping at coming and sacrifice their lives in Zimbabwe. The people left in Zimbabwe were overwhelmingly weak. They were being starved out of existence and 1,5 million adults, the very group that would normally be on the streets, were HIV positive and very sick. Furthermore it is important never to confront any opponent in the territory it has the most expertise in.

The opposition were up against a formidable regime that was spoiling for a fight as it knew that was the only thing that could save it. If it had the distraction of conflict it would then be able to blame the economic collapse on that. The regime had no one to blame but the West and no one believed that. The regime also knew that it would enjoy the absolute support of its neighbours in crushing any violent opposition. But it had been perplexed by the non-violent methods used by the opposition to date. In other words aside from the morality of a commitment to use non-violence, the promotion of methods that may result in violent struggle was not even pragmatic. In short the abandonment of non-violent methods may even set back the struggle to bring democracy to Zimbabwe.

Thus, Mugabe was holding all the aces. The Zimbabweans in the Diaspora were clearly an unhappy lot. But there was nowhere else for them to go. However, it was the hope of those inside Zimbabwe that those who had fled would attempt to attack Mugabe from outside the country and thereby spark civil War that could overthrow Zanu. Most of those in the Diaspora were in their late 20's and early 30's physically fit and mentally they were motivated for military duty. Underneath all the civility and diplomacy was a lot of frustration, a deep desire for Mugabe and his party to be toppled.

Since South Africa would always support and prop-up Zanu, Zimbabweans were being backed into a corner from which they would well have to fight out. There could be a peaceful solution to the Mugabe problem if all stakeholders play their part even handily. Most believed in this cause, in the struggle on to the end regardless; they did understand that there was no revolution in history that started out with an easy chance of victory; no victory had ever come easily.

Militarily defeating Mugabe would be easy as the vast majority of the population were already opposed to him. There were 2 million capable Zimbabweans in South Africa, 1,5 million in Botswana and over 400,000 million in the UK. Plus on the other hand the soldiers could see the suffering of the people and they could theoretically turn on Mugabe. Corruption was rife in the Armed forces and this was of concern to the ordinary low ranking foot soldiers. A UNAIDS survey undertaken in 1999 showed that 55% of the then 36,000-strong army were HIV-positive and three-quarters of soldiers died of AIDS within a year of leaving the army. ZDF troops had allegedly been used as bandit soldiers to provide security to shady companies and groups plundering the Congo, which in turn had paid huge sums in bribes and kickbacks to some senior Zimbabwean government officials and ZDF commanders. They were not very amused by that.

Another mechanism which had been widely used by Mugabe involved the deployment of young Ndebele soldiers in conflicts where Zimbabwe was involved. In the early 1980s hundreds of soldiers died after they had been deployed against the RENAMO (MNR) along the Zimbabwe-Mozambique Border. Hundreds more of those who had survived the conflict died of mysterious illnesses associated with the drugs that had been administered on them before being deployed. All this was raising frustration in the army as well as lost pride of being the most professional and feared armies in Africa.

Apart from the grounded hawk fighter planes, a parliamentary committee expressed concern at the sorry state of military equipment in general, the shortage of accommodation and health equipment, the dilapidated army barracks and the collapsing sewerage system at almost all the army bases it visited. As a result of the huge number of soldiers, the ZNA had to accommodate some of its soldiers in former horse stables. Khumalo Barracks in Bulawayo were in a sorry state of dilapidation and disrepair. The new planes purchased from China had not yet been commissioned into the strike forces. It would take time to retrain pilots and integrate them into the existing Westernised air force.

What was needed in Zimbabwe was a dramatic event that would inspire an effective military challenge to the Mugabe regime. It could be a coup as thousands of soldiers were resigning from the army, signalling low morale and a rising dissatisfaction with Mugabe. These disgruntled solders could provide the backbone for a more organized civilian resistance to Mugabe. It could also be, as in Kenya, a group of dissatisfied Zanu MPs crossing the floor and effectively bringing down the Mugabe regime; university students and youths around the country staging mass demonstrations, or civil servants going on an indefinite strike, effectively shutting down government. Mass protest was still possible in Zimbabwe.

The World: the way forward

Voltaire said: "I may disagree with what you say, but would defend to the death your right to say it".

"I decided to be free. I have been here 18 years and I think that's a lot of time . . . I think I have attained the normal age for retirement, if I were a civil servant. It's time to retire… I think we (African leaders) should not be scared of not being heads of state or government . . . life goes on and there's a lot to do." Chissan, former president of Mozambique, 2004

The world had learned some things. We even have some valuable case law, from the Nuremberg trials to the Truth and Reconciliation Commission in South Africa to the trial and subsequent hanging of Sadam Hussein. But we haven't yet managed to persuade those who think they can slaughter people as a matter of policy that they will inevitably pay a price for doing so. True, there is justice sometimes. Killers from the Bosnian war were serving long sentences. Gen Pinochet may not have tasted prison, but he had not been able to live untouched by the consequences of what he did. The Argentine military leaders who ordered the deaths of 15,000 young people in Argentina between 1976 and 1982 had rarely been free of problems. Some form of tribunal was under way in Cambodia 2005.Many of those who took part in the Rwandan genocide had been arrested.

No one had yet convinced Mugabe and his cronies that they would be held to account for destroying their country and ruining the lives of their fellow citizens. Mugabe had been a welcome guest in France, and was at the funeral of Pope John Paul II in the Vatican even though tens of thousands of Zimbabwean Catholics were being oppressed and its own archbishop of Bulawayo was being personally ridiculed by Mugabe as evil.

The five "white" world powers clang to their weapons of mass destruction, refused to have them inspected, denying everyone else not "white" the right to have nuclear weapons and attacked other nations killing thousands of civilians on a vain global search for oil and liberalism. First communism and then terrorism became an excuse to kill with impunity as Sudanese, Bosnians, Afganistans, Iraqis and Iranian civilians were bombed and shot to death; imprisoned, tortured and killed as the sole superpower abused its position.

As international law stands, the main obstacle to getting rid of tyrants who kill thousands of their own citizens is state sovereignty. However, this concept is overrated. Invisible lines on the earth's surface have no moral standing and can't trump moral standards that are of universal application.

Part of the problem is that there is still no real consensus about what constitutes a crime against humanity. Some people think Argentina and Chile are better off without the generation of left-wingers who disappeared in the 1970s. There are those who think that people like Gen Mladic and Mugabe and those behind the Janjaweed in Darfur have merely had a bad press. The United Nations has been pretty feeble at dealing with crimes against humanity, because few subjects have more political resonance.

It is true that parts of the world have, on rare occasions, stepped up and said no to despots' mass killings. Successful interventions include Vietnam's invasion of

Cambodia in 1979; Tanzania's intervention to remove Idi Amin from Uganda in the same year and Nato's invasion of Yugoslavia in 1999. The success of these interventions and the absence of criticism of such action demonstrate that state sovereignty is no barrier to humanitarian interventions.

So when is humanitarian intervention appropriate? Humanitarian intervention should be mandatory in cases of large-scale government-sanctioned killings. The Security Council should be given the authority and responsibility to supply the necessary resources. If it fails in its role, citizens from countries ruled by despots should be conferred automatic citizenship rights to Security Council member nations; nothing like self interest to stimulate action. In the end, talk of no tolerance towards despots is just that.

African leaders tend to rally behind their colleagues, even against the persecuted people of those countries. Listening to Geldof and Gordon Brown was almost embarrassing in that their simple-minded approach to solving what they referred to as the 'luminous continents' problems smirked of racism. Choose any of six nations currently on their relentless slide into disaster and at the root you will find corrupt ruling classes fanned tribal animosities and ignorance to be the two main contributors to those nations' decline.

It appears that Geldof and Brown were yet another one of those self-loathing guilty, wealthy Western liberals who thinks that Europeans are responsible for all the world's evils and believes that only actions by the West will ultimately solve the continent's problems. The whole idea of predicating the solution of Africa's problems to Western nations sending bales of cash is an insult to the hard working people of Africa and, a form of insidious racism, assuming that Africans are incapable of solving their own problems. This patronizing attitude has long been the staple of Western liberals, whose core belief is that native peoples are similar to helpless children and as such need the resources of the industrialized West to solve their problems. It's beyond arrogant to expect the West to take responsibility for monsters like Idi Amin, Haille Mengistu, Dos Antos, Kabila, Doe and yes, Mugabe.

Aid gives Western politicians a starring role and it can lend a moral dimension to governments, which is often sorely lacking especially after an illegal Iraqi war. And if it is done with enough zing, it can divert attention away from failings at home. Give a little to charity, get a lot of political mileage: it's a seductive win-win equation that has been adopted world over. And we can see this theory at work today when Western politicians, needing a reputation lift, head quickly to Africa.

The secret of cause-related marketing is proportion. The act of fundraising creates a profile far greater than the good actually being done; but the target audience is often more interested in the idea of helping a good cause than doing any sums. In the end, African home industries flop due to cheap donations from abroad and slack demand; Africans acquire a dependency syndrome they cannot shake off; Governments lose on tax revenue; donation-distribution-conflict increases; post-donation the countries suffer even more.

The British-sponsored commission dodged an unambiguous demand for every African regime to constitutionally and judicially embrace democracy and fight corruption. More depressing was the report's coverage of corruption. In a continent where Gen Abacha, the late Nigerian dictator, was able to steal £4 billion in less five years, Dos Santos' Angola siphoned off $2 billion in one year, it urged Western countries to take "all necessary" measures to repatriate illicitly acquired funds and assets held in the financial systems of their countries. What about insisting that African governments stop those "illicitly acquired funds" from being looted in the first place.

Of course, it is true that Western countries rig their economies to keep out cheap African agricultural produce. The developed world funnels nearly one billion dollars a day in subsidies to its own farmers, coincidentally enabling them to dump artificially cheap, poor quality food in poor countries, resulting in yet more poverty. The World Bank estimates that if the rich nations would only stop their farm subsidies and tariffs, the poor nations would benefit by as much as half a trillion dollars and lift 150 million people out of poverty.

There is a solution in Africa's own hands. The nations of sub-Saharan Africa do very little trading with each other. Why not form an African Common Market, raise a universal tariff wall to outsiders, but cut tariffs rapidly between the African states themselves, very much as Europe did. That's the use of trading blocs anywhere.

Global quantitative targets as espoused in the British Commission's Report are wrong as they bare no relationships to recipient countries ability to use these resources effectively and they incorrectly imply that foreign aid alone can eradicate poverty. Foreign aid is a small part of a large pool of resources from varying sources that must be tapped for development. By adopting British Commission's recommendation to write off the bad debts of many African states, it may endorse past theft. Wiping out Africa's national debt would obviously make some very greedy men breathe more easily as they are holding billions of loot abroad. And who wants to forgive the bad debts of Zimbabwe's Mugabe?

The fact is Britain is still in the process of learning just what really happened during the colonial period. It is not so much the West's lectures about human rights abuses that irritate Africans. It is that they are delivered selectively and are based on ignorance. All too often the admonitions smack of hypocrisy, coming as they so often do on behalf of powerful men who may wield big sticks, but are moral dwarfs.

The Chancellor promised to give 0.7% of the UK's national wealth in donations. This was a pledge which the Heath government committed Britain to in 1970. However, Africa's main problem is not poverty, but corrupt dictators. The real problem is that countries cannot generate wealth for themselves, and handouts from the West will not solve this. The economic vandalism of Mugabe in Zimbabwe had already destroyed more wealth in five years than Britain had given to the whole of Africa since 1945. Against such odds, it is far from clear what a new era of handouts can achieve.

There is a positive story in Africa and it's one that involves no politicians or charities. The Africa Economic Outlook projected economic growth of 5%; twice the speed of Britain's. Foreign investment, which dwarfed aid in developing countries, was paying off. Trade was entrenching stability and wealth and it was a formula that, with a little help, could allow Africa to find the answer itself. Oxfam calculated that if Africa could increase its share of world trade by 1%, it would be worth £45bn a year, more than Brown hoped to raise by his convoluted International Finance Facility scheme.

Capital is a cowardly bird unless if it is Chinese. It flies to safer places where it expects to earn better returns. 40 percent of Africa's private investment takes place outside of the continent, while only 3 percent of Asia's investment takes place overseas. If there is to be any hope for long term prosperity in Africa, Africans must be given the predictability that comes with the rule of law, the protection of private property and free markets, and decentralized management of resources. This will harness local knowledge along with the creativity, diligence, and thrift that is natural to Africans.

It is easy for donors to ignore the obvious. Most Africans can survive through the most severe drought and donors show little interest how survivors do it and instead concentrate on the failed pastoralists, the losers and the destitute. During the 1980-81 drought, 90% of Africa's cows were killed by disease not hunger or thirst and hence widespread vaccination was required not boreholes.

Huge dams of course are potent symbols of economic virility and political prestige as they are clearly visible, concrete and demonstrate a basis for future economic and social development. Wilful ignorance of Africans is a long-standing component of Western donors as 60% of the World Bank's live stock projects, between 1967 to 1987, used no anthropological research at any point in the life of the research.

And of course African societies are different. Subsistence peasants have very little interaction with the world outside their farms or homesteads. It is only when they go to hospital that they may have something to do with government institutions. Barring accidents they don't even need hospitals because they doesn't fall sick so often. Under normal circumstances, to think that a Masai roaming the plains with his cattle is going to go into the streets because you have isolated the government of Kenya is naïve. All he needs from the government is to allow him to take his cattle to the market. He finds beauty in having a large herd of cattle; he doesn't want to have anything with street protests. So isolating a despot may work in urban areas, but the rural population anywhere in Africa far outnumbers the urban population. And this is precisely what happens, you go to elections tomorrow, the government loses in urban areas but the rural areas continue to vote for it, and the government remains in power.

Most, if not all, donors know nothing about the people they pity and assume that any way of life that periodically allowed large numbers of people to starve was not worth understanding. Donors feel nomadic pastoralism is a lowly stage in human development well below settled farming as practised in Europe and America and that native Africans are stupid (if they are not they wouldn't starve would they?) and hence Europeans and Americans come all the way to Africa and work around this stupidity and teach them how to be like Europeans (have piped water, toilets, paddocks, electricity, shops, family planning, schools, roads, telephones etc). It is self-flagellation to development, as they want not to just rehabilitate but to elevate. The sun shouldn't be so hot; the soil shouldn't be so poor; there shouldn't be so many flies; life shouldn't be so hard.

However losers, the destitute, the old and too young in camps are the only Africans donors get to meet or know. During famines and wars, African men and some strong women send their children, old and infirm to feeding camps for free meals and medicines while they stay behind to protect their ancestor's graves, animals and their properties. This saves their stores of food and water for cows and their calves.

Most donor projects are designed by foreign based engineers, rely on heavy machinery and complicated pumps with no regular supply of spare parts and backup. They treat local peasants, the beneficiaries, as farm animals and most projects fail even before the donors leave. Some of these schemes actually discriminate against women giving most of the equipment to men and hence causing prostitution to blossom.

Without livestock a traditional African cannot become a man, cannot marry and cannot form meaningful bonds with other clan members. Cattle gifts are used to hedge against localised drought. Stopping a man from rearing a head of cattle undermines family ties. Further Africans supplement their staple diets with fish, wild meat, insects, honey, tubers, wild cabbages and flowers. African seas and lakes are rich in fish.

But then Africans are pleased to supplement their normal diet with free cornmeal, high energy cooking oil and whatever the suntanned white people happen to be giving away in camps. All donor development strategies implicitly exclude the large majority of the economically active work force and culturally significant part of the population. Further all donor aid schemes are almost always top-heavy requiring lots of literate administrators that appeal to overstaffed cash-strapped African governments looking for ways to pay salaries, buy voters and buy loyalties.

About 80% of Japanese aid was spent bringing Japanese goods and services into poor countries; America 20% and Italians insisted that Italian contractors carried out projects. Norad projects would continue to fail as they were based on no coherent plans and the Norwegians lack experienced technical and informed managerial teams with key local contacts; though Norad is legally forbidden to favour Norwegian commercial interests.

Hence lending countries get a two-fisted return from big projects: they supply all the material and expertise and they get repayments plus interest on the loans and the local rulers get the customary 30% kickback. And all the school children chugged out by these donor projects on education graduate to become buggers as they are not taught how to survive in Africa but how to do so in Europe. The education cuts the margins of survival as most boys are herders.

The West invented "white guilt" and political correctness that made truth-telling a crime if it was in any way construed as one-sided racism. They stoked up the Swiss bank accounts of looters with unmonitored funds that were actually intended for aid and development programs. They are the ones, under veils like NEPAD, African Commission, who still think that throwing more money in the same direction will make any iota of difference to the general African syndrome of self-inflicted demise.

The likes of Blair and his promotion of conscience cleansing are willing to further nurture evil in Africa rather than expect the non-achievers and plunderers to actually do something recognizable to justify external support. Blair typically had not realised that leopards do not change their spots. The oracles of evil of yesterday are ordinarily proven to not be the deliverers of vision and statesmanship tomorrow.

What the emerged world has failed to come to real terms with is the fact that African leaders like Mugabe, Nujoma, Kaunda, Mandela, Dos Santos, Kabila, Museveni and Mkapa typically display cultural identity confusions. As the occasion suites them, they try to blend Marxism, struggler mentalities, liberal socialism, extinct ethnic culture promotions, capitalism, tribalism, embittered agendas and the pretences of understanding the real fabric of modern society and democracy.

African regimes should never again be allowed to excuse their monumental failings behind rhetoric about the evils of colonialism. If they fall short of the standards that Western citizens and AU agreements demand of their own governments, they must be condemned and isolated. But most of all, the West and China must only offer more aid if African governments reform and improve. Aid must be an incentive for better behaviour, not an unconditional handout as most of the funds poured into Africa as aid end up with arms dealers and murder on a grand scale. African leaders have to know that being reminded constantly of one's painful past will not solve anything. It will only sow seeds of hatred in it citizens against those who wronged their forefathers.

Several African leaders purport to comprehend proven values of morality, democracy, human rights, standards, international charters and law. When measurements are made, one sees that they are continuously dropping the high-bar. What is now not surprising but still most alarming is the fact that they still do not seem to have the intellectual acumen and maturity to realise their mental deficiencies.

This is not to say that Gordon Brown lacked a genuine desire to help Africa. Aid, like vouchers, is like a pyramid scheme which, to achieve the maximum effect, must be carried out in ignorance of the true economics at play. This is the aid versus trade debate. Trading with Africa has no role for politicians - other than for them to get out of the way.

Africa's hopes lie on the emergence of a breed of young, educated, technologically aware Africans who, less burdened by the rigid demands of tribal loyalty and free of the inferiority complexes of the colonial era, will stride confidently towards the future. Africa was stuck in an uneasy interim, where the remnants of the dinosaur breed of Omar Bongo in Gabon, Paul Biere in Cameroon, Mugabe clinging on to power by their fingertips.

The long walk to freedom

"Darkness cannot drive out darkness; only light can do that. Hate cannot drive out hate; only love can do that. Hate multiplies hate, violence multiplies violence, and toughness multiplies toughness in a descending spiral of destruction....The chain reaction of evil-hate begetting hate, wars producing more wars - must be broken, or we shall be plunged into the dark abyss of annihilation". Martin Luther King, Jr., Strength to Love, 1963.

Ultimately life is a nuisance of time. The history of nations is informed by the actions of each generation. Like a relay, one generation expects to inherit a legacy from another generation. With respect to Zimbabwe, the baton remained locked firmly in the hands of one generation and one mad man to the exclusion of other generations.

Political patronage has opened up opportunities for instant wealth for a small number of Zimbabweans. Yet even this feeding trough is shrinking. Arbitrage opportunities will also disappear as faith in the depreciating local currency lead to dollarisation. This economic fact of life, not the pleas of foreign diplomats, will inevitably change things in Zimbabwe. This would take time so long as the economy is still earning enough foreign exchange through remittances as well as mineral and some tobacco exports.

Thereafter recovery will be painfully slow, contrary to local, international and opposition hopes. The history of aid bringing development and recovery to Africa is poor to the point of pathetic. The economic censure most difficult to change is that imposed by free markets and investors. When Zimbabwe's economy reaches the bottom and Mugabe is finally ejected, the painful process of economic recovery will take at least as long as the decline, more than two decades.

To a great extend, Zimbabweans have to grow up and own up. They let Matibili-Mugabe steal the torch and run away with it right under their noses. He sent soldiers to Mozambique without parliament approval. They don't even know how much was spent there, even the number of casualties. They remained quiet. He did the same with the war in the DRC. When they got independence they received a lot of money such as that from ZIMCORD. Zimbabweans don't even know how much it was, only Mugabe and Chidzero did. Even the actual number and names of those who fought for the country was never divulged nor did they care. There was looting of state funds by Zanu from NSSA, NOCZIM, GMB, various levies for Aids, draught and ZIMDEF without them questioning.

Elections were stolen, people disenfranchised, kicked out of the country, their citizenship stolen, entire families broken up, journalists, students, women of WOZA and leadership people abused in newspapers, tortured and killed; newspaper printing presses, trains, police stations bombed by a mad thug; an entire province of Zimbabwe put on the move without food or medication or logistics. They kept quiet. For Zimbabweans, as long as its not you personally involved, then it seems it's all right. As long as you got away into the Diaspora then it's OK. Look at Venezuela. The government there closed down a radio station and the whole nation said NO with one big voice.

"When a leopard wants to eat its young, it first accuses them of smelling like goats," is an African saying. Africa is sick and tired of being ruled mostly by narrow, violent minded, egotistical, selfish and twisted barbarian brains who find it fashionable to rob and kill their own brothers and sisters with impunity, with pride and without mercy, only to feed Swiss people and other foreigners through their stolen loot investment in those countries.

How can African banks do well when most funds are heaped in foreign banks? What's the rationale of Mugabe's 300 trips to London, Paris and New York which cost US$25 million, inconveniencing passengers on Air Zimbabwe, when he had never visited Munyaradzi Rural District hospital which could have cost less than US$1000 for all those 300 trips? How can Matibili-Mugabe be regarded best customer of Swiss Banks in the 1990s when all the banks in Zimbabwe were collapsing?

Africans must get rid of this destructive mindset of so many African leaders that says "charity" should begin abroad. Africa must destroy its inferiority complex, mental slavery and colonial mentality. Those involved in the destruction of Africa must know that investing African resources in Africa is the only way for Africa to be respected. In corrupt societies in Asia, such as Indonesia, Bangladesh and Pakistan the citizens still prosper because the corrupt elite keeps most of their loot at home. They invest in new mobile phone networks; build private hospitals and tourist hotels.

If Western powers can do all the damage to Zimbabwe that Mugabe claims, then surely they are very brainy people, able to do so much from so far away. If he is so clever as his puppets claim, why has he been unable to do anything about it? He says the West wants to re-colonise Zimbabwe. Who would want Zimbabwe in the condition it had been reduced to? As for sanctions on Zimbabwe, Matibili harps on about them in order to hoodwink people. The sanctions, in fact, benefit Zimbabwe as they saved foreign currency that would otherwise be spent by these people on overseas jaunts.

As for degrees held by our president and government officials, what good have any of them done for the country? The only proof we had of any of them was in violence. The most important assets necessary to run a country, or anything else for that matter, are know-how, common sense and honesty. Our Matibili-Mugabe showed none of these attributes.

Mugabe blamed the international media's "negative reportage" for his bad-boy image. This was garbage of the highest order. What stands true is that the international media never came to Zimbabwe and enticed his officials to be corrupt, crafted the malevolent Posa, Aippa or the Interception of Communications Bill. They had not emasculated the judiciary and stuffed its benches with Zanu sympathisers, neither had they bombed and closed five newspapers. Nor did they beat up Morgan Tsvangirai and his crew.

Who in their right mind would come to marvel and photograph a populace that has been reduced to beggars? Sightseeing poverty is depressing and is certainly not most people's idea of a holiday. Pot-holed roads, dry Zinwa taps and dark cities cannot be advertised as part of packages to attract tourists. Neither are images of battered opposition leaders.

There is no reason why Africans should stand by and be silent when those who have benefited from the struggles of the 20th Century espouse the very racist evils everyone fought against in the 1960's across the world. Black racism against whites in Africa is no more acceptable than white racism in Europe or the USA against the minorities in those communities.

We need to work as a nation state for the common good even if we disagree about how to achieve this. We may disagree about the means, but not about the end. People need to have a sense of ownership and citizenship. They must identify with the whole country and accept all fellow citizens. If they submit out of fear to the notion that only the current leaders own the country, then they are not citizens but slaves.

The facts of politics, which the AU, SADC and Zimbabweans must now face, are that racism has no place in modern countries and that in order to win an election, one must assume that the government is willing to lose. If a government is not willing to lose power, and does not hold the same values of democratic change, surely it is a waste of time to argue the case. "How can you lose if you are counting the votes," is a Malawian 'joke'.

We have to accept that Africans are dealing with a generation of leaders that have no shame. All Africans must accept that we are our own liberators. Mbeki and the rest of the African leaders believe that black oppression is acceptable as long as it's done by another African of black pigmentation and this is in the nature of reality. No strong help to any oppressed African can be expected from African leaders as long as the current mob of corrupt dictators and despots continue to prosper and support each other.

Most revolutions are just to get rid of the people who are considered the wealthy elites and replace them with another group of wealthy elites who have supported the leader of the revolution. The world is changing and the Zimbabwean revolution hopefully will be the last as it is always the poor who suffer in a revolution. Repression is slowly and painfully being drawn back due to the principled bravery of a few and their determination to re-build shattered lives in a new Zimbabwe characterised by peace, prosperity, security and opportunity for all.

If Zimbabweans can unite and get serious, it can rebuild a great country. In a reconciliatory climate both sides can acknowledge mistakes and make concessions. In a climate of accusations, groups move away from each other and harden their viewpoints, leading to greater polarisation. In such a climate each side automatically emphasises more radical viewpoints. In all communities there are radical opinions.

Zimbabwe is breeding some of the worst racists leaders and youths ever found in Africa. The gravest threat to any democracy is frequently not government action. It is, rather, inaction by other players in a nation state, from civil society to business to labour and ordinary citizens.

Our African governments suffer from the illusion that their policies are inherently correct, equitable and justified, so they must govern unchallenged. The only defence against this encroachment is open, direct and sometimes confrontational engagement. This necessitates critics having the courage to raise their heads above the parapet. Unfortunately we have very few of these types of black people.

It is time to admire African leaders based on problem-solving abilities, rather than merely on how well they articulate resentments whose origins many already understand or don't care to understand. But their articulation not only does not at all help us move forward, but actually keep us feeling sorry for ourselves; wallowing in stagnation or regression. Words alone are not going to do anything to the West; if they are useless, why say them. In order to run any country, one needs an educated solid middle class that understands the implications of rising interest rates and the attendant pitfalls of a depreciating currency, lawlessness and the implications of tyranny.

The truth is that those who were looking for immediate change in their circumstances once Mugabe left had to re-consider their views and accept that there was going to be a long way of hard work and sacrifices ahead. Zimbabwe had been set back 50 years. It would need that and more to recover. Only a leadership that had a good grasp of these complexities could address the competing interests. The leadership must have a good understanding of the local, which is hard enough but they must also be ready to handle the powerful external factors, which can be more tricky and challenging.

It is my hope that a successful political settlement will be agreed upon (with the active support of SADC, UN, Commonwealth, AU and South Africa) by the two main parties in Zimbabwe and then at last the population can come to fully participate in their destiny after 140 years of torture, wars and destabilisation by a band of corrupt foreigners.

It is up to us to be winners and not losers and strive for what is ours. When the bureaucracy collapses, law-enforcement agencies and the military will become less disciplined and it is at that stage that the current political warlords responsible for the chaos may be replaced by military warlords who have the power to pervade every aspect of Society.

The prize is too great to give up. We are at the edge now and must keep pushing the monument and the evil serpent will topple into the abyss below where it belongs crushed never to arise again. To stop now would mean giving up an exciting future to be built on solid values where hard work, honesty and fighting spirit is rewarded. To stop now would be tantamount to stripping the honour from those before who gallantly and selflessly fought for our independence and continent in so many different ways. It would dishonour those brave democrats that continue to die in the quest to secure a future filled with aspirations that we all share; a future that will penalize those that do wrong and protect those who uphold the system. We must accept the challenge to succeed in what we feel so deeply about..........

Long live the sons and daughters of Africa!

Pasi nekutambura

Say, "NO!" to crooks and murderers

Aluta continua!

Printed in the United Kingdom
by Lightning Source UK Ltd.
132098UK00001B/49/A